RETRO
FURNITURE
CLASSICS

THIS IS A CARLTON BOOK

Design copyright © 2007
Carlton Books Limited
Text copyright © 2007 Fay Sweet

This edition published in 2012 by
Carlton Books Limited
20 Mortimer Street
London W1T 3JW

10 9 8 7 6 5 4 3 2 1

First published as *Vintage Furniture* in 2007.

ISBN: 978-1-78097-171-1

Printed and bound in Dubai

Senior Executive Editor: Lisa Dyer
Managing Art Director: Lucy Coley
Design: Barbara Zuñiga
Copy Editor: Lara Maiklem
Picture Researcher: Jenny
Meredith
Illustrator: Adam Wright
Production: Janette Burgin

RETRO FURNITURE CLASSICS

FAY SWEET

CARLTON
BOOKS

Contents

Introduction   6

Early Modernism   10
The Scandinavians   46
Mid-Century Modernism   76
Pop & Post-Modernism   112
Late Modernism   148
The New Millennium   184

Buying & Collecting   210
The Directory   214
Index   217
Picture Credits   223

One of Finn Juhl's most famous and rare designs, the sofa was originally created in 1939 and manufactured by Niels Vodder in the 1950s. It is made from walnut with upholstery over plywood. The Finn Juhl teak coffee table from 1951 features a rounded triangular top with a raised wooden rim and an inset laminate surface supported on tapered legs and carved stretchers.

Introduction

Go into almost any major auction house these days and you'll be sure to find special sales dedicated to modern design. This is a relatively recent phenomenon, but vintage furniture by twentieth-century design heroes such as Charles and Ray Eames, Arne Jacobsen and Ludwig Mies van der Rohe, along with contemporary designers such as Ron Arad and Marc Newson, now have the power to attract larger crowds and higher bids than many traditional furniture sales. Mainstream shops are also full of these classics – sometimes they are the original designs made today under license and sometimes they are cheap, but convincing, imitations – so it is clear that the appetite for modern furniture is greater than ever.

This burgeoning interest in modern classic furniture has come about as a result of a growing and widespread appreciation of good design and a general fascination for Modernism. It is a century since many of the high priests of Modernism were born, but at last we are fulfilling their visions of living in well-designed, simple interiors that are furnished with elegant, but often mass-produced and affordable, furniture. At last the best-quality design is no longer just the provenance of the wealthy.

The taste for modern furniture is as varied as the designs themselves. For some people the objects of greatest appeal are the experiments in tubular-steel furniture, the so-called industrial aesthetic, of the Bauhaus designers; for others it is the sculptural and beautifully crafted designs in wood that are associated with the Scandinavians; there are those who prefer the colourful plastics of the Pop era, or perhaps the work of just a single designer.

Most recently, the mid-century and postwar era has attracted the greatest attention. Along with a resurgence of interest in retro fashion, music and art from the 1950s, 1960s, 1970s and 1980s has also come a taste for retro interiors and furniture. Open any home-design magazine and you will soon spot a couple of Eero Saarinen Tulip chairs, the Atomic clock by George Nelson, or perhaps some fabrics by Lucienne Day. The furniture looks great in smaller spaces and it is a badge of our connoisseurship. As Eero Saarinen said, 'A chair should not only look well as a piece

below

Some examples of 'blobby' 1960s design in fibreglass by Eero Aarnio for Asko: two Pastil chairs from 1967 appear centre front, and the Globe, or Ball, chair from 1965 is shown right.

of sculpture in a room when no one is in it; it should also be a flattering background when someone is in it.'

Other factors that have influenced the recent increase in interest in modern classics is the fact that originals and early production models are highly collectable, they are still affordable and are proving to be a good investment. Along with furniture, there are plenty of opportunities to buy related items, such as studio ceramics and glassware, fabrics, lighting, radios and even original artworks. The abundance of TV collecting shows demonstrates that there is fun to be had searching through secondhand shops, flea markets and local auctions to discover those elusive bargains. The success of Internet auction sites, such as eBay, is a further testament to this. With the potential of beautiful and affordable bargains to turn into valuable collector's pieces, we are eager to learn more about the great Modernists and the designs they created. It is also important to be able to distinguish between the originals and the imitations – a genuine vintage version in good condition will

hold and increase its value, where the imitation will not. For those with a taste for more recent designs, there is also a growing market for first editions by contemporary designers.

Just like the art world, interest in modern furniture also follows trends. Exhibitions, for example, will often have an impact on prices. A retrospective dedicated to the work of Finnish maestro Alvar Aalto is quite likely to send prices rising, which is great if you want to sell your much-prized Aalto collection, but not so great if you've been thinking of investing in a few pieces. In the same way, high-profile books on particular designers can awaken new interest and boost prices. Always bear in mind, however, that like all forms of collecting, markets can go down as well as up, so the advice from modern furniture experts is always to buy what you like, look for the best quality and enjoy living with the work.

What makes modern furniture so interesting is that its history is also the history of the modern western world – each piece tells a story. At every major intersection of change, furniture designers and producers have responded by creating exciting and ground-breaking new forms for the altered world. The chain reaction is fascinating, and it is easy to trace the ripples of influence around the globe. It would be impossible, for example, to imagine the technically sophisticated work in fibreglass and aluminium created by Americans Charles and Ray Eames without the influence of the visionary Bauhaus school in Germany. Equally impossible to produce would be the brightly coloured, injection-moulded, all-in-one plastic chairs of the Danish designer Verner Panton without the advances in technology and materials that took place during the Second World War and the influence of Pop Art.

It is a fact that time simply doesn't stand still, and in the past century or so we have seen more rapid and extensive change than in the many centuries that have preceded it. Our story is a microcosm of world events that begins with the Industrial Revolution, moves through the social drive to improve the lives of ordinary people and includes the impact of increasingly informal postwar lifestyles. Today, our focus is on climate change and the effect we are having on the natural environment; this, too will help to shape the furniture of the future.

below

The Lombrico sofa, designed by Maro Zanuso for B&B Italia in 1967 was constructed of modular units that could be combined to any length. The seating was upholstered polyfoam and the base was made from moulded fibreglass. Several designers, such as Pierre Paulin and Jørn Utzon, produced similar modular projects.

right

The 1951 Lady armchair, also by Zanuso, is a curvy, welcoming upholstered easy chair made in collaboration with Pirelli – as Arflex – for its new innovation of the time, foam rubber. This design won first place in the 1951 Milan Triennale due to its innovative use of the foam.

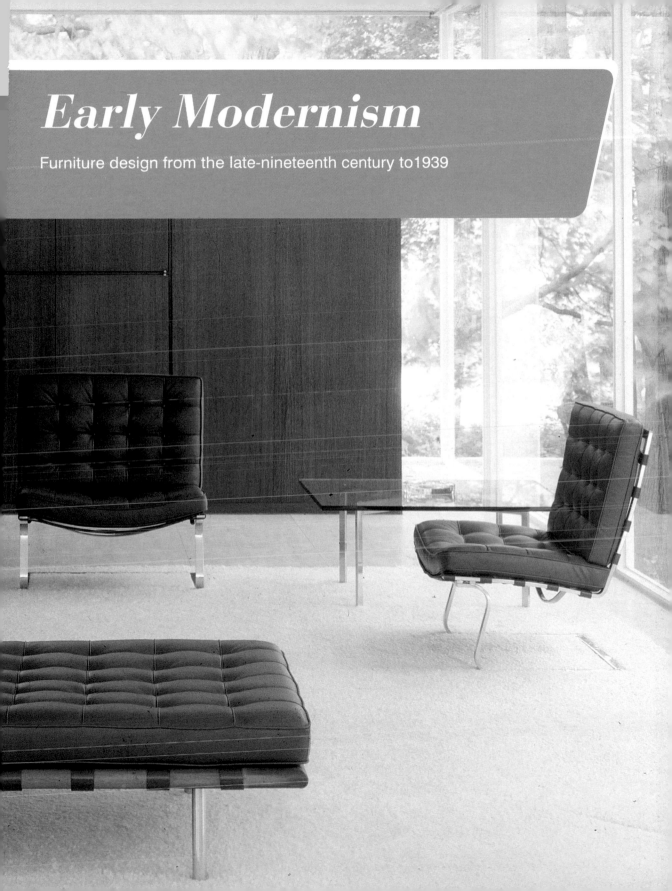

Early Modernism

Furniture design from the late-nineteenth century to1939

There has never been a more exciting period for furniture than the Modern era. The start of the twentieth century heralded an explosion of creativity inspired by new materials and innovative manufacturing techniques that combined with fresh ideas to produce a profusion of brilliant designs. Virtually every area of our lives has been touched by this sweeping change, from our homes and office interiors to hotels and restaurants, airports and schools, libraries and even cafés.

This new world of collectable designs includes such pieces as tables and desks, shelving, storage cupboards, textiles and lighting. Chairs, and seating in general, however, have been at the heart of the most of the innovation. Here designers have mapped the increasing informality of life by providing new ways to sit and take our ease. There are designs for a whole raft of formal occasions, too, for offices, conferences, concerts and dining. More recently, the form of chairs has been influenced by concerns for our health and wellbeing – the study of ergonomics, and today, environmental considerations also play their part in the story of furniture by placing a new emphasis on the wise use, and reuse, of the world's resources. In the space of just one century, seating has evolved for every imaginable purpose: from sprawling in front of the television to providing an imposing power base in the boardroom.

The Start of the Dream

Springing from the Industrial Revolution, the Modern age moved furniture production out of the small workshops, where hand-crafted pieces had been made for centuries, and into the factories for production on a grand scale. In this new setting, as Henry Ford demonstrated with his Model T motorcar, standardization was all. The same design could be assembled piece-by-piece and repeated endlessly to create a reliable and desirable product for the mass market.

Arguably, the first Modern piece of furniture was Michael Thonet's (1796–1871) Model No. 14 café chair, which entered production in 1859. Working in Austria, this Prussian-born furniture maker experimented with techniques for bending and gluing wood, and eventually hit on a design that would become one of the most successful chairs of all time. Formed from solid and laminated beech wood, which he steamed and bent into shape, it is an instantly

overleaf

The 1920s and 1930s were fertile times for furniture designs from Ludwig Mies van der Rohe. Following his success at the International Exhibition in Barcelona in 1929, he worked on a private residence called the Tugendhat house. The cantilevered chairs shown here, Model No. MR70, date from this project of around 1929–30. Van der Rohe also designed the simple day bed and glass-topped table, all shown in the setting of his famous Farnsworth House, Illinois.

below

This page from the 1895 Thonet catalogue shows part of the range of decorative bentwood chairs. By the end of the nineteenth century, early forms of mass production turned out designs in ever-greater numbers.

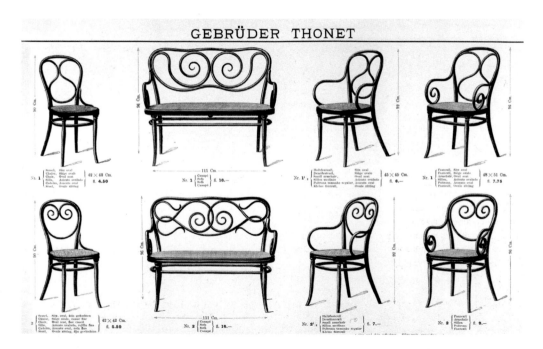

recognizable classic, with its double-hooped backrest and circular
seat. Everything about the chair foreshadows the Modernist dream
of furniture being light, functional, durable, simple to transport and
assemble, and inexpensive. Its success story is astonishing, with
around 30 million chairs sold within the first 60 years of production.
Even now, in the twenty-first century, the same family-run firm is still
making chairs.

Among the admirers of the Model No. 14 café chair was Modernist
master Le Corbusier (1887–1965), who said of the armchair version,
developed by Michael Thonet's son, August Thonet (1829–1910),
'Never has anything been created more elegant and better in its

conception, more precise in its execution, and more excellently
functional.' Le Corbusier was so inspired that he featured the
armchair against the utterly Modernist backdrop of his seminal
Pavilion de L'Esprit Nouveau at the 1925 Paris Expo.

Fear and Loathing

However, industrialization and mechanization were not welcomed by
all. In Britain, detractors included John Ruskin (1819–1900), William
Morris (1834–96) and proponents of the Arts and Crafts Movement,
who feared that the machine would not only kill creativity and craft
skills, but it would also lead to items, such as furniture and textiles,
being stripped of their very soul. As a result, craftsmen and -women
would lose their jobs and the satisfaction of making beautiful
and useful items, and the public would be denied the pleasure of
handmade objects.

This was a concern shared by many countries undergoing their
own transition to industrialization. In Scandinavia, for example,
national craft societies were established to nurture and encourage
traditional skills such as furniture making and weaving. In Austria,
the Wiener Werkstätte (Vienna Workshops) was founded in 1903
as a crafts-based group to promote skills in handmade jewellery,
fabrics, ceramics and furniture, all for a select market. There was Art
Nouveau, too. Flourishing throughout Europe in the late nineteenth
and early twentieth centuries, this formed part of the bridge between
the old and new worlds. Largely associated with interior decoration,
it was rooted in the deployment of human skills to paint and weave, to
forge iron and make furniture, all featuring non-linear, organic shapes.

However, it wasn't long before the opportunities offered by the
machine proved irresistible, and various strands of the general
Arts and Crafts Movement started to adopt its use. The ideal
was to match craftsmen and -women with the machine, using
mechanization to relieve the tedium of mundane tasks. Instead
of making human beings a slave to the machine, its rightful place
was subordinate, to serve. Gradually, industrial processes and
human skills moved closer together, as epitomized by the Deutscher
Werkbund (German Work Federation), founded in 1907 by a group
of architects, designer and industrialists. Here, traditional crafts
became integrated with mass production as part of a national
drive to boost the economy and to ensure that German products
could compete in the growing global marketplace.

Brave New World

Modernism had a complicated gestation and birth. The formulation
of Modernism as a single concept took a long while to emerge, and
debate ranged far and wide throughout the United States, western
Europe and Scandinavia on how and what the new impetus for the
'Brave New World' should be. The single shared goal was to cast off
the inequalities and old-fashioned ideas of the past and create a new
Utopia, to harness the opportunities offered by industrialization and
the spread of new technologies such as electrical power, and to forge
a better quality of life for a larger number of people. This upbeat,
progressive and idealistic vision embraced new buildings that could
be built with standardized components and improved transportation
and communications facilities. These better-quality homes were
beautiful and hygienic and contained affordable furnishings.

left

Michael Thonet experimented with his innovative
bentwood process to produce chairs in many different
forms. Here, he created an elegant folding chair with
woven-cane seat and backrest, dating from around 1890.

below

Sitzmaschine

A highly original design by Josef Hoffmann for an
armchair in around 1905. It is called the *Sitzmaschine*,
that is, the 'machine for sitting', and was designed by
Hoffmann for his Purkersdorf Sanatorium in Vienna.
Featuring an adjustable backrest, it was made by the
bentwood furniture specialists Jacob & Josef Kohn and
was first shown at an exhibition in Vienna the same year.
Inspiration is thought to have come from British Arts and
Crafts furniture.

above

Hill House Chair

One of the high ladderback chairs (1903) designed by
Charles Rennie Mackintosh and inspired by Japanese
design. It was made for Hill House, outside Helensburgh
in Scotland, which Mackintosh created for publisher
Walter Blackie in 1903. Not content with designing the
house, Mackintosh designed the complete interior, too.

left

Another version of the ladderback chair, also by Charles Rennie Mackintosh, thought to date from 1903. Built in ebonized oak with a rush-upholstered seat, these chairs were designed for the Willow Tea Rooms in Glasgow. Notice the horizontal strut at the top of the curved chair back; it has been added for extra stability.

The Mavericks

While the debate continued and designers gathered in groups to discuss their plans and ideas for the future, numerous mavericks were busy producing their own contributions to the Modern era. In Scotland, Charles Rennie Mackintosh (1868–1928) was one of these idiosyncratic early-twentieth-century pioneers. He produced highly original designs for homes and interiors of the sort that had never been seen before. His so-called Glasgow style mixes elements of Art Nouveau with the geometries of Modernism and the simple elegance of Japan. His house designs were commissioned by business people who wanted to demonstrate their success and their abilities for forward thinking. Among his most distinctive furniture designs are his chairs, many of which continue to be in production today. Using ebonized wood (often oak) and powerful geometric lines, he produced ladderback dining chairs in 1903 and distinctive high-backed, half-circle seats in 1904, both created for

the Willow Tea Rooms. Along with the equally geometric Hill House chair of 1903, with its strong vertical emphasis, all of these still look fresh today, with older editions being highly prized.

Meanwhile, sharing that admiration for Japanese elegance and simplicity, in the United States Frank Lloyd Wright (1867–1959) possessed a powerful vision that not only produced a new form of housing – featuring simplified and open-plan interiors with, of course, his own designs for furniture and lighting – but he also experimented successfully with new building types, specifically offices for major companies such as Johnson's Wax and the Larkin Company. Dating from the early 1900s, his furniture designs, mostly in oak, include armchairs and dining chairs with powerful vertical lines. Original pieces are extremely sought after and little of his furniture is still in production today; it is possible to find a few items still being made, including the cherrywood Husser table of 1899, Robie chair and table from 1906, Aurora desk of 1912, and his famous Barrel dining chair from 1927.

left

An imposing office armchair by Frank
Lloyd Wright. Constructed from painted
steel with leather upholstery, it was
designed for the Larkin Company
Administration Building in Buffalo, New
York, which he designed in 1904. There are
also versions with four legs and castors. In
this groundbreaking office building, the
chair was designed to be functionally and
aesthetically unified with the architecture.

right

Barrel Chair

Frank Lloyd Wright's Barrel chair from
1937–9, created for the house called
Wingspread that was designed for Herbert
Johnson. Made from natural cherrywood
with an upholstered seat, it has a strong,
embracing form.

left
The open-plan upper floor of the Rietveld Schröder House in Utrecht, designed by Gerrit Rietveld in 1924 for the Schräder-Schröder family. The the only building ever fully based on the architectural principles of De Stijl, it features the classic De Stijl primary colour scheme of red, blue and yellow, in combination with white, grey and black, which is repeated in Rietveld's Blue/Red chair, opposite.

Outside Influences

The decades around the turn of the twentieth century were a hugely creative period. This great energy was fuelled by the desire to cast off the shackles of the outdated past, and was driven by the urge to move swiftly and optimistically onwards. Confident in their skills to build the new world, architects played a key role in the impetus of Modernism. With their palette of new materials, they were able to fuse art and engineering to make innovative structures, such as iron bridges, skyscrapers, railway stations and even the Eiffel Tower. These began to shape towns and cities in previously unseen ways, but the architects were not alone; intellectuals, scientists, writers, composers and artists were all in the frame, too, challenging the status quo. These were the exciting avant-garde.

Seismic changes in the art world also had a major impact, France being at the heart of the action where the Impressionists began the liberation by painting outdoors and using visible brush strokes of thickly applied colour. They also introduced the notion that humans did not see objects, but rather saw light. Symbolism, too, with its tendency to deconstruction and abstraction, suggested fresh ways of thinking and looking. Constructivism in Russia was devoted to complete abstraction, Expressionism drew its inspiration from emotion, and then Pablo Picasso (1881–1973) and Georges Braque (1882–1963) pushed yet further away from realism and figurative painting with Cubism, which utterly rejected traditional ideas of perspective and representation.

Gradually, step-by-step, in the space of the few years from the 1870s to the 1910s, the old order was disrupted, dismantled and dismissed. The chrysalis of Modernism was starting to unfold, and so, armed with new materials, manufacturing processes, colours and shapes, furniture designers were free to introduce change. In fact, it was almost their duty to produce new forms.

The Shape of Things to Come

The single, most outstanding and original piece of furniture to emerge from this creative turmoil is Gerrit Rietveld's (1888–1964) Red/Blue chair of 1918. Nothing quite like it had been seen before. It was the three-dimensional embodiment of an abstract design, or perhaps an abstract painting by fellow Dutchman Piet Mondrian (1872–1944). Its geometric shape, exposed joints, angled backrest and flat seat all combined to make it a chair like no other. If Thonet's Model No. 14 café chair was the first to be produced in a modern way, this was the first to be designed in a modern way. The chair could be built from standard and inexpensive, factory-made beech and plywood components, it was free from ornament and upholstery, and it was even colourful, being painted in its famous blue, black, red and yellow livery. The prototype was designed around 1917 and given a natural wood finish; it wasn't until around 1922 that it received its famous colouring, after Rietveld had joined the De Stijl (The Style) movement. While Rietveld's own workshop was producing the chair on a small scale, few were made. However, in the 1970s mass production began with the Italian firm Cassina, and

Red/Blue Chair

Still eye-catching a century after it was first conceived in 1918, this chair by Gerrit Rietveld broke new ground. Not only was it sculptural and colourful, but also, stripped bare of upholstery, it dared to show off its construction. While it started out with a natural wood finish, the bold colours were added in around 1921. The early twentieth-century world had seen nothing quite like it before.

it continues to this day. Cassina also produces Rietveld's Schröder side table of 1922–3, which is an abstract composition of a circular base and square top with interlinked rectangles to form the stem; his sharp-angled Utrecht armchair and sofa of 1935; and his exciting Zig-Zag chair, circa 1932. Formed of just four planes, the Zig-Zag chair stands like a dramatic bolt of lighting captured in wood.

The design collective called De Stijl, which was founded in 1917, is hailed as a pioneering force in Modernism. The group's founding father was the painter and designer Theo van Doesburg (1883–1931). Influenced by Cubist painting and devoted to finding a new aesthetic, De Stijl members included avant-garde intellectuals, designers and artists who believed in cutting away from the past, leaving behind ostentatious ornament, adopting the use of straight lines and bold primary colours, and striving for purity and simplicity. Through its magazine, also called *De Stijl*, the group was able to promote its strong Utopian, moral, social and even spiritual agenda, wanting somehow to make reparations after the First World War. The group eventually faltered in 1931 with the death of van Doesburg, but its ideas lived on in many ways, particularly in Germany, where the design influence can be seen in works from the early days of the Bauhaus.

Gerrit Rietveld (1888–1964)

Gerrit Rietveld was a visionary designer who was responsible for altering our perception of furniture – chairs in particular. He challenged tradition by deconstructing familiar designs, removing ornamentation and dispensing with stuffy upholstery. In their place, he created pieces that were geometric, sculptural and fit for mass production. His designs were ahead of their time and must have looked quite startling compared to conventional and traditionally made furniture.

Born in Utrecht in the Netherlands, Rietveld had a thorough understanding of how furniture was made, having trained as a young man in his father's cabinet-making workshop. His fascination with structure was further enhanced when he put himself through evening classes to learn about architecture. He set up his own furniture-making business in 1911, and six years later, after numerous experiments, he produced his innovative Red/Blue (*Rood/Blauwe*) chair. Based on a simple structure of struts and panels with a clearly visible frame, it is made of 15 lintels and two planks – one for the seat and one for the back. The famous colour scheme has all the uprights in black with their ends in dazzling yellow, the backrest in red and seat in blue. It was not intended to be a fine piece of craftsmanship, but instead was a piece that could be easily replicated by machinery. It is clearly influenced by the new art movements of the time, especially the work of fellow countryman and artist Piet Mondrian and the De Stijl group, which was founded in 1917 and of which Rietveld became an early member in 1919. Mondrian described his abstract painted canvases as 'compositions', and this is a fitting description for Rietveld's furniture, too.

Images of the Red/Blue chair were published in the magazine *De Stijl* (The Style) in 1923, which ensured that a wide international audience who was interested in new ideas saw it. There were also connections with influential schools such as the German Bauhaus – records show that De Stijl founder and artist Theo van Doesburg visited the Bauhaus school in the early 1920s, when it was based in Weimar, and the Red/Blue chair was included in an exhibition at the Bauhaus around the same time.

Always eager to experiment, Rietveld also produced a highly original pendant lamp dating from 1920–24. Again, what you see is what you get: he has succeeded in reducing the design to the functional basics and built the lamp using a series of geometric elements. This time he used standard tubular light bulbs and hung them vertically and horizontally, like a kinetic sculpture. Walter Gropius, the German architect and founder of the Bauhaus school, also experimented with designs using tubular lighting at a later date.

Rietveld's lamp design was used in the experimental house he created in Utrecht in the early 1920s for his client Mrs Truus Schröder-Schräder and her three children. Here, Rietveld was the first to apply the principals of De Stijl to architecture. Like a huge, three-dimensional sculpture, the walls and floors of this strikingly modern building, now known as the Schröder House, are composed of vertical and horizontal white planes. It stands in complete contrast with the more traditional brick buildings of the neighbourhood. Along with looking extremely modern, it also had an unconventional layout inside, with all of the living space downstairs as normal, but with an open-plan upper floor with sleeping areas

marked by movable screens. On many occasions, comparisons have been drawn between the house and a piece of furniture because of its great attention to detail. The house was clearly suited to the family: Mrs Schröder-Schräder lived there from its construction in 1924 until her death in 1985.

Also assembled from simple geometrical forms and designed specially for this house is Rietveld's Schröder (sometimes seen as Schroeder) table. As unconventional as the house itself, its Cubist asymmetrical style starts with a circular base, climbs through a stem composed of two interlocking rectangles and terminates with a square top. Like the Red/Blue chair this also has a complex colour scheme, with the square and rectangles given one black side and one white side, and the circular base finished in red and white.

Just before the Second World War, Rietveld won several commissions for private houses, worked as a teacher, and produced another groundbreaking furniture design. This time it was the Zig-Zag chair from 1932–34. An intriguing version of the cantilever idea, it is austere and economical, built in a single material – wood – and composed of just four rectangles to make a base, support, seat and back. The joints at the base and seat are reinforced with long triangular blocks. The design is very satisfying and is a precursor to the single-piece constructions of the 1960s made using plastics.

The war years were lean times for Rietveld, but in the years after he was able to pursue his progressive ideas for mass-produced social housing. Just before his death in the 1960s he began work on designs for the Van Gogh Museum in Amsterdam, which was completed almost a decade after he died in 1973.

left

Gerrit Rietveld musing over a model of one of his experimental housing designs. Tiny miniatures of his Zig-Zag chair can be seen in a couple of the rooms.

right

Zig-Zag Chair

With its powerful graphic outline, Reitveld's Zig-Zag chair from 1932–4 is an intriguing version of the cantilevered structures explored by other designers. It is created from four planes of wood: two horizontal, one vertical and one oblique. However, the construction of the piece is complex and belies its simple form. Extra triangular wedges have been included at the base and under the seat for additional strength.

above
The interior and furniture in this consulting room
was designed by Walter Gropius between 1910
and 1923 for a lawyer's office in Berlin. From 1908
to 1910 Gropius designed offices and furniture for the
Lehmann department store in Cologne, before setting
up an architectural practice with Adolf Meyer and
becoming a member of the Deutscher Werkbund.

To Germany and the Bauhaus

The horrors of the First World War added extra urgency to the effort already invested in the pre-war striving towards a new world. Suffering from defeat and with an unstable economy, Germany became the focus for Modernism with the Bauhaus. Perhaps the most famous art and design school of the modern era, its name derives from *bauen*, the verb meaning to build, and *haus*, meaning house.

From here came a raft of ideas and designs that have infiltrated our lives. There were modern ideas about colour theory, the use of tubular steel for making furniture, table and ceiling lamps that still look fresh today, and steps towards standardization and prefabrication in making new homes.

Based in the city of Weimar, and merging the Weimar School of Arts and Crafts and the Academy of Fine Arts, the school was founded in 1919 by architect Walter Gropius (1883–1969). He wanted to create a new form of art education that would lead to a new kind of society. The early ideals carried the baton of the Arts and Crafts Movement, where craftsmen and -women would work side by side with artists, students were seen as apprentices, and where creativity and manual skills were prized over the machine; it is believed that Gropius' experience as a cavalry office during the war initially led him to be wary of the destructive power of the machine. However, the Bauhaus soon embraced mechanization as it enabled designs to be mass-produced. The school hoped that by selling its own goods, it could raise funds that would enable its adherents to be free from state subsidy, and therefore also free from state interference.

below left

Model No. S33

This timeless and elegant cantilvered chair by Mart Stam dates from 1926. It is based on a frame made from a length of bent tubular steel and is finished with a seat and backrest made from a simple panel of leather. It is an iconic classic, much copied.

below

This extremely modern-looking, geometrically shaped armchair was designed in 1923 by Walter Gropius for the Bauhaus at Weimar. It was intended for Gropius' office as director of the school, and archive photos show it *in situ*, but with mustard yellow upholstery on the seat, back and arms. It has an unusual cantilevered construction.

The Bauhaus attracted as impressive list of talented teachers, from Gropius, himself an architect and furniture designer, to the painters Paul Klee (1879–1940) and Wassily Kandinsky (1866–1944), graphic designer László Moholy-Nagy (1895–1946), metalworker and photographer Marianne Brandt (1893–1983), lamp designer Wilhelm Wagenfeld (1900–90), architect, furniture designer and last director of the Bauhaus Ludwig Mies van der Rohe (1896–1969) and furniture designer Marcel Breuer (1902–81).

Among the most iconic furniture designs are the chairs built using lengths of tubular steel that have been bent to form frames, often with a cantilevered seat. The pioneer in this field was Dutchman and Bauhaus professor Mart Stam (1899–1986), whose workshop experiments with bending and shaping gas piping led him to create the S33 cantilevered chair in 1926. A milestone in modern furniture design, it utterly transformed the look and construction of a chair, and inspired an entirely new generation of furniture design. Still in production today, made by Thonet, its frame is made from a single piece of bent tubing, and rises from a square-shaped base up through the two front legs, then horizontally to make a seat and vertically for the backrest. The original upholstery was in woven fabric strapping.

Among the many to take inspiration from this innovative concept was Marcel Breuer, who in 1927 devised his B33, a cantilevered chair in tubular steel with a leather or canvas seat and backrest. Moving on from Stam's design, this steel frame was not reinforced and so, when sat upon, had an appealing springiness for extra comfort. A year later came his B32 and B64 models that used a similar style of tubular steel frame, but they were given a seat and back constructed from a bentwood frame, which was then finished with woven cane.

below
Continuing his experiments with tubular steel chairs, Marcel Breuer created this ingenious desk in the 1930s as one of a series for the manufacturer Thonet. The flowing, continuous line of tubular steel rises to frame the stained wood desktop and then drops to hold the wooden drawer cabinet.

Wassily Chair

Designed for his friend and colleague the artist Wassily
Kandinsky around 1925, this chair by Marcel Breuer
has become an icon. Also known as Model No. B3,
it marked an historic moment in design history, using
tubular steel and leather strapping to make a modern
and comfortable armchair.

above

Landi Chair

An astonishingly advanced piece of design for its period, the Landi chair was created by Hans Coray in 1938 for use at the Landesausstellung, an exhibition held in Zurich. Use of aluminium makes it very light and durable. The perforations serve a dual function: to reduce weight and allow rainwater to drain away when it is used outside.

Also using tubular steel, but predating the cantilever, is Breuer's classic B3 chair, also known as the Wassily. This was designed in around 1925 for fellow Bauhaus master Wassily Kandinsky, and features the steel frame with a deep leather seat and leather straps for back- and armrests. One of the twentieth century's best-known chairs, this has been much copied and is still made today. Among others quick to experiment with tubular steel and the cantilevered idea of Stam was Mies van der Rohe. His early chairs, the MR10 and MR20 from 1927, adopt more flowing lines, with front legs forming an arc as they rise between base and seat.

Other highly collectable pieces from this school include metalware by Marianne Brandt, including a teapot and ceiling lamp that are produced today by Tecnolumen, and the 1924 metal table lamp WA24 (sometimes known as the MT8) with semi-spherical white glass shade by Wilhelm Wagenfeld, also made by Tecnolumen.

Although its impact on modern design is immeasurable, the life of the Bauhaus was short-lived. It moved to a new location in Dessau in 1925–6 into the Modernist building designed by Gropius, but was eventually closed in 1933 by the Nazis, who suspected its leaders of communist leanings and accused the school of being 'unGerman' and 'decadent'. Such drastic action was intended to quash the rise of Modernism, but it had entirely the opposite effect. Key figures, including Gropius, Moholy-Nagy, Mies van der Rohe and Breuer, headed for America, many of them via Britain, and so the teachings of Modernism were soon to spread across the western world.

above

Sandows Chair

Dating from 1928 and one of a series designed by Rene Herbst, the clever feature here is the use of an elasticated cord to form the seat and backrest. The chair frame is simple and elegant, using tubular steel.

left

From the same series as the chair above, Rene Herbst made a continuous seat and back with the elasticated cord for this version. The chairs required a considerable amount of intricate hand finishing. They were described by one design commentator as 'amusing'.

below

Wassily Chair

This highly sculptural chair, Model No. B3, was designed by Marcel Breuer around 1925. It enjoyed a huge renaissance of interest during the late twentieth century when it became an icon of the loft-living generation. Dozens of manufacturers produced poorly made, cheaper copies that flooded the market.

opposite

Breuer takes a well-earned break and sprawls out in the Butterfly chair of 1938, designed by Jorge Ferrari-Hardoy, Juan Kurchan and Antionio Bonet. It is also sometimes known as the BFK chair, using the initials of its designers. The all-in-one seat and back is made in the form of a leather sling hung from a slender, bent-metal frame. This design is based on traditional wood-frame models.

Marcel Breuer (1902–81)

Marcel Breuer is the king of early tubular steel furniture. Almost a century after they were first conceived, his designs continue to look fresh even today, and many are still in production. This furniture truly came into its own with the loft-living generation in the late 1990s and the early years of the new millennium; inside the stripped-back converted industrial buildings, the furniture designs came to symbolize modernity. Among his most iconic works are the Wassily, Model No. B3 (1925), with its open frame of bent tubular steel, legs that become a horizontal base, and simple leather seat and backrest, it utterly changed ideas about what a chair could look like and should be made from. Shortly after this came his timeless cantilevered dining or office chair, Cesca, Model No. B32, 1928, with its tubular frame and woven-cane seat. For all his success, Breuer was convinced that the Wassily chair design would invite harsh words and said, 'I thought that this, out of all my work, would earn me the most criticism, but the opposite of what I expected came true.'

Marcel Lajos Breuer was born in Pécs, Hungary, in 1902. As with so many of the great Modernist furniture designers, he was also an architect, but unlike most of them he started out as a furniture designer. After completing an introductory course at the Bauhaus, he became one of six apprentices to join the new furniture workshop in the summer of 1921 and excelled in virtually everything he did from the day of his arrival. He was greatly influenced by the De Stijl movement and the work of Gerrit Rietveld – his first furniture designs clearly pay homage to the Dutch designer with their deconstructed frames built from straight wooden struts in an intersecting vertical and horizontal abstract composition. Despite its rigid appearance, the armchair of 1922, sometimes known as the *Lattenstuhl*, or Slat chair, was given a backrest and seat in fabric for extra comfort.

His student years were followed by a brief and unhappy sojourn in Paris, and in 1925, when the Bauhaus director Walter Gropius invited him back to head the furniture workshop, he returned to Germany immediately. Always industrious, he soon began working on his first bent tubular steel chair, the Wassily. A reinvention of the traditional club chair, it was designed for the artist and fellow Bauhaus master Wassily Kandinsky. Unusually light and easy to assemble from ready-made steel tubes, the chair was the result of Breuer's years of experiments with bending steel and was immediately hailed as an important breakthrough in furniture design. Breuer also caused a stir with his director Gropius because he produced the chair outside the school through his own manufacturing company, Standard-Möbel.

Breuer went on to produce dozens of experimental chairs and tables, but his other high-profile design came in 1928 with the models B32 and B64, cantilevered chairs in tubular steel with seats and backrests made in bentwood and cane; the B64 was the armchair version. They involved an intriguing mix of hard and soft material, old and new techniques and became known as the Cesca, after Breuer's daughter Francesca. That same year he left the Bauhaus to practice architecture in Berlin, then in 1933 moved to Switzerland. Here, he continued working on designs for metal chairs and began exploring the use of aluminium by designing a dining chair, Model No. 301, and a chaise longue, Model No. 313. They were put into production by metal manufacturer Embru-Werke, Switzerland. With the rise of Hitler, Breuer avoided returning to Germany and in 1935 moved to Britain. Aided by Walter Gropius, who had also moved briefly to Britain, he began working for the Isokon Furniture Company, established by Jack Pritchard to promote modern designs. While he wanted to create metal furniture for this company, he was soon persuaded that wood would have greater appeal to the British audience, and he produced five designs, including the reclining Long chair in 1936, with echoes of the designs of the Finn Alvar Aalto, and a set of Nesting tables in 1936. All were in moulded plywood and are still made today.

Following his short stay in the UK, Breuer continued his peripatetic movement westwards, this time to the United States. He joined Gropius at Harvard University, where he became professor of the School of Design. Among his pupils were Paul Rudolph, Edward Barnes and Philip Johnson, all of whom went on to become important American Modernists – Johnson, in particular, was responsible for the International Style exhibition at the Museum of Modern Art in New York in 1932. Breuer continued teaching for many years and set up in partnership with Gropius in Cambridge Massachusets, to form an architecture practice that lasted until 1941. During the 1950s, his architectural designs for private houses were much in demand and he established Marcel Breuer Associates in 1957, completing over 70 bespoke homes and winning many high-profile commissions, including the UNESCO headquarters in Paris and the Whitney Museum of American Art in New York in the 1960s.

E-1027 Side Table

Designed by the great Modernist Eileen Gray, this tubular-steel-and-glass, adjustable table from 1927 was created for the seaside villa she built on the coast at Roquebrune Cap Martin in the South of France, which she shared with her husband and fellow architect Jean Badovici. The villa was also called E-1027, a cipher for the architects' intertwined initials: following the E, the numbers 10, 2 and 7 represent the order of the letters J, B and G in the alphabet.

right

Transat Chair

Loosely based on the traditional deckchair, this design from around 1927 by Eileen Gray features an open frame with a slung seat and separate headrest. For ease of transport and storage, it comes apart and can be broken into several pieces. It was also designed for the villa at Roquebrune Cap Martin.

Putting on a Show

Along with architects and designers spreading the word among themselves about their new designs and ideas, exhibitions provided a route to a wider audience. In a world before mass communications, vast international trade exhibitions in the early twentieth century provided the forum for nations to show off their wares, their design prowess and their economic confidence. Among the biggest and earliest was the vast 1851 Great Exhibition, which was staged at Crystal Palace in London. It gathered together the latest ideas and products from all over the British Empire and its protectorates, and showed them off in the innovative glass and steel exhibition hall designed by Joseph Paxton (1803–63).

By 1900 the idea of an exhibitions had evolved, and one of the first shows of the modern era was staged in Paris in 1900. Here, at the Exposition Universelle (World Fair), Art Nouveau was introduced as a significant new style in architecture and design. Visited by 51 million people, the fair included Art Nouveau architecture, furniture, jewellery, ceramics, posters, glass, textiles and metalwork. The story had moved on a little by the time of the World's Fair in St Louis, Missouri, in 1904, with great set pieces such as the Summer Residence of an Art Lover by German designer Joseph Maria Olbrich (1867–1908), which showed how designs were becoming simpler and more streamlined. The fairs continued around Europe, Australia and the United States, introducing new products and inventions, from moving pictures and the escalator to the ice-cream cone and wireless telegraph.

For Modernist design and architecture, the great Paris fair of 1925 was a major event. Called the Exposition Internationale des Arts Décoratifs et Industriels Modernes (International Exposition of Modern Industrial and Decorative Arts), its name was shortened

above

Blending glamour and comfort, this Art Deco club chair with deep upholstery and a soft cream-leather cover was designed by Émile-Jacques Ruhlmann.

left
A richly decorated interior by Émile-Jacques Ruhlmann from the late 1920s. This study is extremely luxurious, with its patterned carpet with a Grecian-style border, exotic wood desk, leather stem chair and heavy drapes beyond.

below
A decorative armchair from around 1925 by Émile-Jacques Ruhlmann. Its simple wood frame is given extra richness with metal-capped front legs, and the golden fabric with its geometric pattern is period-perfect.

and applied to the decorative style we now know as Art Deco. This elegant, glamorous area of design has its roots in a number of sources: the 'primitive' arts of Africa, South America and even Egypt, and the streamlining tendencies of early Modernism with its applications in the new technologies of radios, skyscrapers, aviation, fast cars and trains. In Art Deco furniture and furnishings, the palette of materials includes aluminium and stainless steel, exotic wood, glass, lacquered finishes, Bakelite and animal skins; repeated motifs are often used and include the sunburst, chevrons, geometric shapes and plenty of sensual curves. Mass-produced furniture, most often by uncredited designers, included lavish bedroom suites with bed, wardrobe and dressing table, and dining suites with matching table, sideboard and chairs and sometimes even a cocktail cabinet. The designs are exuberant and upbeat, and had wide appeal throughout the United States and northern Europe.

The few named designers of this period to look out for when collecting pieces from this period include Émile-Jacques Ruhlmann (1879–1933), Eugène Printz (1889–1948), Pierre Chareau (1883–1950), Jean Dunand (1877–1942), Eileen Gray (1878–1976), Edward Maufe (1883–1974) and manufacturers including Heywood-Wakefield, Epstein and Lalique. Ruhlmann designed carpets, textiles, lighting and furniture as the Établissements Ruhlmann et Laurent with Pierre Laurent. Influenced by French Art Deco in the 1920s, by the 1930s his furniture forms became increasingly Modernist.

Grand Confort Sofa

Often attributed to Le Corbusier, this sofa forms part of a series of designs completed by him with Charlotte Perriand and Pierre Jeanneret. The clever design, also known as the LC2, is based on an external frame of tubular steel, into which are slotted large square and rectangular leather-covered cushions.

Alongside the excitement of this popular style, on show in Paris in 1925 stood the Modernist gem of a pavilion designed by the Swiss-born architect Le Corbusier. Called the Pavilion de L'Espirit Nouveau (Pavilion of the New Spirit), the white Cubist villa with its vast square windows and flat roof was considered so provocative by the exhibition organizers that it was located in a quiet corner of the exhibition site, sandwiched between trees, and is reported to have been hidden behind a wooden fence for the opening. Le Corbusier had already designed some experimental housing, but had yet to start work on his memorable white villas and larger projects. And yet here in Paris he expressed his ideas about idealized living with an open-plan living room featuring modern built-in shelving and cupboards, Cubist and abstract paintings on the walls and minimal furniture. He also featured his favourite Thonet bentwood chairs of half a century earlier, alongside his own early prototype furniture designs that included room-divider shelving and cupboards that were all manufactured in metal and formed part of his rational idea about how to 'equip' a home to make the best use of space.

While Le Corbusier is best known as one of the high priests of Modern architecture, his small collection of furniture designs remains ever-popular. Designed in and around 1928, and with assistance from his work colleagues Pierre Jeanneret (1896–1967) and Charlotte Perriand (1903–99), he produced a handful of iconic items that were all made with tubular steel frames. The collection includes the chaise longue, Model No. B 306, with a headrest pillow called the 'rest machine' (see below); the Basculant chair, with its calfskin seat and backrest; the Model No. B302 dining chair with circular seat and wraparound padded leather backrest; and the Grand Confort armchair with its tubular steel frame designed to accommodate five large upholstered leather cushions. These must all have looked astonishingly radical and intriguing to homeowners in the late 1920s, and it took some decades before they assumed iconic status. However, today the designs have truly come into their own. Although the furniture designs are much copied, those made to original designs are manufactured by Cassina.

below

Chaise Longue

A fresh take on the traditional chaise longue, the Model No. B306 design by Le Corbusier with Charlotte Perriand and Pierre Jeanneret, from 1928, has a base that acts as a cradle for the upper section. The leather-covered bolster adds extra comfort as a headrest. Finishes include ponyskin, very popular in the late 1920s and early 1930s, or black leather.

Le Corbusier (1887–1965)

One of the high priests of Modernism, Le Corbusier made a huge and indelible impact on the changing face of the twentieth century. Primarily known for his highly original and often controversial architecture, he was responsible for such groundbreaking Modernist homes as the purist, white-box Villa Savoye at Poissy just outside Paris, the Unite d'Habitation tower block (apartment house) in Marseille, and the massive government buildings in Chandigarh, India. Along with his architecture came his radical ideas for town planning, his numerous polemical books, his paintings and his furniture.

Born in Switzerland in 1887, Charles Edouard Jeanneret was a prizewinning watch engraver until his delicate eyesight led him to reinvent himself. He changed his profession and his name to become the renowned architect and designer known as Le Corbusier. The pseudonym was derived from his cousin's name 'Lecorbezier' and the French word *corbeau* (for crow), and adopted around 1920.

Around 1908 he went to Paris to attend lectures by the great architect Auguste Perret (1874–54) – the first man to exploit reinforced concrete. Two years later he became apprentice to the visionary Peter Behrens in Berlin, where both Walter Gropius and Mies van der Rohe were also training. After this formative experience Le Corbusier returned to Switzerland to teach and practice architecture. He started work on private villas and began to evolve his ideas about mass housing. The Maison Domino comes from this period; it was unbuilt but designed as a system for fast-track housing after the First World War, to be made from concrete, prefabricated and with open-plan spaces that were highly unusual at the time. In peacetime Le Corbusier moved to Paris, where he spent much of his time painting and developing his own theories for the modern world. This culminated in 1919 with the launch of a magazine called *L'Espirit Nouveau,* which explored the possibilities of industrialization and mass production to create a more efficient environment and higher standards of living.

By the 1920s Le Corbusier had set up in practice with his cousin
Pierre Jeanneret and produced a series of homes for private clients.
He also took part in big design exhibitions, including the 1925 Paris
world show called the Exposition Internationale des Arts Décoratifs
et Industriels, where his all-white Modernist Pavilion, de l'Espirit
Nouveau, won him international attention. As co-founder of the
Congrès Internationaux d'Architecture Moderne (CIAM), he promoted
his personal philosophy of architecture as part of what he called 'the
machine for living', an inextricable component of life and living.

Remarkably, his furniture design work took place in just one year,
1928, and was the result of a collaboration with Pierre Jeanneret
and Charlotte Perriand. Perriand had gained experience of working
with modern materials, and before joining Le Corbusier's office
had exhibited furniture made from steel and aluminium. This new
furniture was as radical as Le Corbusier's architecture and used
new materials, primarily metals, modern manufacturing techniques
and embraced radical ideas. The work is still fresh and desirable
and embodied part of the practice's ideas about creating 'interior
equipment' for homes.

Among his instantly recognizable pieces is the B306 chaise longue,
based on a recliner tracing the shape of an outstretched body and
sits on a H-shaped cradle – a single long cushion forms the headrest.
There's also the Grand Confort chair and sofa designs, featuring
a slender geometric framework of bent tubular steel, which is then
upholstered and given shape with large rectangular leather cushions.
It is a radical design that puts the frame on the outside – by making
the upholstery deep and luxurious, the designs challenged ideas that
only traditional furniture could be comfortable. Other designs from
this series include the Basculant chair, Model No. LC1, a tubular metal
frame with panels of leather for the seat and backrest; a small side
chair with circular padded seat and padded back rail, Model No. LC7;
and glass-topped tables, including the dining table LC6.

As Le Corbusier's reputation grew, so did his ideas. During the
1930s he continued developing his theories about modern city
planning. He put his work on hold during the Second World War, but
picked up immediately afterwards when he completed the United
Nations headquarters in New York in 1947. He also became involved
in rebuilding France with his ideas for mass housing executed in
such landmark projects as the Unite d'Habitation in Marseilles –
the 'streets in the sky' where more than 300 apartments, shops,
a gymnasium, a cinema and even an hotel were all contained in
the same 17-storey concrete building. Gradually, his straight-line
Modernist ideas turned more organic, and his sculptural Notre Dame
du Haut chapel at Ronchamp, Northeastern France, also in concrete,
was completed in 1954. Throughout the 1950s he also worked on the
complex of government buildings in Chandigarh, India.

By the end of the decade Le Corbusier had become increasingly
withdrawn, particularly following the death of his wife in 1957, and
he entered partial retirement in the South of France. There, he
continued to work on a mixture of disparate projects, including
a convent, a customs house, more Unite apartment blocks and
university buildings. Le Corbusier died suddenly while swimming
in the Mediterranean in 1965.

The International Style

By the late 1920s and early 1930s, the assorted strands of Modernist theory and practice were drawing together across the world from Moscow and Milan to Manhattan. It was possible to see emerging a cohesive style of architecture and design, underpinned by the shared beliefs in functional and rational design, the use of new materials and manufacturing techniques, and full acknowledgment of the new ways of living. Of course the most obvious, high-profile manifestation of this new world was in architecture: in buildings with sheer, unadorned walls, large, plain windows to let in the sunshine, flat roofs, and open-plan interiors with stripped-back finishes free from decoration.

To furnish these spaces, new types of furniture evolved that echoed the aspirations and style of the buildings. One of the most complete and best-recorded examples of an early, fully-fledged Modernist interior is the German Pavilion shown at the International Exhibition in Barcelona in 1929. Designed by Ludwig Mies van der Rohe, this pavilion was the distilled essence of the times, with its long, rectangular plan, flat roof, floor-to-ceiling windows, open-plan interior and furniture also designed by the architect to match. For this project Mies van der Rohe created his ever-popular Barcelona chair, also known as the MR90, which has been much admired by generations of architects ever since, and is often to be found in their reception areas.

The chair is formed from a steel frame, which makes an X shape in profile, with one upper arm of the X folding down to make the

below

Barcelona Chair
Designed by Ludwig Mies van der Rohe, this beautiful chair went on show in the German Pavilion at the Barcelona International Exhibition of 1929. Also known as Model No. MR90, it is based on an X-shaped frame with leather strapping to support the plush, leather-covered cushions for the back and seat.

seat and the other raised for the backrest. The frame is then given a webbed seat and back, onto which are placed two large, upholstered leather cushions. It is elegant and simple in form and epitomizes the spirit of Modernism by displaying its structure and being machine-made. However, the industrial production of this design has never been entirely automated; even today the production process involves considerable hand finishing. Original chairs are extremely rare, and it has been much copied, but bona fide versions are still produced today by Knoll, along with other items from the pavilion, including the Barcelona stool and Barcelona sofa.

Marking the maturing of Modernism as a recognizable new form of building and design came the 1932 exhibition at the New York Museum of Modern Art called 'The International Style'. Here the organizers Philip Johnson and Henry-Russell Hitchcock and the museum's director Alfred Barr drew together examples of the new architecture from the decade starting in 1922. Barr devised the title 'International Style' and formalized it with capital letters. To compile their exhibition, the three of them toured Europe 'just plain looking' and photographing every example they found, from office buildings and banks to the Mies van der Rohe pavilion in Barcelona to the Bauhaus school in Dessau. Occasionally they stopped to admire the furnishings, and the exhibition included images of a Marcel Breuer-designed bedroom in Berlin complete with tubular-steel-framed bed, desk and stool, along with a modern study furnished by Mies van der Rohe in New York. The exhibition was pivotal. By collecting so many examples of this innovative and distinctive work, it somehow solidified the notion of a fully formed new style which had captured the imagination of architects around the globe and seemed fit for the purpose of building a better world.

British Modernism

Modernism was slow to be welcomed over the threshold in Britain. Although a scattering of flat-roof white villas was built in the 1930s, it wasn't a style of architecture that was relished by the majority of nostalgia-loving Brits, who preferred pitched roofs and bay windows. Aside from these private villas, only a very few large buildings appeared in the new style: the pavilion at Bexhill-on-Sea, a beach-side café at Canvey Island, the Highpoint apartments in Highgate and a few office buildings, factories and cinemas. Generally, enthusiasm ran low, and if the British appetite for modern buildings wasn't limited enough, the taste for modern furniture and furnishings was virtually non-existent. It was widely believed that steel-framed chairs and tables belonged in the office as utilitarian objects.

Several British designers tried their hand at following their colleagues on the Continent with radical furniture in interesting new shapes and materials, but it was of very little public interest. A distinct breakthrough came, however, in 1933 when the work of Finnish Modernist architect Alvar Aalto (1898–1976) was exhibited in London. His appeal was instant; in his version of the look, contemporary style was made not in metal, but in wood – Modernism had become soft, tactile and appealing.

There were few champions of Modern design in Britain, but among those forging the new path was the company Isokon, which was set up a year before the Aalto show by furniture manufacturer Jack Pritchard (1899–1992) and architect Wells Coates (1895–1958), who was a Canadian born in Japan. They worked together on the designs for the Le Corbusier and Bauhaus-inspired Modernist Lawn Road apartments in north London. The pair were well connected, and acted as a magnet for Modernists. Lawn Road appealed to the avant-garde, and residents included Walter Gropius and Moholy-Nagy, who stayed briefly on their flight from Germany during the Second World War. Curiously, residents also included the novelist Agatha Christie. The communal bar was designed by Marcel Breuer.

Isokon produced a number of Breuer's latest designs. Following the British affection for wood, in 1936 he designed a beautiful sofa and armchair with wooden arms, a dining chair and a chaise longue made in birch – all of which are in production today. The Viennese designer Egon Riss (1901–64), created the best-selling Penguin Donkey, a small book and magazine rack constructed from plywood and designed to hold up to 80 Penguin novels. It was an instant bestseller and has spawned several more recent designs created in homage to the original, also made by Isokon.

Home-grown British Modernist talent was in scarce supply, but furniture-maker Gerald Summers (1899–1967) was determined to experiment with the International Style and set up his own company, called Makers of Simple Furniture, in 1932. One of the company's most fascinating pieces from the 1930s is his plywood armchair. Designers had long been intrigued by the possibilities offered by plywood, and here, in 1933–4, Summers took a single sheet of the material and successfully bent and curved it to form a chair with four legs and a continuous seat and back. It used the latest technology to shape the sheet material.

right

Penguin Donkey
A simple and practical solution to keeping books and magazines tidy, this small storage unit by Egon Riss, 1939, was called a 'Penguin Donkey' because it was exactly the right size for storing Penguin paperbacks.

Modern styles of furniture and home furnishing formed only a small part of the British market in the years before the Second World War. Serving the 'discerning' buyer, some enlightened retailers such as Heals, Waring and Gillow, and Maples in London, carried small ranges of the daring new designs created by Summers and fellow Modernists such as Oliver Bernard (1881–1939), Denham McLaren (1903–89) and Gordon Russell (1892–1980) (an arch Arts and Crafts follower who turned to Modernism in the 1930s), and manufacturers including PEL, the Good Furnishing Group and Makers of Simple Furniture.

However, with the advent of the Second World War, the march of Modernism in Britain was put on hold and it wasn't until the mid-1940s that the story continued.

above

Bent Plywood Chair

A dazzling piece of plywood design by Gerald Summers from 1933-4. This chair, including its arms and legs, is formed from a single sheet of plywood. It is a highly economic, rational and satisfying piece of design.

◀ **Cantilevered Chair, 1926**
Mart Stam's Model No. S33 tubular bent-metal chair for Thonet is designed as one fluid piece: the tubular metal joins the back with the floor support. Highly influential, the design led to others by Mies van der Rohe and Breuer.

▶ **Lloyd Loom Chair, circa 1922**
The chair was created by William Lusty, after a collaboration with Marshall Boyd Lloyd, the inventor of the twisted-paper weaving loom. First used to make baby carriages, the twisted paper-and-wire process has proved flexible enough to make a range of elegant and durable furniture that is still manufactured today.

Key icons of
early
modernism

▼ **Writing Desk and Drawers, 1930**
Designed by Piero Bottoni for Comacina in 1930 and much copied today, the tubular-steel supports create a streamlined piece that is still in production, manufactured by Zanotta.

▲ **Red/Blue Chair, 1918**
Designed by architect Gerrit Thomas Rietveld in 1918, the Red/Blue chair exhibits the straight lines and primary colours advocated by the De Stijl art movement. Rietveld wanted to design a chair that could be machine-made but it was never mass-produced.

▶ Cesca Chair, 1928

Designed by Marcel Breuer and manufactured by Desta and then Thonet, the Cesca, or Model No. B32, was the most refined of the pioneering cantilevered chairs produced in the late 1920s. Made from long lengths of chromium-plated steel, lacquered beechwood and cane, versions are still being produced.

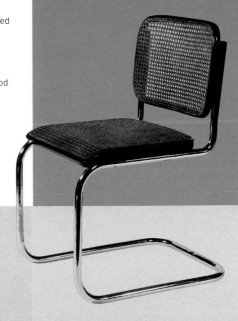

▲ Grand Confort, 1929

Created by Le Corbusier, Pierre Jeanneret and Charlotte Perriand as part of an interior created for the Salon d'Automne in Paris, the armchair's chrome-plated tubular-steel frame holds five orthogonal cushions.

▶ Barcelona Chair, 1929

The classic x-frame chair, designed by Ludwig Mies van der Rohe and manufactured by Knoll, is also known as Model No. MR90. Buttoned leather cushions rest on straps that are attached to the horizontal bars.

▲ Bentwood Café Chair, 1918

Designed by Michael Thonet, this version of the Model No. 14 bentwood chair is still manufactured today by the Thonet company as Model No. 214. Made of only six components, the design has remained virtually unchanged for nearly 150 years.

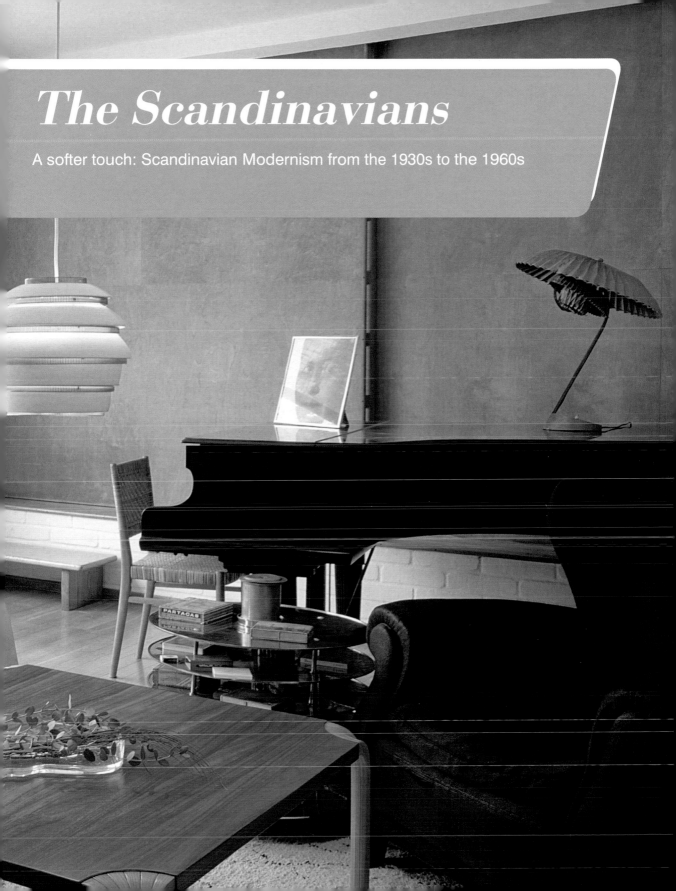

The Scandinavians

A softer touch: Scandinavian Modernism from the 1930s to the 1960s

overleaf

The living room of Alvar and Aino Aalto's home and office in the Helsinki suburb of Riihitie, completed in 1936. This modestly furnished space includes the armchair Model No. 400 (also known as the Tank) from 1936, a coffee table, Model No. X800B from 1954, and pendant lamp A331 in white-painted aluminium with brass rings, also from 1954. The home is open to the public.

above

Finn Juhl's highly original sofa, designed in the late 1930s and then produced in the 1950s. It is distinguished by the unusual organic shape and separate horizontal headrest stretching along the length of the back of the sofa, then wrapping round above the arms at both ends. Contrasting coloured upholstery adds interest. A classic organic table and chairs from the same period complement the piece.

The Scandinavian countries of Denmark, Sweden, Finland and, to a lesser extent, Norway, have made an impressive contribution to the history of Modernism and modern furniture design. The Scandinavians produced a brand of accessible, soft Modernism that was tactile, comfortable and had an instant appeal. For anyone who found the hard-edged industrial aesthetic of the Bauhaus difficult to embrace, here was a type of Modernism they could relate to. It is a remarkable endorsement of the greatest Scandinavian designers that large numbers of their products not only succeed in looking stylish, relevant and fresh many decades after they were first made, but also that they are still in production and continue to appeal to new generations of home-makers. While some of these design classics date way back to the 1930s, they have a timeless quality and look as good in the most minimal of loft apartments as they do in a family home.

A Period of Change

To understand what underpins this Scandinavian design phenomenon, the answers can be found in the past. In the early years of the twentieth century, each country was in the process of reinventing itself. In 1905 Norway won its freedom from the union with Sweden, leaving both Norway and Sweden to redefine themselves. Meanwhile, in 1917, Finland gained its independence from Russia and also began to seek a new identity, and Denmark was growing accustomed to life with new social -democratic politics. In each case, Modernism provided the opportunity for a fresh start,

and well-made modern goods would also help to boost the flagging economies. The focus was on high-quality, easily exported, high-value products that included furniture, ceramics, glassware, jewellery and metalware, tools and textiles, to be followed later by electronics, cameras and telephones.

It wasn't long before Scandinavian design became a byword for superb quality, with exemplary household names such as Volvo, Saab, Aga, Marimekko, Electrolux, Hasselblad, Lego, Bang & Olufsen and, more recently (with the most populist agendas), companies like Ikea and Nokia.

Industrialization came late but fast in Scandinavia. The speedy introduction of electricity, roads, rail and factories brought about vast change, and as more people were attracted to the cities looking for jobs, so overcrowding, disease and social unrest grew. Again, Modernism was enlisted to come to the rescue with well-designed and quick-to-construct new homes.

The housing issue soon became the centre of political debate in Scandinavia. In Sweden, for example, it was agreed that the health of the nation as a whole was built on the health of the family, and that meant making a comfortable, hygienic, well-furnished home – thus the need for good design was firmly added to the new political agenda. Combined with the new social-democratic politics, modern design could offer the opportunity of an improved life at home and shared prosperity, and to this day the home remains absolutely central to the focus of Scandinavian life.

Building the New Utopia

In common with the Arts and Crafts Movement in Britain, the Deutscher Werkbund in Germany and Wiener Werkstätte in Austria, the Scandinavian social reformers believed that design could be used as a force for good and as an instrument of change, and that by improving living conditions, society as a whole would benefit. Numerous liberal-thinking architects were motivated to start planning how people might live in a new and improved world. They were interested in making homes free of the old-fashioned trappings of wealth, to make them simpler, more hygienic, more in tune with the natural environment.

left

Finn Juhl's home in a Copenhagen suburb was designed in 1942. This light-filled interior includes a built-in sofa at the lower level and steps up to a dining area. Rooms are divided by a glass shelving unit. In true Scandinavian style, wooden floors, stairs and ceilings are left in their natural state.

Creating the most potent vision of the new Utopia in Scandinavia were Swedish artists Carl and Karin Larsson (1853–1919 and 1859–1928). At the end of the nineteenth century, they transformed their countryside home into a simple, but beautiful rustic dwelling with painted furniture, bright fabrics, woven rugs and painted wall decorations. The Larssons took much inspiration from William Morris and the Arts and Crafts Movement, and it is known that they were subscribers to the Arts and Crafts magazine, *The Studio*. Carl's watercolours of the interiors were published in 1899 in the book *Ett hem* (*A Home*), which sold extensively. The apparently effortless style captured the imaginations of many, including social reformers such as Ellen Key (1849–1926), who was moved by seeing Larsson's watercolours at the Stockholm Exhibition of Art and Industry in 1897. Key joined Larsson in believing that the power of art could improve health and wellbeing. In 1899 she expressed these ideas in her own popular and influential publication, *Skonhet for Alla* (*Beauty for Everyone*).

During this period of reinvention and modernization, numerous national design organizations, including Svenskt Form in Sweden, the Dansk Design Centre in Denmark, Norsk Form in Norway and Design Forum Finland, all worked hard at ensuring traditional crafts skills were not lost in the rush for the new world. In each country indigenous skills had evolved to make best use of local materials, from timber and metals to leather and wool. These organizations encouraged new generations of designers to learn from the past, not discard it, and to build on the bedrock of the skills base. It is clear that design gurus like Alvar Aalto looked to ancient Finnish furniture for inspiration from its simple forms; he made the most of the Finnish forests for his supply of birch, and is reputed to have echoed the irregular outlines of lakes in his famous glass vases. Many other early Modernist furniture designers worked with wood as their main material, drew inspiration from the organic shapes in nature, and borrowed its colour palette and patterns.

Northern Modernism

Modernism was embraced by the Scandinavians early in the twentieth century. While the philosophy was rooted in the works and ideas of the high priests Le Corbusier, Peter Behrens (1868–1940), Walter Gropius and the Bauhaus, the northern style evolved rapidly in its own way. Early indicators of this new direction included the fresh architecture of the Nordic design giants. These included Erik Gunnar Asplund (1885–1940) in Sweden, who designed Stockholm's city library in the 1920s in a pared-down and simple geometrical style; the Dane Arne Jacobsen (1902–71) who, in the late 1920s, won a House of the Future competition with a radical circular home complete with flat roof and sundecks, a carport and huge picture windows; and Alvar Aalto in Finland, who was working on his landmark Paimio Sanatorium – a crisp white building of rectangular blocks with sunny open terraces and new-look furniture.

While the Scandinavian countries are certainly geographically remote from the heart of Europe, their architects and designers have always remained closely in contact with global events, avidly devouring international books and magazines, and travelling extensively. At the heart of the success of Scandinavian Modernism has been the ability to assimilate, to take the stripped-back simplicity and machine-made efficiency of mainland European Modernism and transform it with a warm and human touch. Right from the start, furniture designers exchanged cold, tubular steel for fine-grained, natural wood; they found ways of making timber pliant and learned how to coax it into the latest shapes. They took the edginess out of the machine aesthetic and softened the corners, added comfort and warmth with textiles and subtle lighting, and generally created human-centric designs that hug the body and ooze sensuality.

Early Scandinavian Icons

The first truly iconic piece of modern furniture design to come from Scandinavia was the chair now known as the Paimio, designed in 1931–2 by Alvar Aalto. It was created for the Paimio Sanatorium, designed by Aalto for patients with tuberculosis.

During the late 1920s, Aalto, assisted by his wife, Aino, experimented with cantilevered chairs and tubular steel frames and also with forms of moulded plywood, but he soon switched to using wood only. There is clear evidence that Bauhaus designers like Marcel Breuer exerted a strong influence on this young Finn.

left

The dining room of Carl and Karin Larsson's late-nineteenth-century home at Sundborn, Sweden. Comfortable and modest, this is the epitome of rustic Scandinavian style, with painted furniture, embroidered cushions and coloured-glass windows.

opposite

Alvar Aalto's hallway at Villa Mairea at Noormarkku, Finland (1938–41). Slender and irregularly spaced columns of natural timber reflect the surrounding pine forest, and chairs and benches are minimal. The brass Model No. A330 pendant lamps from the 1930s are also by Aalto.

right

right

Two early designs from Alvar Aalto. On the left is Kakkonen from 1930 and on the right is Aulatuli, a version with armrests from the same year.

above

Neat rows of seating under the undulating timber ceiling in the Lecture Room at the Viipuri Library by Alvar Aalto, opened in 1935. Birchwood three-legged stools, Model No. 60 from 1932–3, feature his trademark curved leg. Towards the far end of the room are rows of birch Model No. 68, from 1933–5.

below

Paimio Chair

Aalto's elegant chair of bent birch and birch plywood, from 1931–2, shows virtuoso handling of the natural material. Called Model No. 4, it was created for the tuberculosis sanatorium at Paimio, Finland, and completed in the early 1930s. Its angled backrest assisted breathing and it was easy to keep dust-free.

One archive picture of his home in Turku from 1929 shows a simple living room, complete with Marcel Breuer's Wassily chair and one of his table lamp designs.

In so many ways the Paimio chair has genuinely stood the test as an all-time classic piece of Scandinavian modern design. It is made with a curvy, shaped laminated wood frame and has an all-in-one seat and backrest made from sheet plywood. Aalto was convinced that the use of wood would be infinitely more comfortable for tuberculosis patients at the sanatorium than the metal-framed designs emerging from Germany. The chair's status as a classic derives from the fact that it has a timeless appeal and remains in production to this day. Built from local materials, in this case Finnish birch, the frame is given a light finish, but the grain of the wood is left exposed. In the true spirit of any design from a people with a sensitivity for the environment and who use precious natural materials sparingly, it is not excessive in any way, and because it is composed of simple elements it is easily mass-produced. It has also proved to be highly adaptable and is made in upholstered versions and even as a sofa. Finally, the Paimio is a conscious piece of human-centric design, the backrest being angled to best support the patients at Paimio and assist with their breathing. Practically, the simple, open, plywood frame was also easy to keep hygienically clean.

This level of design care is quite astonishing in such a young designer. Aalto was only 29 when he won the competition for his great landmark of architecture, a gleaming, white multistorey building set in the forest where tuberculosis sufferers could enjoy the clean, rural, fresh air. He worked on the building and all its fixtures and fittings with his wife, Aino, lavishing attention on every detail, from door handles designed so they didn't catch the sleeves of staff or patients, to washbasins made with a deep, rounded bowl to avoid the irritating sound of rushing water.

Aalto held on to his position in the spotlight throughout the 1930s, and along with a full order book of buildings, his furniture design work continued apace. Among his other great classics from this decade is the Model No. 60 stool from 1933. This modest and delightful stool is again built in birch, again constructed of simple components and again, with its curved leg, involves new technological advances in shaping wood. In the same year as this stool first appeared, Aalto gained international recognition with his first retrospective show in the UK. It was staged in the unlikely setting of London's Fortnum and Mason store, but attracted enthusiastic crowds and ensured him lifelong popularity among British admirers of Scandinavian modern design.

Alvar Aalto (1898–1976)

Alvar Aalto was the father of Scandinavian Modernism, a distinctive type of 'soft' Modernism inspired by organic forms and based around natural materials. The most important Finnish architect of the twentieth century, Aalto is best known for the Paimio Sanatorium (1929–33), the Viipuri Library (1927–35) and the Finlandia Hall (1962–71), along with a collection of influential individual houses. Also a prolific furniture and lighting designer, his groundbreaking work continues to be popular today.

Born in Kuortane in Finland, Aalto studied architecture at Helsinki University of Technology. He set up his practice in 1923 in Jyväskylä, shortly after Finland gained independence from Russia. The country needed to reinvent itself, and its cultural and economic renaissance followed two routes – one was the rediscovery and reassertion of national identity, the second was the pursuit of industrialization and Modernism to become a world player. Confident and hardworking, Aalto was perfectly placed to create a new national architecture and to help rebuild his country for the twentieth century.

Aalto's architectural practice was busy even in the early days, but his big break came in the late 1920s and early 1930s when he won two major commissions: one for the Viipuri Library (now inside the Russian border and in a perilous state of dilapidation) and the other for the Paimio Sanatorium. The two projects provided Aalto with the opportunity to show off his mastery of the new International Style. The buildings are white and cubic with flat roofs and large expanses of glass; both are unmistakably progressive, functionalist and part of the new world.

The Paimio Sanatorium, in particular, attracted national and international attention and was hailed as a Modernist masterpiece. It was designed both inside and out by Aalto with his designer wife, Aino Mairiso-Aalto. They attended to every detail, from the special door handles, light fittings that didn't collect dust, built-in wardrobes and storage and, of course, the furniture. One chair in particular is iconic. Now known as the Paimio chair, it takes inspiration from the mid-1920s bent tubular steel work of Bauhaus designers including Marcel Breuer – archive pictures show that Breuer chairs took pride of place in the Aaltos' own home. The Paimio chair from 1932 was a groundbreaking design, not just for its innovative handling of bentwood and moulded plywood that achieved greater appeal than the cold metal tubing of the Bauhaus designers, but also because it was conceived to take account of tuberculosis patients' posture and was intended to help them breath easily.

Furniture designs formed an integral part of the Viipuri Library job, too, and famously produced the 1933–5 Model No. 69 chair and the 1933 Model No. 60 stool, both made using Finnish birch and incorporating Aalto's development of the bentwood

Paimio Chair

A period version of this classic armchair. The frame is constructed from bands of heat-formed laminated birch while the seat and back are made from a continuous strip of shaped plywood, here in a contrasting black. More recent versions have a series of decorative horizontal slits at the top of the backrest.

above

Model No. 100 Screen

An early screen from 1933–6, designed by Alvar Aalto.
This highly flexible, freestanding screen or room divider
is made from narrow strips of lacquered pine. The
narrowness of the pieces means the screen is very
flexible and can be wrapped around tight corners.

L-leg. The popularity of this furniture led the Aaltos to set up the manufacturing company Artek, which continues to this day. Throughout his career Aalto produced a vast catalogue of furniture designs, from the famous chairs and stools to lesser well-known items such as tables, trolleys, a desk, a bed and lighting. He also designed the iconic Savoy glass vase in 1936.

Aalto founded Artek in 1935 with art collector and promoter Maire Gullichsen (1907–90) and the art historian Nils-Gustav Hahl (1904–41). Maire gave her name to the much-admired Villa Mairea in Noormarkku, which was designed by Aalto for Maire and her husband, Harry, in the late 1930s. It has been compared in quality and innovation with the famous Fallingwater house by American architect Frank Lloyd Wright (1867–1959), which was completed at around the same time in the United States. These were enlightened clients: Harry Gullichsen was an industrialist and Maire had trained as a painter, they shared an interest in the avant-garde and wanted a house that was both Finnish and modern.

By the mid-1930s, and with growing fame, the Aaltos sought a more metropolitan life and moved from Turku to set up home and office in Helsinki. Here, Alvar Aalto designed his home

below
Experiments in plywood by Alvar Aalto. The material has fascinated designers for decades. Along with this chair and trolley is the well-known Model No. X601 stool. Produced in 1954 with an fan-leg design for Artex, it is made in birch.

and studio where he was based for the rest of his life and where Aino Aalto lived until her death in 1949. The place was restored around the turn of the millennium and is now open to visitors. For an architect with such a big reputation, it is surprisingly modest.

With the world economic recession of the 1930s work began to slow, but despite this Aalto continued to grow his reputation, not least with his show-stopping Finnish Pavilion at the 1937 Paris International Exposition, which even drew praise from Le Corbusier. The following year he completed interiors for the upmarket Savoy restaurant in Helsinki, which is still intact today, and in 1938 he was honoured with his own exhibition, entitled Alvar Aalto: Architecture and Furniture, at the Museum of Modern Art in New York. This delivered a whole new audience of American admirers, and by the mid-1940s he was working as a visiting professor in the United States and designing buildings for the Massachusetts Institute of Technology.

In 1952 Aalto married the architect Elissa Mäkiniemi (1922–94) and built a beautiful brick rural house for them in Muuratsalo. While his practice remained busy after the Second World War on such high-profile commissions as the Opera House in Essen, Germany, a college and library in Oregon, USA, the Finlandia Hall in Helsinki and dozens of churches, libraries, town halls and housing schemes, Aalto never quite regained the dazzling brilliance of his earlier work. In 1957 he was awarded the Gold Medal by the Royal Institute of British Architects, and he died in Helsinki in 1976. His legacy lives on today with countless young architects acknowledging his influence.

Swedish Modernism

The organic interpretation of Modernism was also being pursued in Sweden during the 1930s. As in Finland, wood was the dominant material in furniture design. Following the early modern architectural successes of Erik Gunnar Asplund, the designer next to emerge with his innovative and eye-catching furniture designs was Bruno Mathsson (1907–88). Where hard-edged, geometric Functionalism had flowered briefly in Sweden, Mathsson swiftly and confidently changed history's course with his soft and flowing lines. Once again, like Aalto, Mathsson was interested in how humans sat and rested in chairs and so his work focused on making ergonomic shapes for maximum comfort.

Among his most famous designs is the Eva chair of 1933, which illustrates his philosophy. It is a comfortable-looking chair with a sinuously curving frame made from solid birch and bent plywood with a deep seat that fit the contours of the body. The chair is finished in an upholstery of woven hemp webbing, the idea being that this would dispense with thick and bulky upholstery, instead replacing it with a lightweight and breathable material. As part of his development of this design, Mathsson also produced in 1944 the Pernilla chaise longue and the Pernilla lounge chair.

After producing this family of elegant chairs, Mathsson dedicated the 1940s and most of the 1950s to his career in architecture. However, in the late 1950s he took over the running of the manufacturer Firma Karl Mathsson, developing furniture with the designer Piet Hein (1905–96). He produced more of his own designs for the manufacturer Dux, which continues to have many pieces, including Pernilla, still in production.

above

Eva Chair

Bruno Mathsson's 1934 Eva chair saw great popularity and has remained an enduring icon of his career. A strong nod to the work of Alvar Aalto, it is a more refined version of his Grasshopper, and eventually evolved into a closely related series of webbed chairs, sofas and ottomans.

left

Superellipse Table

An elegant table in maple with steel-rod legs designed by Piet Hein and Bruno Mathsson. Often used in conference rooms, in more recent years this design has become a popular dining table.

Chieftain Chair

In luxurious teak and leather, this comfortable throne-like armchair was designed by Finn Juhl and made by Niels Vodder in 1949. The open style of structure is highly sculptural, and early models of each chair were exquisitely handcrafted. All vertical elements, including the legs, are made in an elegant tapering shape.

Danish Modernism

The thread of modern production that was started in Europe by Michael Thonet with his bentwood café chairs of the mid- and late nineteenth century, was picked up and carried forward in Denmark after the First World War. The Danish manufacturer Fritz Hansen experimented with its own bentwood furniture, and in 1930 put into production one of the first modern Danish designs, the DAN chair by Søren Hansen (1905–77); Hansen was a descendant of the company's founder. This chair is simpler and more refined than its Thonet predecessor, the key to this dazzling piece of bravado being the single length of bentwood that forms the deeply curved backrest and two rear legs. It is not just a highly expressive piece of design, but also a technical masterpiece and goes down as one of the first markers in the story of Danish Modernism.

While many producers continued with their experiments, Denmark's greatest contributions to early Modern design appeared more than a decade later. Despite the country being occupied by German forces, Denmark's brilliant young designers were hard at work developing their own distinctive brand of organic Modernism. Two of the outstanding exponents from the 1940s were Finn Juhl (1912–89) and Hans J Wegner (1914–2007). While a Modernist in spirit, Juhl had a passion for fine craftswork and collaborated closely with cabinetmaker Niels Vodder (1918). Together they produced limited ranges of designs, often in fruit woods and exotic hardwoods, especially teak, that were highly original, sculptural and clearly of the modern age. Juhl's own favourite chair was the NV44, from 1944. Made in rosewood, its curved back continues its embrace in the armrests, which then drop to form the front legs. It is clearly a fine piece of craftsmanship. These were not the stuff of factory mass production, but were instead handcrafted in small batches – some designs barely made it into double figures. The chair known as NV44, for example, was originally produced in a batch of just 12. The small numbers of these originals make them very collectable; however, it is worth noting that the designs were later adapted for mass factory production by the American firm Baker Furniture and so occur in more profusion. Among Juhl's other works from this American producer is the highly expressive two-tone upholstered sofa with its wraparound backrest.

Juhl's most famous design, however, came from the postwar years and is the Chieftain chair from 1949. Again made in rosewood, this intriguing design can be interpreted as an assemblage of spears and shields and is said to have been inspired by the shields of African

Lounge Chair

This sculptural and intriguing bent and folded plywood chair from 1963 is by Grete Jalk. The design is produced from just two elements: the base and seat is bolted to the back, close to the floor at the rear.

tribesmen. It is a low-slung lounge chair with a dark wood frame, round, tapering legs, and a seat, back and armrests in sculpted leather – most of the original edition of these chairs were destined for Danish embassies around the world and are highly collectable. Later in his career, Juhl worked in upholstered furniture. Among the most distinctive is the Pelican chair of 1940; with its great swooping 'wings' that wrap protectively round the sitter's body it must have been quite startling to behold in the 1940s. Many of his designs are made today by Hansen Sørensen.

A contemporary of Juhl and fellow countryman was cabinetmaker and architect Hans J Wegner. He shared Juhl's passion for high-quality craftsmanship and often looked to traditional designs for his inspiration. His most iconic design is the Peacock armchair of 1947. With its great hooped, slatted and splayed back resembling the peacock's open fan of tail feathers, this chair is actually Wegner's interpretation of the famous English Windsor chair, and while it looks handcrafted it was in fact designed specifically for factory production. Wegner's other great design classics are the Round chair, also called Model 501, from 1949, and the Y chair or Wishbone chair from 1950. The Round chair found favour with overseas buyers and was particularly popular in the United States, while the Y chair is still a perennial favourite with design aficionados and has featured in hundreds of magazine features as the epitome of Scandinavian Modernism.

The Scandinavian Phenomenon

The popularity of the new Scandinavian style in furniture and homewares reached its peak in the middle of the twentieth century. In 1949 *Time* magazine featured a cover image of a chair by Danish designer Hans Wegner, flagging its main story about the 'Scandinavian design phenomenon'. In 1951 the fashionable Heal's department store in London hosted an exhibition called Scandinavian Design for Living, which partnered the British Council of Design show, Scandinavia at Table, in the same year. Designs from Denmark, Sweden and Finland drew huge crowds and a clutch of awards at the high-profile Milan Triennale exhibitions of 1951 and 1954, where people clamoured to see the latest interiors filled with light and elegant furniture; multifunctional design; stacking, space-saving and flat-pack ideas; innovative glass objects, ceramics, textiles and more besides. Between 1954 and 1957, a touring exhibition called Design in Scandinavia made its way around the major cities of America and Canada, and in 1957 the Dane Jørn Utzon (1918–) won one of the most high-profile architecture competitions of his generation: to build Sydney Opera House in Australia.

right

Wishbone Chair

Sculptural and classic, Model No. CH24 Y-Stolen by Hans Wegner, from 1950, has been a firm favourite for more than half a century. The name derives from the wishbone-shaped strut at the back. With its woven seat, the frame is now made in a range of woods from light maple and ash to dark walnut.

above

Wing Chair

In a move away from his chairs in wood, Wegner produced a handful of upholstered armchair designs around 1960. This timeless, high-backed armchair, Model No. 445, sits on a tubular steel base. It has recently been reissued.

right

Ox Chair

Wide and welcoming, this armchair, also known as Model No. EJ100 Pollestolen, has a high back and headrest. It was designed by Wegner in 1960. Sitting on a low base of tubular steel, it is extremely comfortable and made in a choice of fabric or leather upholstery. There is a matching footstool, too.

Hans Wegner (1914–2007)

Widely admired by the design community for his originality, and ever-popular with the public because of his accessible designs, Hans Jørgen Wegner was a towering figure in twentieth-century Danish design. He was an innovative and prolific furniture designer with more than 500 pieces to his name. Many have been continuously in production, while a new surge of interest in his work in the late 1990s led to others being re-released. His great skill was in fusing modern design and organic sculptural forms with outstanding craftsmanship. Above all, he made modern design tactile and comfortable. The work, often in beautiful hardwoods including cherry, walnut and oak, epitomized the mid-century Danish style, which captured international attention. His most famous pieces include the 1947 Peacock chair, a modern reinterpretation of the traditional English Windsor chair, and the 1949 Y-Stolen or Wishbone chair, which has become a true modern classic.

Born in Tønder, in southern Jutland, the son of a shoemaker, the young Hans Wegner was apprenticed to a master cabinetmaker. After a brief spell of military service, he returned to his education at Copenhagen's School of Arts and Crafts in 1936, where he trained as an architect. After graduating, he put his combined skills to the test by working in a couple of design practices before joining the office of architects Arne Jacobsen and Erik Møller (1909–2002) in 1940. He designed furniture for several of Jacobsen's projects, including the Aarhus Town Hall (1937–42). Although the style of the moment was for the bent tubular steel and the functionalist lines of the Bauhaus, Wegner was drawn to working with wood and reinterpreting Denmark's crafts heritage, and he often spoke about his desire to make wood 'come alive'. His fascination for purity and distilling designs to their essence was finding favour and so, too, was his interest in the sculptural potential of furniture.

Throughout the 1940s, working from a studio at home, he designed modern and affordable chairs intended for small postwar apartments and began a long association with the small craft-based manufacturer Johannes Hansen. In 1947 he produced his stunning Peacock chair, whose design was clearly rooted in the great Windsor chair. This fresh reinvention, with its splayed back and woven cord seat, has the appearance of being handcrafted, but was in fact designed for mass production. It is made today by the Danish firm PP Møbler, which makes most of Wegner's designs. His next great piece was the now-famous 1949 Round chair, also known just as the Chair. This model, which he was to revisit and reinterpret many

above

Hans Wegner with a model of one of his wooden chairs, the 1978 PP112, many of which took their inspiration from traditional pieces of furniture. He worked with Erik Møller and Arne Jacobsen on the Arhus Town Hall and ran his own design studio in Arhus in the 1940s; by the 1950s he was a leading exponent of Scandinavian design.

right

Flag Halyard Chair

One of Wegner's most unusual and captivating designs, this laid-back chair design from 1950, Model No. PP225 Flaglinestolen, is constructed with a tubular steel frame on which is woven a rope seat and back. There is a separate headrest pillow, and draped over the whole is a fluffy sheepskin.

left

Rocking Chair

A late work by Hans Wegner, this 1984 rocking chair (PP124) has a distinctly Shaker feel. It is made from solid ash with a backrest of woven rope. One cushion is for the seat; another acts as a headrest.

below

Teddy Bear Chair

Playful and organic, this PP19 chair from 1951 got its name after a critic referred to its armrests as 'great bear paws embracing you from behind'. In recent years, the Teddy Bear chair has been one of the most popular of all Wegner designs. A matching footrest, PP120, was also designed by Wegner in 1954.

times, was featured on the front cover of *Interiors* magazine in America in 1950, with the caption 'The World's Most Beautiful Chair'. This helped to catapult Wegner to international fame and ensured a spotlight on Danish – and more generally, Scandinavian – design for the following decade. In the same year came his equally iconic Wishbone chair. Produced by Carl Hansen, it is distinguished by its turned and tapering legs, a gracefully curved backrest and the forked vertical back support, which resembles a chicken's wishbone.

Among his most novel pieces is the 1950 Flag Halyard chair, a highly original piece of design in the form of a laid-back armchair with a metal frame, woven rope seating and a backrest finished with an animal skin as upholstery. Then there was the Valet chair of 1953, made in carved wood. Its unusual and playful shape, with sloping 'shoulders', strange horizontal struts at the back of the seat and under-seat storage, is designed for hanging and storing every piece of a man's suit of clothing. Then in 1960 came the extremely comfortable Ox chair. Moving away from wood, this armchair sits on bent tubular steel legs and has a deep-upholstered chair shell with distinctive 'horns' as the headrest.

During the last two decades of his life, Wegner worked in partnership with his daughter, Marianne (1947–). In recent years, his designs have found a new and enthusiastic audience, and there has been a surge of interest in collecting both original and new pieces. His work forms part of a prominent new display of Scandinavian design at the refurbished Museum of Modern Art in New York (reopened in 2004) where his chairs are not only on display, but they are also used in the museum's restaurants.

below

Egg Chair

Fabulously rounded and enveloping, the Egg's shell of a body sits on a neat stem and cross-shaped base. The shape was derived from a plaster sculpture created by Jacobsen in his garage. Today it is made with a leather cover or fabric and available in a spectrum of colours.

right

The Egg, or Model No. 3316, was designed by Arne Jacobsen in 1958 for the lobby and reception areas of the Royal Hotel in Copenhagen shown here. The hotel was built between 1956 and 1961.

The Fabulous Fifties

As Scandinavian design was enjoying global attention throughout the 1950s, the design scene on home turf was dominated by the Danish designer Arne Jacobsen. He began his career as a strict Modernist architect and was responsible for projects including the 1930s white-liner-style Bellavista apartment building and Bellevue theatre and restaurant complex at the seaside suburb of Klampenborg outside Copenhagen. With its sharp lines and crisp profiles, this was very much in the International Style of Le Corbusier. However, after the Second World War it was clear that Jacobsen had changed direction; using softer lines and curves he was on a different and more human-centred course.

Among Jacobsen's great furniture-design triumphs of the early 1950s are the Ant chair of 1952 and the Series 7 chair from 1955. Both are still in continuous production and are manufactured by Fritz Hansen. The Ant has a huge personality, with a simple rounded seat that flips up and continues to form the backrest, a nipped-in waist and an elliptical back – almost like a head on a body. Here Jacobsen continues that great Modernist obsession with the possibilities of plywood, with his Ant chair taking its place in this particular hall of fame. Following experiments by other designers, notably Charles and Ray Eames (1907–78 and 1912–88), Jacobsen treated the plywood seat separately from the legs. Initially this design was

conceived with three tubular steel legs, but later models were given four for greater stability. The mass production of these designs now runs into many millions.

Again the plywood seat of Jacobsen's Series 7 chair sits on legs made separately, but the design is more restrained than the Ant. The chair is a perfect fusion of the Scandinavian Modernist ideal, with its slender, tubular steel legs and the timber softness of the curvy, enveloping, all-in-one moulded plywood seat and backrest. The Series 7 chair achieved fame, and even notoriety, when a copy of the design was used in a photograph of the British model Christine Keeler, who had caused a scandal in her affair with British Conservative politician and Secretary of State for War, John Profumo. The photographer was Australian Lewis Morley, who created a humorous version of the shot much later with Dame Edna Everidge, played by the comedian Barry Humphreys, in the hot seat.

Following these experiments with moulded plywood, Jacobsen was quick to respond to the possibilities of new materials and manufacturing techniques, and by the end of the decade he was working on his iconic upholstered chairs. Called the Egg and Swan, these chairs appeared right at the end of the 1950s and formed part of his design work for the SAS Royal Hotel in Copenhagen. Not only did he design the handsome multistorey tower, still one of the city's tallest landmarks, but he also completed the interior design, including these exceptionally voluptuous and beautiful chairs.

As its name suggests, the Egg, from 1958, is a round shell shape, an all-in-one piece rising seamlessly from a bowl at the seat to the curved armrests and then the rounded back with its 'wings' at the top. It is reminiscent of the classic English wing chair, but reborn as a piece of sculpture. The seat's shell is made in moulded fibreglass, then padded with upholstery and covered in fabric or leather with a cushion for the seat. The whole unit sits on a short stem that terminates in a four-point, cast-aluminium base.

The Swan, from 1956, also follows this sculptural style. It is a smaller chair with a wide and deep seat from which the two arm elements rise like wings either side of the backrest. Again, the basic shell is made from moulded fibreglass that has been given foam upholstery and then a leather or fabric cover. This chair first appeared in the SAS Royal Hotel's lobby and is still manufactured by Fritz Hansen in its original chair format and extended as a sofa.

While Jacobsen was truly a creative force to be reckoned with, he didn't have the 1950s all to himself. Fellow Dane Poul Kjaerholm (1929–80) was producing very different but equally eye-catching work. An architect and carpenter, one of the hallmarks of Kjaerholm's work is its structural innovation. Among his earliest pieces, for example, is the PK25 chair from 1952, which has a slender, almost spindly, steel frame with a seat and backrest made from rope. The following year came his utterly different, but equally intriguing PKO chair: a sculptural three-legged model constructed from two sections of moulded plywood, one of which forms the front leg and backrest, the other forms the seat and two back legs. This daring design did not enter production, however, until the late 1990s and, after a decade, is now out of production once again.

Kjaerholm bucked the trend set by so many Scandinavians, as his work has a much greater emphasis on using metal than wood. His most famous design is the PK22 from 1956: a low-set side chair without arms, this has a chromed flat steel frame and legs with all-in-one leather seat and backrest. While it looks utterly different from Mies van der Rohe's Barcelona chair, it is reminiscent of its elegance and presence.

below
Elegant built-in furniture by Danish designer Børge
Mogensen (1914–72). These day bed and table designs
were first shown at the Nordiska Kompaniet exhibition
in 1959. Although very simple in style, there is great
complexity in the clever use of contrasting woods.
Mogensen trained under Kaare Klint and was known
for his reinterpretations of traditional forms.

Arne Jacobsen (1902–71)

Denmark's most outstanding architect of the twentieth century, Arne Jacobsen, completed such landmark buildings as the SAS Royal Hotel (1956–61) and National Bank in Copenhagen (1966–78), an entire seaside quarter called Bellevue at Klampenborg (1932–5), dozens of groundbreaking schools, town halls, one-off houses and housing schemes and, in the United Kingdom, St Catherine's College, Oxford (1960–3). He was also fascinated by product design and was responsible for some of the world's bestselling modern chairs, along with textiles, wallpapers, innovative lighting, tableware, cutlery, taps (faucets) and even door handles.

Born in Copenhagen in 1902, Jacobsen's first taste of the building trade was as an apprentice bricklayer, and his love of materials, particularly brick, remained constant throughout his career. He studied architecture at the Academy of Arts in Copenhagen and, as a student, traveled around Europe to see the work of the emerging Modernists, including Le Corbusier, Walter Gropius and Ludwig Mies van der Rohe. He attended the landmark Paris Exposition Internationale des Arts Décoratifs in 1925 and won a prize for a chair design; here, too, he also admired Le Corbusier's Pavilion de l'Espirit

left

Complete with his trademark pipe and bow-tie, Arne Jacobsen is shown alongside an image of the fantastic sculptural, six-storey-high glass and steel stairway of his National Bank in Copenhagen, completed in 1971.

right

Ant Chair

In its original guise with just three legs, Model No. 3100 Myren was revolutionary for its time, formed from a moulded plywood shell on tubular steel legs. A four-legged version, Model No. 3101, was added in 1980 after Jacobsen's death.

opposite

The famous Room 606 at Copenhagen's SAS Royal Hotel has been preserved with the original 1960s décor. Although the hotel was refurbished around 2000, this suite was left intact and is available for Jacobsen fans wishing to stay there. Furniture includes the Egg and Swan chairs, along with the less well-known Drop chairs and the 3300 sofa.

Nouveau. Back in Copenhagen, he set up his practice in 1930, where he worked for the rest of his life, apart from a brief spell in the mid-1940s when, as a Jew, he was exiled to Sweden during the Nazi occupation of Denmark.

During the early part of his career, the rational straight lines, geometric blocks, flat roofs and white walls of the International Style were his stock-in-trade. His large 1930s Bellevue seaside development, just north of Copenhagen, exemplified this with its white liner-style blocks of apartments and a Modernist theatre, restaurant, petrol station and even beach changing huts. However, it wasn't long before the lines softened to become curvy, voluptuous shapes and his palette of materials changed from smooth, white plaster to brick, ceramic and timber. Along with fellow Modernists in the Scandinavian countries, Jacobsen was pioneering a softer, more organic type of design.

Jacobsen's most prolific period was after the Second World War. His housing schemes won international attention; the homes were modern and simple, but also very appealing, with sloping roofs, chimneys and a generous use of brick. Jacobsen moved into one of his modest houses, built around 1950 at Søholm, just north of Copenhagen, and stayed there until his death in 1971.

The early 1950s also saw him experiment with furniture design. He knew the work of the Americans Charles and Ray Eames, and produced his own intriguing moulded plywood designs, which have since sold in their millions. The first of these, produced in 1952, was the Ant, or Myren. The moulded plywood seat was separate from the slender, tubular steel leg structure – it was lightweight and designed for stacking. Along with his technical skills, Jacobsen's genius was in giving his designs great personality, seen in the Ant with its nipped-in waist and generous rounded backrest. Designed for the Danish furniture maker Fritz Hansen, the first production of Ant chairs, made with three legs, was used in the canteen of the healthcare company Novo. A four-legged version was put into production after Jacobsen's death.

Following the Ant, Jacobsen worked on a range of shaped plywood chairs, creating the other great classic design, the Series 7, in 1955. Once again the seat and back were all in one piece, supported on four slender, tubular steel legs. However, this time the body of the chair was more classic in shape, the nipped-in waist swelling into a curved and fan-shaped backrest. Over the years, this design has sold in millions and is available in numerous versions: with or without armrests; as an office chair on a stem base; and with or without upholstery. It is also available in around 20 colours.

From 1956–61 Jacobsen worked on one of his largest commissions: the SAS Royal Hotel in Copenhagen, a soaring, 22-storey tower on a rectangular base. It remains one of the city's landmark buildings to this day, and was, for Jacobsen, an opportunity to work on a major project down to every last detail. The two most famous chair designs to come from this project are the sculptural and organic Egg and the Swan, both 1958. Jacobsen unleashed his love of sculpture and carved the prototypes for these generous and embracing shapes from lumps of plaster, shaving away a millimetre here and there to achieve the perfect curves. The Egg, with its embracing head- and armrests, was intended to be used in a group, where the high back would help to enclose the space when the chair was in a large room like the hotel lobby, whereas the Swan, with its more open structure, is ideal for smaller rooms like a bar. Originally moulded in styropore, today the shell is made in polyurethane, padded in foam and then covered in fabric or leather.

Other great designs from this project include abstract-patterned textiles, wineglasses, ashtrays, candlesticks, salt and pepper shakers, pendant and floor lamps and the famous door handle, which is made from cast metal and fits perfectly into the palm of the hand. Another great design of note is the stainless-steel AJ cutlery from 1957, which is still made today by Georg Jensen. Even a decade later it was considered so futuristic that it made its screen debut in Stanley Kubrick's futuristic film, *2001: A Space Odyssey* (1968).

The scale of this work was only matched by one of Jacobsen's last commissions, St Catherine's College in Oxford, England. In its sensitive historic setting, the elegant, modern brick building keeps a modest profile. Again Jacobsen reveled in detail; the chair designs to come from here are known as the Oxford series. From 1965, they are a collection of understated office chairs with a choice of either high or low backs, arms or no arms, finished in black leather upholstery.

Jacobsen continued experimenting with materials and production methods right up to the end of his career. His final years are marked by the beautiful stainless-steel Cylinda-Line tableware from 1967, a family of jugs, coffeepots, teapots, and containers, and the much-imitated, minimalist Vola series of taps (faucets) and shower fittings from 1969.

above

The bar at the Bellevue Restaurant in Klampenborg, designed by Arne Jacobsen in the 1930s as part of a vast scheme for this seaside town, and complete with theatre, seaside apartments and beach huts. Refurbished in the early 2000s, the restaurant was renamed the Jacobsen.

opposite

Egg Chair

The 1958 Egg chair, in soft white upholstery fabric, is a perennial favourite as a sculptural object in corporate settings, such as this wonderful lobby. It looks equally good in a small-scale domestic setting.

The Complete Home

While this period of Scandinavian Modernism is populated with furniture designs of outstanding originality and beauty, the decades between the 1930s and the start of the 1960s are also filled with other exquisite designs for the home. From the 1930s, the Finn Aino Aalto (1894–1949) not only worked alongside her husband, but also created her own designs. Still in production by Iittala are her ridged glassware, now called 'Aalto'. Also by the same company is Alvar Aalto's world-famous Savoy vase. Meanwhile, from Sweden came the classic Aga cooker in the late 1920s, invented by Gustaf Dalén (1869–1937), and in Norway Jacob Jacobsen (1901–96) produced the desk lamp Luxo-L1 in 1937.

In the 1940s came the innovative and interchangeable Kilta tableware by Finn Kaj Franck (1911–89) for Arabia. He designed a range of bowls, dishes and plates in geometric shapes that were available in a range of mix-and-match colours. Made from heat-resistant earthenware, they could be used in the oven or as tableware – a radical idea for the time. In the same decade Finn Gunnel Nyman (1909–48) produced some of her most beautiful glassware, as did fellow Finn Tapio Wirkkala (1915–85) and the highly collectable Swedish designer Sven Palmqvist (1906–84).

In the 1950s, Poul Henningsen (1894–1967) produced a series of classic lamps for the Danish manufacturer Louis Poulsen. His most memorable design is the PH Artichoke of 1958, made from layers of 72 metal 'leaves' that filter the light. Arne Jacobsen produced designs for Poulsen, too, including AJ floor and desk lamps and the AJ Pendant, both from 1957. Also in the same year came Jacobsen's famous AJ stainless-steel cutlery, which made a starring appearance in Stanley Kubrik's futuristic film, *2001: A Space Odyssey* (1968). Another great lamp producer of this time was Le Klint, also of Denmark, established by Peder Vilhelm Jensen-Klint (1853–1913). The company's trademark was its decorative folded, pleated and die-cut paper lanterns, which included, in the 1950s, designs by Esben Klint (1915–69). Many are still in production by the company.

By the end of the 1950s, Scandinavian modern design was known throughout the western world. The furniture and furnishings had been featured in magazines and advertising. Hans Wegner's Round chair even got top billing on the now legendary CBS televised debate in 1960 between Richard Nixon and John F Kennedy – the TV company had ordered a dozen of the chairs to dress its studio set. In that same year Jackie Kennedy bought seven colourful outfits made by the Finnish textile company Marimekko while on holiday in Cape Cod. The company was riding the crest of a wave with its bold and colourful designs by the likes of Maija Isola (1927–2001) and Vuokko Eskolin-Nurmesniemi (1930–). Other companies producing beautiful textiles included Svenskt Tenn in Sweden, with fabulous colourful, detailed, nature-inspired designs by Josef Franck (1885–1967). It was official: Scandinavian design was cool and highly desirable, but this was also the peak of its popularity. While designers have continued in the decades since to produce their appealing and high-quality furniture and furnishings, the work was about to be upstaged by an explosion of irreverence, energy and colour.

above

A Savoy vase, designed by Alvar Aalto in 1936. Its wobbly sides are thought to be evocative of the undulating coastline of Finland's lakes. The piece is blown by craftsworkers into the mould (an example shown here), from which it takes its shape.

opposite

In this unusual setting of a converted water tower, the circular room is furnished with 1949 PP503 Round chairs by Hans Wegner. The circular table was designed by Marianne Wegner, who worked with her father and now runs the Wegner Design Studio. Based in Wegner's home town of Tonder, the tower contains a permanent exhibition of his furniture.

left

With direct inspiration from nature, this leaf-shaped wood platter, designed in 1951 by Tapio Wirkkala, is made from laminated birch.

◀ Spokeback Sofa, 1945
Børge Mogensen subtly incorporated new ideas into his revisitation of traditional forms. This sofa featured leather ties that allowed the sides to be dropped.

Key icons of

the

Scandinavians

▼ Peacock Armchair, 1947
A natural ash hooped chair; radiating flattened spindles that resemble a peacock's feathers give the chair its name. One of Hans Wegner's most iconic pieces, it was designed for Johannes Hansen.

▲ Model No. 98 Tea Trolley, 1935-6
Manufactured by Artek, Alvar Aalto's famous Model No. 98 tea trolley features his innovative side frames, made of moulded, laminated birch, and the disc wheels. Several versions were made.

◀ **Series 7 Chair, 1955**
By Arne Jacobsen for Fritz Hansen, the Series 7 is also known as Model No. 3107. A sleek variation of Jacobsen's Ant chair, it became notorious in the 1960s, when a portrait of the British model Christine Keeler posing naked on a copy of the chair was widely published during the UK government's Profumo scandal.

▼ **Model No. PK22 Chair, 1955**
Discrete, elegant and portable, the PK22 was designed by Poul Kjaerholm and stands as an icon for his work. Steel-framed, it was designed so that the seat could be made from leather or cane. It was made by Fritz Hansen.

▲ **Swan Chair, 1957**
Made for Fritz Hansen and designed for the lobby and lounge areas of the SAS Royal Hotel in Copenhagen, the Swan showed Arne Jacobsen's love of organic forms. The supports are cast aluminium with red upholstery.

Mid-Century Modernism

The postwar landscape from 1939 to 1959

It took mainland Europe many years to recover from the devastating effects of the Second World War. Cities were in ruins, economies were destroyed, and ordinary people had somehow to try to piece their lives back together. In this climate of trauma and austerity, furniture production was at a low ebb. The war had effectively killed off many furniture producers, and for those that were left there was great hardship. They faced skills shortages, a scarcity of materials, the need to invest in and re-equip their factories and a flat consumer market where buyers had little money to spare on such luxuries as new furniture. With Europe suffering the brunt of the postwar privations, the focus of innovation and excitement in modern furniture design moved across the Atlantic to the United States. Although the country was still emerging from its cataclysmic Depression of the 1930s, it had been spared the worst effects of war and now there was the potential to make use of the new materials and technologies produced during the conflict. There was a spirit of optimism in the air – the United States had played its part in defeating the enemy, national pride was in the ascendant, and the design and architecture schools were bursting with the necessary energy and innovation to satisfy the pent-up consumer demand.

overleaf
In a welcoming canteen, PAC-1 upholstered plastic-shell chairs sit on stem bases, with laminate-top dining tables from 1958, by Charles and Ray Eames for Herman Miller. The moulded plastic shell armchairs were first designed in 1948, using moulding processes developed during the Second World War; they were the first chairs to be mass produced.

above
Complete with a wall of fitted wooden cupboards with sliding and fold-down doors, this living room is furnished by George Nelson. The unit conceals a built-in radio and bar. Furnishings include a Nelson-designed wood-frame armchair and his club chair in mustard-yellow upholstery.

left

Butterfly Chair
Also known as the BFK chair and the Hardoy, and designed by Antonio Bonet, Jorge Ferrari Hardoy and Juan Kurchan in 1938, this chair has a leather seat slung on a metal frame. Knoll acquired US production rights in 1947 and brought the design to an international audience.

Modernist Family Tree

While this newfound American vigour was refreshing and inspiring, it did not happen in isolation from the rest of the world. As a consequence of the rise of Adolph Hitler and the war, the family line of the Modernist movement had shifted continents, but remained unbroken as it crossed the Atlantic to take root in the US.

Even before the outbreak of the Second World War in 1939, many of the high-profile designers from the Bauhaus had made good their escape from the Nazis. They were potential victims of persecution, not just because several were Jewish, but also because the Nazis feared intellectuals and socialists and branded them as degenerate and 'un-German'. Some, like Walter Gropius and Marcel Breuer, stopped over in the Britain for a couple of years; others went directly to the United States. By the 1940s, their presence in the American colleges and design schools was substantial.

In 1933 Joseph Albers (1888–1976) and his wife, the weaver Anni Albers (1899–1994), moved to North Carolina. Joseph and Anni had been students at the Bauhaus, and from 1923 Joseph taught furniture design and drawing there. After leaving Germany and arriving in the US, Anni taught weaving and practised as an artist while Joseph began his long American teaching career at Black Mountain College, and later at Yale's Department of Design. The Hungarian Laszlo Moholy-Nagy left the Bauhaus and headed for the Midwest, via London, where he established the New Bauhaus in Chicago. This went on to become the greatly respected Institute of Design, where Moholy-Nagy remained director until his death in 1946. Meanwhile, from 1937 Walter Gropius became a professor of architecture and chairman of the Department of Architecture at Harvard in Cambridge, Massachusetts; his protégé, Marcel Breuer, joined him there as associate professor of architecture. Ludwig Mies van der Rohe also immigrated to the United States in 1938, and headed for the Midwest and Chicago, where he took up the post of head of the architecture school at Chicago's Armour Institute of Technology (later renamed the Illinois Institute of Technology). At the same time, despite being aged over 50, he set to work rebuilding his architectural career and went on to produce some of America's most iconic early Modernist buildings, from the modest but hugely influential Farnsworth House in Plano, Illinois (1951), to the high-rise Seagram Building (1958) in New York. However, while the influence of these Europeans was considerable, particularly in the realm of Modern architecture, their energy was not focused on producing groundbreaking pieces of furniture design.

Scandinavians at Large

Among the most intriguing furniture pieces in the early part of this mid-century era were designs by Scandinavians who were living in the United States. Again, the threads of Modernism continued to be woven together, and following the great 1939 New York World's Fair, where the crowds went wild for Alvar Aalto's Finnish Pavilion, the Americans started to develop a taste for all things Scandinavian.

Arriving like a blast of fresh North Sea air, the Side chair, from 1941–2 by Danish-born Jens Risom (1919–), was the first chair to be produced by the New York-based German émigré Hans G Knoll (1914–55). Risom immigrated to the US in 1939 and, after meeting Knoll, the pair travelled across the country to investigate the new design scene that was gradually emerging. They became convinced that the upcoming generation of homeowners was ready for modern furniture designs, and so they set to work producing them. When Knoll issued his first catalogue in 1942, more than half of the 25 items in production were Risom's designs and included armchairs, stools and lounge chairs. Initially, because of wartime restrictions, the furniture was made from cedar wood with cotton webbing material, but gradually, as restrictions were lifted, other materials began to be used.

Today the Side chair is made of maple and continues to be manufactured by Knoll. It is a timeless classic; its spare and elegant frame features tapered legs and an angled backrest. The unusual upholstery is woven webbing that had made an appearance the decade earlier in the furniture of the Swedish designer Bruno Mathsson. The chair was conceived for mass production, made from a simple kit of parts, and had inexpensive and lightweight upholstery. It was perfectly suited to the new age.

Home-Grown American Talent

Leading up to the mid-century years, the American public had been introduced to modern designs in many aspects of everyday life. Cars, trains, clocks, vacuum cleaners, refrigerators and even aeroplanes all came from the drawing boards of such legendary designers as Raymond Loewy (1893–1986), Henry Dreyfuss (1904–72) and Norman Bel Geddes (1893–1958). While they were busy reshaping their industrial products, all of which were distinguished by their long, low shapes and sleek streamlining and laced with a hint of speed, they left furniture design mostly to architects.

It wasn't long before two of America's greatest multitalented designers, the husband-and-wife team Charles and Ray Eames, made their debut on the scene. In the late 1930s, Charles Eames entered Cranbrook Academy of Art in Detroit, Michigan. Here, not only did he meet fellow student and his future wife Ray Kaiser, but he also became closely associated with the Finnish-born architect Eliel Saarinen (1873–1950). Saarinen, a teacher and later president of Cranbrook, had come to the United States in 1923 after winning second place in the major competition to design the Tribune Tower in Chicago. By the late 1930s he had set up a practice with his architect son Eero Saarinen (1910–61). Following his studies, Charles worked for a while with the father-and-son team, where he soon became firm friends with Eero and was seduced by the potential of Modernist design.

Charles Eames first attracted public attention in 1940 with the furniture he designed with Eero Saarinen that won the Organic Design in Home Furnishings competition organized by the Museum of Modern Art in New York. Ray Kaiser worked on the presentation drawings for the graphic display panels. Around this time manufacturers and museums staged many of these competitions, and government encouraged them. The idea was to stimulate the American design scene, reinvigorate industry and demonstrate to the public that good design could improve living standards.

Among the main furniture pieces from the Eames and Saarinen team were three chairs. They were all in organic sculptural shapes, had moulded plywood seats finished with upholstery, and all of them were conceived for informal sitting – they were called Relaxation, Conversation and Lounging. The submission for the competition also included intriguing storage and display cabinets that combined drawers, doors and open shelving in the same unit; there were also several tables and a small home desk. So fresh and outstanding were these designs that they succeeded in marking a new era in the very concept of how furniture could be. Eames and Saarinen took the two top prizes, one for seating and the other for storage design.

These chairs opened a new chapter in furniture-design history for three main reasons. Firstly, they acknowledged the increasing informality of modern life and provided more relaxed ways of sitting. Secondly, the designs took the use of plywood into a new realm and beyond the success of Alvar Aalto by moulding and shaping it into complex, multidimensional forms to best support the body. Many designers at this time were experimenting with plywood because solid timber and countless other materials

were in short supply as a result of the war. However, among all of those working with this pliable material, Ray Eames is credited with making greatest advances in the use of plywood for modern furniture. She developed and honed her skills in shaping and forming the material while producing a series of elegant undulating and abstract plywood sculptures. Thirdly, the chairs by Charles Eames and Saarinen featured a new type of construction, actually a deconstruction, by creating the seat as a single-form shell and producing it separately and quite independently from the legs and supporting structure. While this exhibition furniture was not put into mass production, it formed the inspirational prototypes for countless interesting designs that were to follow.

left

Lounge Chair

The Model No. 670 lounge chair, a luxurious moulded plywood and leather easy chair from 1956, was the culmination of the Eames' efforts to create comfortable and handsome lounge seating using production techniques that combined technology with handcraftsmanship.

left

Storage Unit

Designed by Charles and Ray Eames in 1950, the ESU 400 unit is based on a modular system of cases, cabinets and drawers in neutrals or bright colours. The design is strong and durable with uprights, cross-supports and perforated panels in zinc-coated steel; cabinet fronts in dimpled plywood; drawer fronts and shelves in moulded plywood and case side and back panels in painted hardboard.

below

Soft Pad Lounge Chair

Part of the Aluminum Group of furniture by Charles and Ray Eames, the Soft Pad is deeply luxurious and equally popular in a commercial or domestic setting. These chairs were originally developed by Ray Eames for a private residence being designed by Eero Saarinen and Alexander Girard in 1958. At the time the furniture was called the 'leisure group' (or 'indoor-outdoor group') since it was intended to address the lack of high-quality outdoor furniture on the market.

Sculpture for Suburbia

For aficionados of modern furniture, Charles and Ray Eames dominated the American design scene during the 1940s. In 1946, the Museum of Modern Art in New York staged an exhibition entitled New Furniture Designed by Charles Eames. The work in plywood had evolved considerably and had been refined to create an entire collection of exceptionally beautiful chairs, tables and a curvy plywood screen. This has come to be known as the Plywood Group from 1945–6. The show's title is misleading, however; according to interviews with many of their contemporaries, the designs were entirely a joint effort, with Charles and Ray Eames working side by side. In fact, with Ray's passion for abstract art and her many experiments with plywood, many believe that she was actually more concerned than Charles with the sculptural qualities of these designs.

The plywood pieces suited the age so well. They arrived at a time when young people were living in modern suburban homes; with limited space for furniture, the slim and elegant designs were ideal. It was also important that, in the free-flowing and open-plan spaces, all the furniture, especially the chairs, looked good from all angles.

And when it was time for families to move house that the furniture was lightweight and easy to pack and transport.

The basic form of these new Eames-designed plywood chairs was the same for the whole collection – an assemblage of abstract shapes. Among the best known are the LCM (Lounge Chair Metal – plywood seat and back on tubular steel frame) and DCW (Dining Chair Wood – plywood seat and back on moulded wood frame). The chairs were made up of a small curved rectangle of plywood for the backrest and a separate, and larger, sculptural piece of plywood for the seat. The all-in-one-legs-and-frame was made in a number of options: bent and curved plywood or shiny tubular steel. Some were made for sitting high and some for sitting low, and where the plywood meets the steel there are rubber discs that give the furniture an element of springiness. These are complex designs that are only made possible as a result of considerable technological research and experimentation, and at the same time are perfectly suited to mass production on assembly lines. At first the Plywood Group was made by the Eameses' own Evans Production Company, but later manufacture was transferred to Herman Miller. They continue to be made by Herman Miller in the US, while Vitra makes the range for Europe.

above

Sofa Compact

The sofa's striking profile and crisp, light scale evolved from a built-in sofa that was designed by Charles and Ray Eames for the living room of their Pacific Palisades home. The 1954 design provides all the comfort associated with traditional sofas and also fits well in smaller spaces.

Charles (1907–78) and Ray (1912–88) Eames

The undisputed heroes of twentieth-century American design, Charles and Ray Eames have acquired legendary status for their vast portfolio of work that shaped the look of the postwar era. They experienced the defining events of the modern United States: the Depression, the Second World War, the rise of modern manufacturing, new technologies and materials, and the growth of corporate America. Throughout this time their creative output ranged from architecture and exhibition design to making films and toys, but it is their furniture for which they will always be best remembered. Their roll-call of design classics is unmatched by any other designer; there are the groundbreaking moulded plywood chairs of the mid-1940s, followed by the single-shell fibreglass chair of the early 1950s, the luxurious lounge chair and ottoman of 1956, and then they set new levels of corporate style in the late 1950s with their sleek furniture designs in cast aluminium and leather. Central to the work of this design duo is the way they combined technological ingenuity with visionary design, and always there was the Modernist democratic agenda of producing the best-possible designs at affordable prices for the mainstream market.

Charles Ormand Eames was born in St Louis, Missouri, in 1907. His father was a keen amateur photographer and worked as a railway security guard – he died when Charles was 12.

Charles worked for several engineering and manufacturing firms before gaining a scholarship to study architecture at Washington University in St Louis. There he met his first wife, Catherine Woermann. After graduating in 1928, the couple married in 1929 and took a honeymoon tour of Europe to look at the architecture of Le Corbusier and Ludwig Mies van der Rohe. Their only child, Lucia, was born in 1930.

Coinciding with the Depression, Charles' early career as an architect was tough, and by 1936 he returned to education at the Cranbrook Academy of Art, Detroit, Michigan, to study photography, ceramics and metalwork. It was here that he met his second wife, Ray. Born in Sacramento, California, in 1912, Bernice Alexandra (nicknamed Ray) Kaiser, came from a creative family: her father was a theatre-manager-turned-insurance-salesman and she was always fascinated by theatre, dance and art. After her father died in 1929, she and her mother moved to New York, where Ray studied art. She became part of Abstract Expressionism and in 1937 was a founding member of the American Abstract Artists group and participated in its inaugural exhibition. After her mother died in 1940 she studied at the Cranbrook Academy of Art where she met Charles Eames. It was a perfect match: abstract art meets industrial production. Charles brought the technical and practical expertise, while Ray's brilliance

below

La Chaise

This beautiful organic and sculptural
reinterpretation of the chaise longue was
designed in 1948 for a competition at the
Museum of Modern Art in New York. Inspired
by *Floating Figure*, a sculpture by Gaston
Lachaise, it is made with a fibreglass shell
that sits on chromed metal rod legs with
a natural oak cruciform foot.

below

DAR Armchair

DAR plastic armchairs with R-wire bases were first shown by Charles and Ray Eames as part of the 1950 Museum of Modern Art Low-Cost Furniture Design competition. The seat shells in the latest polypropylene were combined with various bases and sold in millions. This one has the Eiffel-Tower legs.

was in experimentation, colour and free-form sculpture. They
worked on several projects together at Cranbrook, most notably the
1940 Museum of Modern Art competition, Organic Design in Home
Furnishings. The following year, Charles divorced Catherine in May,
and married Ray in June. They left Cranbrook together on a long
honeymoon drive across the country to Los Angeles.

They joined millions of American pioneers who headed west in
search of a new life and a job. The US defence industries were based
in Los Angeles, and it wasn't long before Charles and Ray Eames got
a job working for the US Navy designing plywood splints for injured
personnel. After building a moulding contraption in their apartment,
they used their combined skills of shaping plywood, won an order
for 5,000 splints, and set up a small production company, Evans
Products Co. Around the same time, they also established their first
design office with collaborators including Harry Bertoia, who they
knew from Cranbrook and who had designed Ray's wedding ring.

Using the experience they gained from the production of splints,
the couple continued to work with plywood; Ray produced numerous
beautiful sculptures, and by 1946 they put their first plywood chair
into production. Having tried unsuccessfully to make the chair shell
from a single piece of plywood, they opted for a separate seat and
backrest, held in place on a simple tubular steel frame. The chair,
along with a range of other pieces in plywood, formed the heart of
the exhibition at New York's Museum of Modern Art entitled New
Furniture Designed by Charles Eames – quite unfairly, Ray was given
no credit for her considerable contribution to the plywood work.
The exhibition was seen by representatives from the manufacturer
Herman Miller and the company soon took over production of the
furniture; thus beginning a long collaboration with the Eameses.

Determined to pursue their quest for an inexpensive, single-
shell chair, Charles and Ray Eames turned to working with
fibreglass-reinforced plastic. They showed a series of prototypes
at the International Competition for Low-Cost Furniture Design,
organized by the Museum of Modern Art in New York in 1948, and
by adapting wartime technology, their moulded fibreglass series
began production in 1950. They were made by Zenith, which had
made parts for warplanes, on behalf of Herman Miller – originals bear
a red, black and white chequered label with the name Miller Zenith.

Charles and Ray's curiosity about design and materials also
spread to architecture. Along with many other young and aspiring
Californian designers, they created their own prototype home as
part of the Case Study Houses project, sponsored by the avant-
garde magazine Arts & Architecture. Using off-the-shelf components,
many from trade catalogues, they built a groundbreaking modern
home in glass and steel in Santa Monica during 1949; they moved
in and stayed here for the rest of their lives, and it is now open to the
public by appointment. The idea of the Case Study Houses scheme
was to find ways of producing affordable, quick-build modern homes
for returning war veterans.

During the 1950s, the couple turned their attention to working with
metals. First came the wire chairs. Again, these built on the single-
shell idea, but by using a wire mesh they created chairs that were
dematerialized. They were see-through, and yet also sculptural, and
ideal for use in smaller homes because they didn't occupy a huge
space. In fact, the success of many of these designs lies in their
versatility. The chairs and other items of furniture looked good in
homes where they were just as stylish around a dining table as they

were when used as bedroom chairs. Because they were durable
and inexpensive, they also worked for office environments and for
institutions like schools and colleges. As a result, they sold in their
hundreds of thousands, first in the United States and then worldwide.

By the later 1950s, the designs became more upmarket and
luxurious. In 1956 came the ultimate chief executive chair in the
lounge chair with ottoman, which was made with a moulded
plywood shell and given deep leather upholstery. The expansion
of their popularity in Europe grew enormously after 1957 when
Vitra became licensed to make Charles and Ray Eames designs
for the European market. In the following year came the launch
of the Aluminum series of chairs, which were rigorous, elegant
and ideal for corporate America.

In the latter years of their business, Charles and Ray Eames
moved away from furniture design to concentrate on exhibition
design, marketing projects for major companies like IBM,
Polaroid and Boeing, and filmmaking.

The Wartime Legacy

In these years shortly after the end of the Second World War, the technologies and materials invented during the conflict began to find peacetime applications. The process of mass production had been much improved and made faster for the construction of everything from planes and tanks to guns and protective clothing. Along with this came advances in moulding and laminating, welding and high-powered glues. There were new lightweight materials, too: fibreglass and resin, plastics and acrylics, cast aluminium and foam rubber. During the 1930s came melamine and Perspex, followed by nylon, which replaced traditional silk for American-made parachutes. Polyethylene, a new lightweight flexible plastic, was instrumental in the development of radar and found a peacetime use at the Tupper Corporation for food and drinks containers called Tupperware. Furniture designers picked up many of these intriguing processes and materials and in these fast-moving times, technology in furniture production seemed to advance with virtually every new design.

One such new design was the 1948 Womb chair by Eero Saarinen. Like the Eameses' Plywood Group, this originated at the Organic Design in Home Furnishings competition of 1940. Clearly, Saarinen's inviting and embracing, soft-form seat has the famous Conversation chair prototype designed by Saarinen with Charles Eames for this contest as its forebear. The design is reputed to have also drawn inspiration from a conversation between Saarinen and Florence (née Schust) Knoll (1917–), a student at the Cranbrook Academy, who said that she was fed up with chairs that held the sitter in a fixed position. The Womb was therefore designed with a wide and deep seat, low-set armrests, and a couple of soft-pad cushions for the seat and back so the sitter can choose to curl up or sprawl in maximum, upholstered comfort. Saarinen deployed moulded reinforced plastic for the chair's body shell, which was then padded with foam rubber and finished with close-fitting fabric upholstery. The legs and supporting structure were in very fine tubular steel with pretty circular pad feet. The chair forms part of a 'Womb family' alongside a footstool and sofa. The design captured imaginations and soon images of this laid-back icon were appearing in the pages of magazines and in advertising. It continues in production today with Knoll.

Emerging Manufacturers

By the late 1940s, Mid-Century Modernism in the United States was well into its stride. Along with the growing roll call of emerging, great designers, also rising to prominence were two hugely important and progressive manufacturers: Knoll and Herman Miller. Knoll was established in New York in 1938 by the German émigré, and son of a furniture maker, Hans G Knoll. Influenced by the Bauhaus, he was driven to produce modern furniture for the home that was not just elegant and functional, but also affordable. After opening a showroom in New York in 1942 and launching his first designs, including many by the Danish-born Jens Risom, he expanded the operation and soon drew on the services of a range of high-profile designers, among them Harry Bertoia (1915–78), Eero Saarinen, Pierre Jeanneret (1896–1967) and Florence Knoll.

Florence Knoll had impeccable Modernist credentials. She had studied architecture with Mies van der Rohe in Chicago, been a student at Cranbrook at the same times as the Eames, and had

above

Womb Chair

This deep and inviting armchair designed by Eero Saarinen in 1948 is formed from an upholstered shell case held in a bent tubular steel frame. Part of the original inspiration came from a conversation with Florence Knoll, who longed for informal and modern seating designs.

opposite

Modern living, with a dining area and home office all in the same matching suite of furniture by George Nelson. The chair in the foreground is the extremely lightweight Pretzel chair from 1957.

left

Lounge Seating

Like so many of her groundbreaking designs, Florence Knoll's 1954 lounge collection has made its way into the pantheon of modern classics. The versatile collection includes a lounge chair, settee, sofa, two-seater bench and three-seater bench. The Knoll Studio logo and Florence's signature are now stamped into the base of the frame.

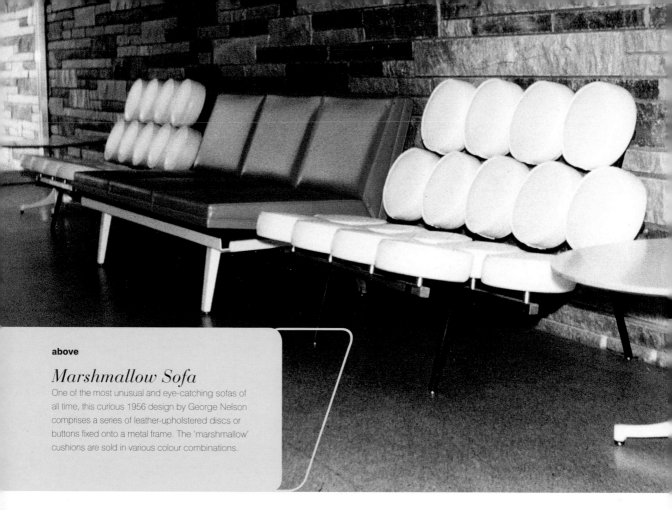

above

Marshmallow Sofa

One of the most unusual and eye-catching sofas of
all time, this curious 1956 design by George Nelson
comprises a series of leather-upholstered discs or
buttons fixed onto a metal frame. The 'marshmallow'
cushions are sold in various colour combinations.

worked for a while with Walter Gropius and Marcel Breuer before
she joined Knoll in 1943 as an interior designer and founder of the
planning unit. Three years later she married Hans Knoll, the firm
changed its name to Knoll Associates, and she went on to become
a tremendous creative force within the company. The company's
major commercial breakthrough came shortly after Hans and
Florence were married, when they were hired to design the
Rockefeller family offices in Rockefeller Plaza, New York. The job
was heralded as a benchmark for office designs of the day and it
became a springboard for Hans and Florence into other high-profile
office-design jobs. Knoll today continues to produce many of the
early modern masterpieces, but it is mostly focused on high-quality
contract furniture production for commercial and office interiors.

Meanwhile, also daring to be different was the Herman Miller
furniture company (now Herman Miller Inc). Based in Michigan, and
founded in the 1930s by entrepreneur Dirk Jan DePree (1891–1990),
it started life producing rather run-of-the-mill domestic furniture in
comfortable and safe styles. However, in 1945 the company had
a dramatic change of heart and adopted the Modernist mantra,
pledging to produce a collection of furniture 'designed to meet fully
the requirements for modern living'. This change of gear is attributed
to the firm's new design director George Nelson (1908–86), a Yale
architect and editor of the *Architectural Forum*. Hardly giving himself
time to settle at his desk, he had soon enlisted the talents of Charles

and Ray Eames and Isamu Noguchi (1904–88). He was no slouch in
his own design work, either, and set to work creating a new logo for
the company, improving the advertising, upgrading the graphics and
producing smart new catalogues.

Nelson's own furniture designs rank among the smartest of
the time, too. Among his primary concerns was storage; he was
the inventor of the storage wall, but also produced designs for
sideboards and media-centre cabinets. His most iconic works
include the Platform bench of 1947, the seductively elegant Thin
Edge bed of the 1950s and the wacky Marshmallow sofa of 1956.
This latter piece is quite unlike anything designed before or since.
It is composed of circular foam pads, often covered in multicoloured
leather and fixed on a metal frame. It still turns heads and makes
people smile, especially in the ever-popular colour combination of
purple, pink and orange, and after a 34-year rest it was reintroduced
into production in 1999 by Herman Miller in the US, and is also now
made by Vitra in Europe.

Herman Miller will always be closely associated with the Eameses'
products. From the Moulded Plywood series through the Moulded
Plastic group, and then the ultra-luxurious lounge chair with ottoman
and the Aluminum Group, this epic collection still stands proud
among the greatest of twentieth-century design, consistently well
produced, always innovative and still in demand today in both the
new and secondhand markets.

right

A complete room set of furnishings by George Nelson from 1958. The sideboard, sofa with side table and coffee table are all finished in rosewood. On the far side of the room are two fabric-upholstered Coconut chairs and a footstool from 1955.

below

Coconut Chair

Like a slice of coconut, with its soft inner wall, George Nelson's 1955 Coconut chair is composed of a single shell form made from upholstered steel, which sits on a slender, wire tripod base.

Noguchi Table

Pure sculpture, Isamu Noguchi's 1948 coffee table is constructed from two pieces of organically sculpted wood, on top of which is balanced a free-form shape of clear glass. 'Everything is sculpture,' he said. His signature is on the edge of the table top and on a medallion on the underside of the base.

Mid-Century Mature

By the late 1940s and early 1950s, it was clear that the Modernism propagated by the Bauhaus and its disciples had moved into a new realm. The hard-edged industrial aesthetic had given way to an unbuttoned, laidback, more expressive, free-flowing kind of style that might be asymmetrical, curvy and even colourful. Of course improved production techniques and new materials played their part in making the innovative designs possible, but inspiration was also drawn from other contemporary cultural sources: from the rebellious spirit of jazz, rock-and-roll and pop; from artists like Jackson Pollock and Alexander Calder; and from science and the atomic age.

The ultimate product of this time is the sculptural and abstract coffee table, now called the Noguchi table, of 1948, which was designed by the American-Japanese designer and artist Isamu Noguchi and made by Herman Miller. The legs are composed of two identical and asymmetrical, biomorphic-shaped pieces of walnut wood, joined together at one point by a pin and supporting an organically shaped top of clear glass. After a spell out of production, it was reissued in 1984 by Herman Miller.

In a completely different vein, but again a piece that is key to this era, is the sculptural and abstract Diamond lounge chair, from 1951–2, by Harry Bertoia, a contemporary of Charles Eames and Florence Knoll at the Cranbrook Academy. The chair looks like a mesh of steel wire that has been pushed into shape to form a seat with wide arms. The shell body sits on a structure of slightly more substantial bent wire that forms splayed legs. Like Noguchi, Bertoia was passionate about sculpture and he saw this chair as an extension of his artistic work. The chair was formed with the help of technicians from Knoll and is an essay in transparency.

below

In the 1950s exhibitions and shop displays set out how to put together the ideal modern room. Horizontal lines dominate. In the foreground the Noguchi table is flanked by plywood chairs by Charles and Ray Eames before a fashionable, long and low sideboard. Striped linoleum completes the effect.

Harry Bertoia (1915–78)

Best known for his collection of wire-mesh chairs, Harry Bertoia was primarily a sculptor. He described his open-weave seating designs as 'mainly made of air', and added that 'space passes right through them'. Working in metal was his passion, and along with the famous chairs Bertoia also produced jewellery and sculpture.

Born in San Lorenzo, Pordenone, Italy, in 1915, he came to America aged just 15 to visit his brother, who was living in Detroit, Michigan. He chose to stay in the US and attended the Cass Technical High School, where he studied art and design and learnt the art of jewellery making. In 1936 he attended the art school of the Detroit Society of Arts and Crafts, but among his most formative years were those spent at the Cranbrook Academy of Arts, Detroit, which he joined on a scholarship in 1937. Here, he not only encountered Modernist designers, including Walter Gropius, Cranbrook director Eliel Saarinen, and his designer son Eero, but he also formed friendships with students Florence (néeSchust) Knoll and Charles and Ray Eames.

In 1939 he opened the metal workshop at Cranbrook, where he taught jewellery design and metal work. With the onset of war, however, metal became a rare and precious commodity, so he concentrated on small-scale designs for jewellery – he designed the wedding ring for Ray Kaiser when she married Charles Eames.

In 1943, after marrying Brigitta Valentiner, Bertoia joined the American exodus to the west coast and found work with Charles and Ray Eames in Los Angeles, California. His projects included military commissions for aircraft components and he helped in the development of the moulded plywood splint that the Eameses were working on. He also worked on furniture projects, including helping the Eameses during the early days of the plywood furniture. However, partly because he felt he was not receiving credit for his input and partly because he preferred working in metal, he left the Eames studio in 1946.

By 1950 Bertoia was living and working in Pennsylvania. He had re-established contact with another fellow Cranbrook Academy student Florence Knoll. An architect and furniture designer, Florence had married manufacturer Hans Knoll and was steering the company in a Modernist direction (see pages 90–2). Bertoia's innovative sculptural vision was just what the company needed. In an act of great faith, the Knolls offered Bertoia a salary and a studio and the freedom to create whatever he wanted. At first he worked on sculpture, but then between 1950 and 1952 he came up with his landmark collection of five wire-mesh chairs. The most iconic piece is the 1952 Diamond chair, an elegantly resolved design based on a square shape when seen from above. The single piece of lattice, made from fine metal rods, has a deep and rounded seat and a frame that splays out at either side to form armrests, while the back climbs to a soft apex. Formed as a single shell, the seat sits on a metal base of bent tubular steel. They are sold today with the option of an upholstery cover or a seat pad.

Nothing quite like it had been seen before, and it was an instant hit that was featured in countless magazine articles and advertisements. Others in his collection are the Side chair, the Barstool, the Bird chair and the Asymmetric chaise, all from 1952. The one cloud on the horizon at this time was the fact that this type of wire design was very close to work produced by Charles and Ray Eames for Herman Miller. A court case ensued, and although Miller won, Knoll retained the right to continue production. The commercial success of these designs, and his royalty fees, gave Bertoia the freedom he craved to devote the rest of his life to sculpture.

left

Harry Bertoia, taken in 1961. Although primarily a sculptor, Bertoia was persuaded to team up with the manufacturer Knoll to produce a series of beautiful and now-classic wire chairs that stand as sculptural seating.

Diamond Chair

Light and wrapped in wire, this 1952 chair is an undisputed masterpiece. The seat shell, mostly assembled by hand, sits on slender tubular steel legs with sledge feet. Versions appear with a simple seat pad or a fully upholstered cover.

left

Bird Chair

Also from 1952, this model is more laidback, with a deeper seat and much taller back. Stubby wings and a rounded 'belly' lend a distinctly bird-like appearance. A matching footstool accompanies it. Upholstered versions are also available.

Festival of Britain, 1951

In Britain, unsurprisingly, public morale was running low after the war. Despite being proclaimed the victors of conflict, in the years immediately after the fighting there seemed little to celebrate. Just like other countries, Britain looked to design as a way of stimulating the economy and boosting national pride. In 1946, at the Victoria and Albert Museum in London, came the Britain Can Make exhibition, which showcased an enticing array of modern consumer goods, from furniture and fashion to ceramics and cookers. It attracted an impressive 1.5 million visitors and generated huge numbers of orders. The following year a similar show, called Enterprise Scotland, was staged in Edinburgh. However, it was in 1951, with the Festival of Britain, that modern design really hit centre stage.

As part of the ongoing need to revive the nation's flagging spirits, where rationing of everyday goods was still in effect, and to mark the centenary of the famous Great Exhibition of 1851, this new Festival of Britain was designed to take place on a large swathe of derelict industrial land on the South Bank of the Thames in central London.

below

BA3 Chair and Table

There is a strong edge of glamour in these chairs that were designed by Ernest Race in 1945. The slim silhouettes, with their nipped-in waists, are made of cast aluminium recycled from wartime use. For ease of transportation, each chair is made in seven parts. They are accompanied by an aluminium table with a contrasting hardwood top.

Here, around two dozen of the country's best young architects and designers were drawn together to put on a show of all that was best in the 'Brave New World' of the postwar years. The sense of optimism was infectious. Dazzling modern, quirky and colourful buildings were constructed in shapes and materials never seen before. They included, most famous of all, the Dome of Discovery – a giant man-made mushroom, clad in aluminium – the great sculptural Skylon and the themed pavilions for Homes and Gardens, Transport and Communications, and Power and Production.

The single most iconic piece of furniture to be associated with this event was the 1951 Antelope chair by designer Ernest Race (1913–64). Spindly and wiry, this enigmatic chair incorporated a moulded plywood seat and a curvy frame made of thin, enamelled steel rods. The legs terminate in small ball feet. Its clever use of limited materials and jaunty design came to symbolize the spirit of the exhibition. After the festival, Ernest Race's manufacturing company called Race Furniture put the Antelope into commercial production and it remains available today.

The other great design that is inextricably linked with the festival is the Calyx fabric pattern from 1951, created by Lucienne Day (1917–). Again, with that classic 1950s spindly theme, it is an abstract design loosely based on botanical shapes. Lucienne was half of the UK's most celebrated design couple of the time, with her husband, the furniture designer Robin Day (1915–). While there have been the inevitable comparisons with Charles and Ray Eames, the Days did not work as a team; Lucienne was, and is, an independent and successful textile designer in her own right. However, they were fêted by the homes magazines of the time, and both believed passionately in the transformative power of modern design to make the world a better place.

In common with so many other European designers, the Days found their careers on hold during the war years, but when life started to get back to normal their energy and enthusiasm was unleashed. In 1948 Robin Day and Clive Latimer won first prize in the storage section of the International Competition for Low-Cost Furniture organized by New York's Museum of Modern Art. Plywood was again a key material. Following this, Robin Day's work attracted the attention of the manufacturer Hille, which was keen to start incorporating modern designs into its portfolio. Among his earliest designs for this company is his Hillestak chair of 1950. It joins the pantheon of mid-century ply and is a charming design, with beechwood frame and legs, and shaped ply elements for the seat and backrest. Best of all, like many of his designs at the time, it was affordable. This was followed by more experimentation in his steel and plywood chair designs that went on show at the Festival of Britain in the Homes and Gardens Pavilion, but among his most successful work of this time was the armchair that was commissioned in 1951 for the Royal Festival Hall. Again, this chair is based on the use of plywood, but it has an upholstered back and seat. Day also designed the hall's auditorium seating, which was refurbished for the 2007 Royal Festival Hall reopening.

Robin (1915–) and Lucienne (1917–) Day

Pioneers of modern design in Britain, Robin and Lucienne Day achieved almost movie-star status during the 1950s for their furniture and fabric designs; their modern-style home was featured in numerous magazines and advertisements. Their greatest early triumph was their work for the 1951 Festival of Britain. Their impact on the British design scene for the past half a century has been astonishing, with many designs for furniture and textiles being reissued and enjoying a renaissance at the turn of the millennium. Their greatest success was to produce and promote a modern style that appealed to the British public, which was notoriously reluctant to embrace Modernism.

While often portrayed as Britain's answer to America's high-profile design couple Charles and Ray Eames, the Days worked in very different ways. While the Eameses were collaborators on most of their projects, the Days have followed their own independent paths: Robin in furniture design and Lucienne in textiles, wallpapers and ceramics. However, there are some parallels to be drawn with these great American designers. Importantly, the Days shared the belief that modern design had the potential to improve the lives of ordinary people. Like Charles Eames, Robin Day had a fascination for new materials and new methods of production, and Like Ray Eames, Lucienne admired and drew inspiration from the abstract art movement and was an expert and inventive colourist. Although their work often carried them in different directions, their originality and shared vision have ensured that the pieces have a creative synergy and always sit together harmoniously.

above

Robin and Lucienne Day at work in London. During the 1950s and 1960s, Robin, a furniture designer, and Lucienne, a fabric designer, set the interior design style for Modern Britain.

right

Polyprop Chair

A selection of classic Polyprop chair designs from 1963 by Robin Day. Versions with and without arms are made and there is a choice of supports, including stems and feet. These chairs have sold in their millions around the globe.

Robin Day was born in 1915 in High Wycombe, Buckinghamshire.
The son of a policeman, he trained as a furniture maker and from
1934–8 attended the Royal College of Art, London, specializing
in furniture and interior design. Lucienne Day was born Désirée
Lucienne Conradi in 1917 in Coulsden, Surrey. She studied at the
Royal College of Art between 1937 and 1940 when she met Robin
Day at a college dance. They married in 1942 and set up home
in Chelsea, London.

During the war years they taught art, and then in 1948 Robin Day
got his first taste of professional success. He and fellow designer
Clive Latimer entered designs for a plywood and aluminium storage
system for the International Competition for Low-Cost Furniture Design,
organized by the Museum of Modern Art in New York. Out of more than
3,000 entrants, they won top prize. British manufacturer Hille spotted
Day's talent and in 1950 he became the company's design director
and launched his revolutionary moulded plywood Hillestak stacking
chair. This collaboration resulted in the production of more than 150
furniture designs for home and office during the following 45 years.

The year 1951 was a major landmark in the careers of both Robin
and Lucienne Day. They exhibited furniture and fabrics at the Milan
Triennale and achieved the twin success of both winning gold
medals. During the same year came the invitation to contribute to
the Festival of Britain, the huge and morale-boosting, government-
sponsored design extravaganza staged on the South Bank of the
Thames in London. Robin was invited to contribute two room sets
– one low cost and the other more luxurious – to the Homes and
Gardens pavilion, for which Lucienne provided the furnishing fabric
called Calyx. The fabric was produced by Heal's, for whom Lucienne
created more than 70 designs in the ensuing two decades. Quite
unlike the stuffy old furniture and dull fabrics of the time, Robin's

sleek and simple furniture combined with Lucienne's plant-based,
abstract fabrics and wallpapers in unusual modern colours attracted
huge crowds. Robin also designed seating for the newly completed
Royal Festival Hall, much of which was refurbished for the reopening
of the concert hall in 2007. The couple attended the grand gala
opening concert.

The Days' success grew during the 1950s and 1960s. In 1953
Robin produced his Q Stak chair with Hille, while Lucienne worked
on her now-classic designs, including Spectators and Perpetua for
Heal's. Throughout this era she was also designing modern carpet
patterns for the likes of Wilton, wallpapers for Rasch and ceramics
for Rosenthal. By the end of the decade, Robin was turning his hand
to consumer electronics, designing stylish televisions, radios and
record players for Pye. In 1963 he launched his now-ubiquitous
Polyprop stacking chair. It was the first shingle-shell chair to be
made using the new injection-moulding material polypropylene, and
it proved to be cheaper and quicker to produce than the Eameses'
single-shell chair that was made in fibreglass-reinforced plastic.

With their reputations firmly established by the 1960s, the Days
worked together on several consultancy projects for clients that
included the British airline BOAC and the retailer John Lewis
Partnership, where they worked on the house style of John
Lewis department stores and Waitrose supermarkets. From 1969
to 1973 Robin also worked as a consultant for the Barbican Arts
Centre, then under construction, and designed much of its seating.

With the tide of Modernism gradually changing tastes in Britain,
the Days' work was joined by generations of new designers.
However, in the late 1990s the quality of their designs was once
again recognized, and a number of companies, including Habitat,
reissued their furniture and fabrics.

left

Antony Chair

Considered by many to be Jean Prouvé's finest design, the Antony chair was created for La Cité Internationale Universitaire at Antony, near Paris, in 1950. One of his last furniture designs, it is distinguished by its unusual construction and dynamic shape. The frame is made from lacquered sheet and tubular steel while the seat shell is formed of plywood.

below

Lady Chair

Exploring early uses of foam, Marco Zanuso wanted to demonstrate how new materials could revolutionize furniture production. His 1951 Lady chair remains an elegant and timeless classic.

On the Continent

France had, of course, suffered badly during the war, but a core of design talent, particularly interior designers, had survived. The single high-profile furniture designer to emerge from this time was Jean Prouvé (1901–84). Driven by the desire to make art accessible, he had trained as an engineer and metalworker and then turned his skills to furniture. In the late 1940s he began a furniture factory and started to experiment with the uses of aluminium, largely for use in his building designs. His furniture designs are unequivocally modern and his best-known work is the Antony chair from 1950, which has a metal structure with splayed legs and an elegant seat and back combined in a single curved swoop of moulded wood.

Meanwhile, it was the Italians who grabbed the mid-century limelight with truly original designs. They launched themselves from virtual obscurity in the pre-war era onto the postwar Modern design scene and pulled off a small miracle. While in the grips of Fascism, under the leadership of Benito Mussolini between 1922 and 1943, the Italian economy had stalled. This had a stagnating effect on the production of consumer goods and modern culture in general. The country had also taken part in the Second World War – at first as allies of the Germans and then, after 1943, occupied by them – but somehow, by the 1950s, Italian spirits were revived and there followed an explosion of quite stunning furniture designs. The growing fame of the Milan Triennale furniture showcase certainly helped to focus ideas and many believe this great spurt of postwar brilliance was made possible by a manufacturing system that was geared up for small-scale production runs. This meant that manufacturers, including many of today's well-respected names such as Tecno, Cassina and Arflex, were prepared to take risks on unusual designs without fear of losing a fortune.

Among the most eye-catching designs of this time was the 1951 Lady chair by Marco Zanuso (1916–): a curvy, welcoming, upholstered easy chair with a deep and comfortable seat on short splayed legs that are made from tubular stainless steel. Zanuso had been working with the rubber giant Pirelli, which had invited him to experiment with the new foam rubber; the Lady chair was one of the results. The chair can be finished in fabric of leather upholstery and continues to be made today by Arflex, set up by Pirelli.

Another great name of the time is Carlo Mollino (1905–73), who worked with Zanotta. Among his most powerful designs is the Arabesco coffee table from 1949. Built from his trademark bent plywood, it features a lavish flourish for the sculptural and organic frame and a simple glass top. In a completely different style is the work of Piero Fornasetti (1913–88), whose work is decorative and classical, but with a modern twist. His ornamented cabinets and chairs remain perennial favourites and the highly collectable originals command enormous prices. Among the best-known pieces are his folding screen covered with architectural imagery, and the trumeau desk and shelving unit called Architettura, covered with black-and-white architectural imagery, both from the 1950s. He designed ceramics, too, which continue to attract collectors.

In the mid-1950s, the architect Gio Ponti (1891–1979) created a scintillating design with his Super Leggera (Super Light). Based on traditional chairs from Liguria, this design has proved to be a timeless classic. Based on his ethos of always making things lighter, cheaper and more convenient, the chair is stripped to its very essentials; it finds that delicate point of balance between lightness and strength.

below

Corinthian Capitello

This striking chair design, from around 1955, features a screen-printed image of a decorative Corinthian column head and was created by Piero Fornasetti. He loved applied decoration, often with an architectural theme. With its neat tapering legs and glossy black finish, this is an extremely elegant chair.

Gio Ponti (1891–1979)

Gio Ponti was a giant of Italy's postwar design renaissance, championing Modern design in his home country for more than half a century. Not only was he an architect, a designer of ceramics, fabrics, glass and interiors, an architecture professor, the founding editor of the internationally influential *Domus* and *Stile* magazines, but he was also a poet and a painter. In addition to this, he also designed a now world-famous, chrome espresso machine for La Pavoni and among his prolific output of furniture designs he created one of the most scintillating chair designs of the 1950s, the Super Leggera (Super Light) in 1957.

Gio Ponti was born in Milan in 1891. He studied architecture at the Milan Politecnico and, after the interruption of the First World War, in which he fought and was decorated for bravery, he graduated in 1921. Throughout the 1920s he worked for the ceramics manufacturer Richard-Ginori, where his designs attracted attention and won him the coveted Grand Prix at the famous 1925 Paris Exposition Internationale des Arts Décoratifs et Industriels Moderne. He produced a huge variety of pieces, from vases and ashtrays to serving dishes and plates. Many feature neoclassical decoration, but he also was also fascinated by sporting motifs and

used stylized images of tennis players, golfers, boxers and even weightlifters. In tune with other pioneering Modernists, he held a firm belief in the potential of mass production to produce high-quality goods for everyone. He declared that 'Industry is the style of the twentieth century'. These sentiments were shared by the Fascist regime of Mussolini at this time; economic self-sufficiency was encouraged and so mass production was hailed as a route to national autonomy.

In 1926 Ponti designed his first house in Milan, and two years later founded *Domus*, which remained Europe's most influential architecture and design magazine throughout the twentieth century. With just one short break, he edited the publication until his death. During the interwar years, as Milan was expanding and becoming established as a design capital, Ponti worked on exhibition designs, including the fifth Milan Triennale of 1933. He also completed a number of architecture commissions, including the mathematics department at Rome University in 1934 and the headquarters of the minerals firm Montecatini in Milan in 1936.

The 1940s began with Ponti leaving *Domus* magazine to set up the rival *Stile* (he returned to *Domus* in 1947). He also started work with the Murano glassware company Venini, producing incredibly beautiful – and now much sought-after – intensely coloured glassware, including stunning vases and chandeliers. Throughout this time, he was also producing dozens of designs for furniture and lighting, and completed the interiors of four cruise liners. His work in industrial design reached its peak with the espresso coffee machine for La Pavoni in 1948. With all the beauty of an Italian sports car, this gleaming, curvaceous chrome machine rapidly found favour in coffee bars and helped to set the style of the 1950s, when Italian *dolce vita* was at its peak.

With an impressive body of work already to his name, Ponti somehow managed to step up a gear in the 1950s. Early in the decade he developed his experience of ceramic design and began work with manufacturer Ideal Standard. In 1953 he produced his highly sculptural and Modernist sanitaryware called Series P. His architecture commissions continued, too. There was the 'Butterfly House', or Villa Planchart, in Caracas in 1955, and one year later the landmark Pirelli Tower in Milan, one of the city's first skyscrapers. Ponti's thoughts were never far from his beloved furniture, however. He had forged a strong friendship with the artist and designer Piero Fornasetti and the two worked together on a long series of projects – Ponti designing the chair or sideboard and Fornasetti adding his trademark, classically inspired and often surreal, decorative finishes. Among their best-known pieces is the Architettura Trumeaux bureau-bookcase of around 1955, which is decorated with a monochrome architectural scene. They also worked together on the interiors of the Casino at San Remo in 1950.

Of Ponti's own furniture designs, his most iconic piece is the Super Leggera. As his inspiration he took a traditional Italian chair from Liguria and pared it down to its very essentials, aiming for it to be as light as possible, while also being strong; publicity photos for the chair show a child or a woman picking up the chair with one finger. Built in ash, the chair is given a dark tint and finished with a woven cane seat. One of Ponti's guiding design mantras was always to 'shift from heavy to light, from opaque to transparent'. Super Leggera is made today by Cassina.

Through the 1960s and 1970s, architecture became Ponti's main focus. Along with his work in 1964 on the beautiful modern interior design for the Grand Hotel Parco dei Principi in Rome, he also designed its sister hotel in Sorrento both inside and out. Opened in 1962, this gleaming-white cliff-top hotel has recently been restored to its former glory and, complete with his furniture, is a haven for Ponti fans.

After completing a series of churches, including Taranto Cathedral, Apulia in southern Italy in 1970, one of his final commissions was for the 1972 castle-like Denver Art Museum in the United States. In 1979, Ponti died at home in Milan.

above

Super Leggera

Always striving for lightness and transparency, Gio Ponti is reputed to have worked on this design for almost a decade. This 1957 chair is based on a traditional design, trimmed and stripped back to the essentials by Ponti. It is built from ebonized wood with a woven rush seat. Today it is made by Cassina.

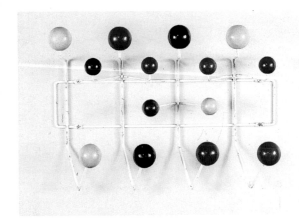

While the high-profile, top-end designers of this time directed a great deal of their creative energy and invention toward chairs in particular and seating in general, others were hard at work on every other aspect of domestic design. For those who were not interested in high design by the Modernist maestros there was plenty of choice. Once plastics, bright colours and asymmetrical designs were unleashed in Europe and the United States, all manner of exuberant and expressive products emerged, from boomerang-shaped coffee tables and animal-print fabrics to Formica-topped tables and any number of weird and wonderful light fittings. For collectors interested in the joys of kitsch, this is a truly fertile period. Sadly, though, in this world of mass production, the designers are rarely credited by name.

Even the design gurus took time out from their core business of designing seating and tables, and clearly relished the opportunities to work in other areas. During the 1940s and 1950s in the United States, Isamu Noguchi produced some beautiful modern lamps, many of which were made using paper and plastic; George Nelson designed his charming Atomic wall clock in 1949, which looked like a molecular structure made with rods and balls; and, in a similar vein, the Eameses made a hanging rack with brightly coloured bobbles held on a metal frame. Called Hang-It-All, it was designed in 1953.

Meanwhile, in Europe, Italian Roberto Sambonet (1924–95), designed exquisite, clean-lined stainless-steel cookware and tableware for his family company called Sambonet, and the Dutch painter Karel Appel (1921–2006) produced fabulous bold fabric designs for the Bijenkorf department store. The great German polymath, Dieter Rams (1932–) was not only busy producing groundbreaking designs for everything from shavers to radios for Braun, but also created the 606 Universal shelving system for Vitsoe in 1960, which remains in production and has earned its place as a Modern design classic.

above

Hang-It-All

This colourful rack was designed by Charles and Ray Eames in 1953 to encourage children to hang up their clothes. The design borrows the atomic or molecular motif so popular in the 1950s. It is made of steel wire with a white coating and painted wooden balls.

opposite

Kangaroo Chair

In reinventing the club chair, George Nelson refined the 1956 Kangaroo chair to its sculptural minimum. Seat and back are made from moulded plywood, padded and upholstered, with the inner and outer surfaces in contrasting fabrics. The shell sits on a lightweight frame of tubular steel. On the wall is Nelson's Atomic, or Ball, clock, one of the best-known designs of the 1950s.

below

An all-time shelving and storage design classic, this 606 Universal modular system comprises shelves, cupboards, drawers, desktops, and more and was conceived by Dieter Rams in 1960. It remains in production today.

above

Designer Eero Saarinen is shown at his home
studio in 1958. The room is furnished with two
of his greatest chair designs: the Womb from
1948 and the Tulip from 1956.

The Shape of Things to Come

By the late 1950s, it was clear that a major shift in design was in
progress. The mid-century experimentation had seen off the austerity
and harsh conditions of the postwar years and the Western world
was moving into a new design phase characterized by ever-more
expressive shapes and colours. Jazz and band music, modern cars
and postwar recovery were being replaced by pop and psychedelia,
the space age and futurism.

Among the early signs of this new expressive age were the
1955 Butterfly stool by Sori Yanagi (1915–). A Japanese industrial
designer, Yanagi had worked with Charlotte Perriand before setting
out on his own and producing a new type of furniture for a modern
Japan. While the stool is Western in style, the beautiful design has
echoes of traditional furniture, but is made with modern processes
and, once again, is based on moulded plywood.

A year later, in 1956, came the Tulip chair by the American-based
Finn Eero Saarinen. It forms part of his last family of designs that
have the most incredible futuristic lines. The Tulip appears to be
made from a single piece of moulded material, which ideally is
what Saarinen would have liked, but the technology was not ready
for him and so the furniture was made in two parts. The moulded
seat was reinforced plastic and the stem aluminium, which was
lacquered to match the seat. Saarinen disliked the visual mess
and confusion created by furniture legs, so this series of designs
saw the successful fulfilment of his dream to rid his world of such
distractions. On a lighthearted and even surreal note, the 1957
Mezzadro tractor seat chair by Achille and Pier Giacomo Castiglioni
(1918–2002 and 1913–68) is novel, fresh and delightfully frivolous. It
fixes a tractor seat to a highly engineered piece of flat steel and ends
in a tapering footrest. This design and his Sella stool with bicycle
seat from the same year influenced the next generation of designers,
and whets the appetite for many of the playful designs that followed.

left

Sella

This curious stool made from a bicycle seat on a stem
was designed by Achille and Pier Giacomo Castiglioni
in 1957. Its surreal flavour provided a foretaste of the
imaginative, and often wild, ideas to come in the 1960s,
1970s and 1980s.

opposite

Tulip Chair and Table

Pointing to the future, these organically shaped and
moulded chairs designed by Eero Saarinen in 1956 were
way ahead of their time. Saarinen's dream was to create
a chair from a single piece of material, but technology
refused to match his ideas and the seat shell had to be
made separately from the stem base. Other versions of
the table include a white marble top.

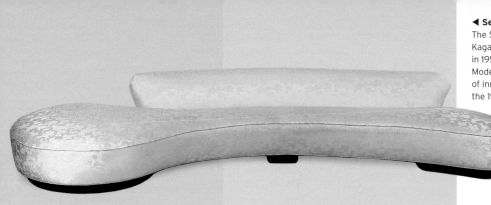

◀ Serpentine Sofa, 1949

The Serpentine sofa, created by Vladimir Kagan and manufactured for Kagan-Dreyfuss in 1950, has sinuous curves and an organic Modernist shape. Kagan is known for a variety of innovative sofa designs from the 1940s to the 1960s, both individual pieces such as the Moon (1949) and the Sloane (circa 1950), and modular units such as the Omnibus (1974).

Key icons of
mid-century
modernism

▲ Time-Life Stool, 1960

A walnut stool by Charles and Ray Eames for Herman Miller. Ray Eames drew on her training as a sculptor to design a new kind of occasional piece for the lobby of the Time-Life Building in New York City.

▼ Lady Armchair, 1951

By Marco Zanuso for Arflex. Among the first designs to use foam rubber as furniture upholstery, the Lady armchair consists of four elements: back, seat and two arms, each upholstered separately.

▲ Credenza Cabinet, 1961

Florence Knoll mixed wood and metal to great effect, as seen here in her four-unit marble-topped Credenza cabinet in wood veneer, made by Knoll.

▶ Butterfly Stool, 1956

By Sori Yanagi for Tendo Mokko. Two identical moulded-plywood elements are linked by a metal stretcher with a sublime oriental beauty.

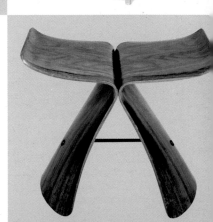

▼ Arabesco Tea Table, 1950

This plywood-and-glass table was designed by Carol Mollino for Apelli & Varesio. The wood base is reminiscent of tree branches or deer's antlers and it is a biomorphic design using moulded-plywood technology.

Diamond Lounge Chair, 1951-2

The airy steel-mesh seat of this elegant chair by Harry Bertoia for Knoll International was sculpted out of steel rods; the mesh was then moulded and secured to a metal stand.

▼ Platform Bench, 1946

Introduced in 1946 as part of George Nelson's first collection for Herman Miller, the Platform Bench, with its clean, rectilinear lines, reflects Nelson's architectural background. The slats are spaced so air and light pass through.

▲ Cyclone Table, 1954

Created by Isamu Noguchi and manufactured by Knoll, these tables in varying sizes are composed of circular bases and tops with spindly metal stems.

◄ Club Sofa, 1962

Britain's original Club sofa was designed by Robin Day in 1962; it was generously proportioned and comfortable.

Pop & Post-Modernism

Into the future: furniture designs from 1960 to 1985

The decade that followed the austere, monochrome 1950s was, by contrast, a Technicolor era of confidence and consumer boom. In the western world, it was an exciting moment to be young; for the first time young people had their own fashions and music, while Pop Art and drug-fuelled psychedelia ensured that the new world was pulsating with primary colours and pattern. In the wider world, the picture was troubled. Shock rippled around the globe when President John Kennedy was assassinated in 1963, and then came another terrible blow five years later when his brother Robert was killed. In 1966 China declared a cultural revolution, and in 1968 the murder of American black civil-rights leader Martin Luther King led to riots in 100 US cities. America was at war with Vietnam, and Soviet tanks rolled into the streets of Prague, Czechoslovakia, to crush a popular anti-Communist uprising.

In the home, there was an explosion of colour, pattern and new materials, especially plastics, which helped to inspire expressive and revolutionary furniture designs. Homes and interiors magazines began to appear that showed readers how to transform their living spaces and put together this new look. Pages of seductive advertising also promoted this modern, aspirational lifestyle; whether for cookers (ovens) or carpets, cigarettes or vodka, the ads generally showed beautiful people draped over the latest furniture. In design, the greatest change was the rejection of and shift away from the International Style. It was no longer the case that functionalism should be the designer's primary concern. As part of this strong reaction against the straitjacket of Modernism, young designers argued that their work could be functional, if it was necessary, and also much more besides. Echoing trends in pop music, fashion and art, furniture began to become more laidback, informal and, above all, fun.

Following the exuberance, and almost sheer joy, of the 1960s, the 1970s took a more sombre course. The dream of endless low-cost energy came to an abrupt halt with the 1973 oil crisis; the price of oil quadrupled and the decade culminated in a second oil crisis in 1979. As a result, petroleum-based materials like plastics became very expensive to produce and the rush to use them slowed down. But the effects of the oil crisis spread beyond the use of plastics, with rising energy prices also boosting manufacturing costs. It soon became apparent that the world was in recession. The effect of world events on designers was profound. Many questioned their role in the consumer society and felt compelled to be more careful with natural resources, to use technology in a more careful way and to think about ways of countering obsolescence and encourage recycling. There was also a move toward producing more human-centred designs, not just for the general public, but also for specific groups such as young children and the elderly.

overleaf
There is something unmistakably glamorous about the organic and freeform shapes of the Pop era. Here, Eero Aarnio's Ball seat from the mid-1960s sits alongside the chaise designed by Charles and Ray Eames with astonishing vision in the late 1940s. In the background are Verner Panton's all-in-one Panton chairs from the late 1960s.

below
The chair and stool below, designed by Nanna and Jørgen Ditzel in 1957 and produced by Fritz Hansen, are typical Scandinavian Pop designs in candy colours. They are shown in Nanna's bedroom in the house in Klareboderne, Copenhagen.

below

Corona Chair

Four elliptical-shaped cushions are held in space on a slender metal frame in Paul Volther's 1961 Corona chair, also known as Model No. EJ 605. Each cushion is based on a piece of shaped plywood that is foam padded and then upholstered. The design is said to have been inspired by the solar eclipse.

Panton Chair

With its glamorous curves and gorgeous colours, the late 1960s Panton chair by Verner Panton has remained a firm favourite for half a century. It is claimed to be the first single-material, single-form injectio-moulded chair, made now in a choice of rigid expanded plastic with a lacquer finish, or, since 1999, in satin-finish polypropylene. There's also a children's version: the Panton Junior.

Tube System

A highly ingenious concept by Joe Colombo, produced in 1970, this modular seating system is based on a series of rigid plastic tubes padded with foam and then upholstered. They can be fixed together in a variety of configurations. One of the most appealing features of the design was that the composite parts were sold slotted inside one another and stashed in a drawstring bag. It was ideal for the new generation of young homemakers.

Italy in the 1960s Spotlight

While brilliant new furniture designs were appearing around the world, the epicentre of energy and excitement throughout the 1960s was Italy. The outpouring of innovation here was unmatched by any other country. Although still recovering from the effects of the Second World War, Italy was at last enjoying a period of stability; in the 1950s it had joined NATO and become a member of the European Economic Community, both events which helped revive the economy. The country had a long-established tradition of furniture-making and there was also a plentiful supply of skilled workers. Because most of the workshops and factories were small, their owners were prepared to experiment with small editions of the new designs in new materials. The country was also able to build on its powerful design heritage, and with its high-quality design education, it produced confident and dynamic designers. Often working in small studios, single designers and groups of collaborators seized on the new plastic and foam materials and wrought them into the most unusual, captivating and sometimes outrageously over-the-top designs.

By the mid-1960s, Italy's Radical design movement was under way. It had a theoretical and philosophical base, which was to encourage the public to question accepted norms. This was to be achieved by taking everyday objects and reconfiguring them in different and surprising ways, and by using new materials. Key proponents included groups such as Superstudio, Archizoom Associati, UFO, Gruppo Strum and individuals such as Ettore Sottsass. Eventually, this questioning would lead on to the Post-Modern movement of the 1980s.

The range and variety of work produced at this time is quite astounding, with many designs challenging such basic notions as traditional furniture construction, the use of materials and the shapes and colours of chairs and tables, even the possibility of making transparent designs. Highlights include the 1961 Ribbon chair by Franca Stagi (1937–) and Cesare Leonardi (1935–), which was made by the Bernini company near Milan. As the name suggests, the main feature of this design is the ribbon-like formation for the seat. Made from moulded fibreglass, a great band of the material has been depressed in the middle to form the backrest and arms; the lower part of the band forms the seat. This fibreglass body sits on a triangular tubular steel base. It is a particularly powerful design because it is so expressive and yet apparently simple.

Fibreglass proved to be a dream material for designers, as it provided a way of making broad curves and large shell-like forms. It was also the material of choice for Joe Colombo (1930–71), with his Elda armchair from 1965. Its great cup-like shell, with a high curved back, is considered to be the first such design in self-supporting fibreglass. It is given deep upholstery and finished in leather and the whole unit sits on an invisible rotating base. Colombo was among the most prolific and inventive of Italy's designers in the 1960s and broke ground with plenty of his designs, using a rich palette of materials from plywood and steel to plastics. Among the most unusual was his Tube system for the Milanese company Flexform. It was conceived as a modular system of different-size tubes, made from rigid plastic that was upholstered in foam and covered in textile – the idea was to link together a sequence of tubes to form chairs, stools and loungers. Modular furniture was a new concept that fascinated many designers at the time. It provided the possibility for reconfiguration, so that owners could change the look of their rooms by rebuilding the furniture. Colombo revisited the theme several times in his career, most successfully in 1968 with the Additional Living System, a series of foam-filled cushions in different sizes that could be assembled in a variety of configurations and held in place on a metal base with metal pins.

below
Two of Verner Panton's fresh and original designs. On the left is the Pantonova Wire chair, with upholstery, from 1966. A cantilevered, upholstered tubular steel chair, right, is from Panton's 1973 System 1-2-3.

Blow Chair

Inflatable furniture captured the public imagination in 1967 with the armchair called Blow by Gionatan De Pas (1932–), Donato D'Urbino (1935–) and Paolo Lomazzi (1936–). Fresh and original, it was made from see-through PVC and was available in many colours.

Experiments in plastics produced a constant stream of innovative designs during this era. In 1964 the Italian Marco Zanuso (1916–2001) and the German Richard Sapper (1932–) launched their brightly coloured child's stacking chair, Model No. 4999/5. When patents expired in the mid-1960s, polyethylene became a much cheaper material to use, and so Zanuso and Sapper decided to explore its potential in the production of furniture. Their child's stacking chair has a distinctive ribbed back and seat, designed specifically to provide a rigid structure. While this was the first chair completed in injection-moulded polyethylene, it was still not possible to make a single-piece design, and the legs had to be made separately. It was made by the large Italian company Kartell, which was set up by Giulio Castelli (1920–2006) in 1949 and set out to introduce plastics into the home; the company continues with groundbreaking designs, mostly in plastic, today. Following swiftly after this, and also from Kartell, Joe Colombo produced his own design for the first adult chair using an injection-moulding process, this time in ABS plastic (acrylonitrile butadiene styrene), a refined material chosen for its superlative surface quality, colourfastness and lustre. Called the Universale, it took a full two years to develop and eventually entered production in 1967. The design is chubby and softly rounded, but once again Colombo was thwarted from making an all-in-one piece and the legs had to be produced separately. Today the chair is made in batch-dyed polypropylene. In fact, by the arrival of the Universale, the first single-piece, plastic chair, complete with four legs, had just been launched at the 1966 Cologne Furniture Fair by the German designer Helmut Bätzner (1928–). His BA 1171 design, also known as Bofinger, used compression-moulded, fibreglass-reinforced, polyester resin.

However, the most iconic plastic chair of all time came in 1968 from the Danish designer Verner Panton (1926–98). Called Panton, it is a single-piece chair with a sweeping curved base, cantilevered seat and rounded back. The designer had been working on the design and trying to solve the technical challenges of production since the late 1950s, but it wasn't possible until the company Vitra came up with a manufacturing solution by using a material called Baydur, a type of hard foam. Originally sold by Herman Miller, the Panton was the first single-piece, single-material, injection-moulded chair and continues to be made by Vitra in a choice of materials: hard-foam plastic finished with a gloss lacquer or the cheaper polypropylene.

Back in Italy, polyurethane foam was seized upon by designers because of the endless possibilities it presented for forming voluptuous, curvaceous shapes from this rigid-soft material that required no framework for support. In 1966 the design group Archizoom Associati designed the Superonda, a rectangular, two-piece unit of interlocking, curvy shapes that could be configured in a number of ways, but most often to create a sofa-style arrangement with seat and backrest. In the same year, architect and artist Roberto Sebastian Matta (1911–2002) produced his 'installation' called Malitte, which comprised five interlocking, curvy pieces of textile-covered polyurethane foam that could be used separately to furnish an entire room, or pieced together to form a sculptural wall. Perhaps

The beanbag, a symbol of the laid-back Pop era, began life as the Sacco in 1968. Designed by Piero Gatti, Cesare Paolini and Franco Teodoro, it was essentially a large bag filled with polystyrene beads. The small beads adapted to the sitter's shape, making it perfect for informal lifestyles.

Ingenious and intriguing, Gaetano Pesce's Up series of seating from 1969 was made from textile-covered moulded polyurethane foam in seductive, rounded shapes. The furniture was sold as a compressed, vacuum-packed slab in a PVC wrapper. Once the wrapping was removed, the furniture filled with air, expanded and literally sprang to life.

most extraordinary of all, however, was Gaetano Pesce's (1939–) Up series from 1969. Made from textile-covered, moulded polyurethane foam in seductive, rounded shapes, the greatest novelty here was that the furniture was sold as a compressed, vacuum-packed slab in a PVC wrapper. As the wrapping was removed, the furniture literally sprang to life.

The Italians seemed irrepressible, and before the decade was out they had produced yet more iconic designs. Inflatable furniture caught the public attention in 1967 with an armchair called Blow by Gionatan De Pas (1932–91), Donato D'Urbino (1935–) and Paolo Lomazzi (1936–). Created in see-through PVC, which was made possible by the invention of new welding techniques for this material, the chair marked yet another departure from the recognizable forms of the past, and one year later another iconic design found its place into the history books. Sacco chair by Piero Gatti (1940–), Cesare Paolini (1937–) and Franco Teodoro (1939–), was perfect for the informality of the times. Essentially a large bag filled with polystyrene beads, it was moulded by the human form and adopted the shape of any sitter. The design has been much copied and became known as the 'beanbag'.

Joe Colombo (1930–71)

above
Joe Colombo was one of the most influential designers of his generation. His work was always fresh and innovative.

Joe Colombo was only in his early forties when he died, but he was already a prolific and influential designer of furniture, storage ideas, lamps, clocks and interiors. He is perhaps best known for his curvy, sensual, glamorous shapes and wild futuristic ideas, and became a key player in the explosion of new Italian design throughout the 1960s.

Born in Milan in 1930, his real name was Cesare, but for most of his life was known by his nickname, Joe. His father ran the family firm manufacturing electrical components and Joe studied painting and sculpture at art school in Milan, then architecture at the Politecnico di Milano, joining the avant-garde group called Movimento Nucleare (Nuclear Painting Movement) in 1951. It was here that he began to evolve his futuristic visions about how society was changing and how people might live in the future; his paintings featured abstract and organic forms – an early manifestation of his dislike for sharp corners and straight lines.

His career in design began in the early 1950s when he created an art installation for the ceiling of a Milan jazz club. He followed this by designing and making a series of television 'shrines' for the Milan Triennale in 1954. It was at this point that he changed career and began to study architecture. By the late 1950s, following his father's death, he and his brother took over the running of the family firm. With his art career on hold, the factory became his new studio where Colombo became fascinated with the potential of plastics and experimented with their properties.

In 1962 he opened his own design studio and worked on interior designs for ski lodges and a hotel in Sardinia. Modern one-piece interiors fascinated him, along with adaptable furniture, and in 1963 he produced the eye-catching Elda armchair made from fibreglass. This represented a remarkable piece of ingenuity; it was a large, high-backed chair in moulded fibreglass, with deeply upholstered cushions and set on a rotating base. It continues to be made today by the Italian company Comfort. Also in 1963 came Colombo's design for the Minikitchen, made in a small edition in 1964 by Boffi. This was a version of the 'hostess trolley', which was so popular at the time, and included a small fridge, a twin hotplate, storage space and pull-out chopping board – all on wheels. The unit has now been updated and reissued by Boffi and made in the modern acrylic material Corian.

In the early 1960s Colombo started experimenting with different materials. His early work in moulded plywood gave way to pressed steel in his 1964 chair called LEM, standing for Lunar Excursion Module because of its resemblance to the machines being used on the moon at the time. The black frame, made from flat metal strips, was finished in chunky, ribbed upholstery for the seat and the backrest covered in black leather. Around the same time, further experiments in moulded plywood produced the chair called Model No. 4801, which had a fluid shape with a rounded back that curved downwards to form arms and then underneath to make the base. The whole structure is made from just three interlocking pieces.

Living Centre Units

Colombo's interest in whole-room environments
and systems found one expression in these
Living Centre units on castors from 1971,
designed for Rosenthal. To the left, a storage
unit is combined with a table with tambour
doors. The chaise with padded seat on the
right features retractable shelves.

below

Model No. 4801

An innovative plywood chair designed in
three interlocking sections by Joe Colombo
in 1964. His first design for Kartell, it was
made in a white, black or natural finish. The
use of fluid-shaped plywood prefigures
Colombo's later use of plastic storage units.

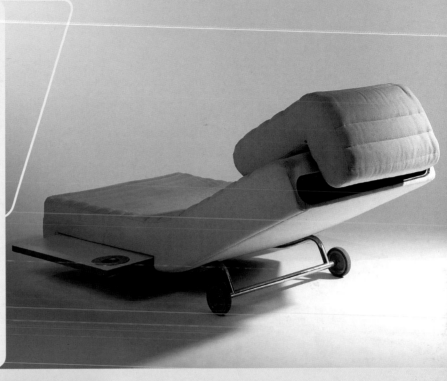

His work in plastic culminated in the mid-1960s with the classic
designs for the Universale chair, Model No. 4860, still made by
Kartell. Although it was originally intended to be made in aluminium,
Colombo eventually settled on injection-moulded ABS plastic. His
goal was to make a chair in one piece, but despite his best efforts,
the legs had to be made separately. He turned this to his favour,
however, by making virtue of the fact that the legs were detachable,
and they were offered in two lengths.

Later in the 1960s he moved into modular furniture design with
the clever Additional Living System (1967). This was based on a
series of polyurethane foam cushions that could be linked together
in different configurations for sitting, lounging or lying. The idea was
revisited in 1970 with his Multi chair, a system based on just two
pieces that could be fixed together or used separately in a variety
of configurations. In the same year came his Optic alarm clock,
now produced by Alessi, and ingenious compartmental plates for
the airline Alitalia.

In 1971 he produced another of his classic pieces, this time
for storage, which remains in production with Bieffeplast. The
Boby trolley is a mobile stacking unit made from ABS plastic and
containing a tower of rotating drawers and shelves on five castors;
Colombo's signature is embossed on the lower shelf. It was featured
on the set of the British science-fiction television series *Space 1999*.
This proved to be one of his last designs: while he was at his most
creative, he died of a heart attack on his forty-first birthday.

A Rich Mix: Primitivism, Plastic, Paper and Plywood

Outside of the excitement that was occurring in Italy, the trickle of new and ingenious furniture and household product designs that appeared in the 1950s became a torrent of ingenuity in the 1960s. Hot spots of invention included the United States, Britain, Scandinavia and France. Bearing little resemblance to traditional and familiar designs, many new pieces were infused with a sense of freedom, energy and excitement; they broke fresh ground in proposing new ways to sit, eat and relax. Designers were not afraid to experiment – quite the opposite in fact. They relished the chance to break away from the past, to try new ideas, borrow from other cultures and experiment with even the most unlikely materials.

In 1960 Charles and Ray Eames drew inspiration from African design with their highly unusual Time-Life stools. In a move away from the hi-tech productions that had marked their earlier career, they took a complete departure from the mainstream and moved towards low-tech simplicity with these solid-walnut wood stools. They are all the more surprising when seen in contrast with the extremely slick and highly technical aluminium series of chairs that the Eameses had produced just a couple of years earlier. Designed for the lobby of the Time-Life Building in New York, the stools were conceived for use as a seat or a table and echoed the widespread fascination at the

below

Rounded and blobby shapes symbolized modernity during the 1960s. Here, seating includes a Tulip chair by Eero Saarinen, 1956 on the left, a couple of fibreglass-reinforced, polyester Pastil chairs from 1967 by Eero Aarnio in the centre, and by the same designer and in the same material, the Ball or Globe chair from 1966, described as a 'room within a room'.

below

Throw-Away Armchair

Along with the new consumerism of the 1960s, came the throw-away culture. Willie Landels designed low-tech and inexpensive disposable furniture, called the Throw-Aways, in 1965. The sofas and chairs were made from block polyurethane foam covered in vinyl or leather.

Bubble Chair

Made in acrylic, the Bubble was designed by Eero Aarnio in 1968, who explained, 'After I had made the Ball chair I wanted to have the light inside it, and so I had the idea of a transparent ball where light comes from all directions. The only suitable material is acrylic, which is heated and blown into shape like a soap bubble… the name was obvious: Bubble.'

Polyprop Chair

The classic multipurpose stacking chair, the Polyprop, was designed by Robin Day in 1963 and made in moulded polypropylene. Its seating shell is separate from the metal legs. These chairs have sold around the globe in millions.

time with so-called primitive art. Underlining her interest in sculpture, Ray Eames is usually credited with their design. The stools feature in numerous photographs of the Eameses' home, which was furnished in a highly original, Modern-Bohemian style, with pieces of their own furniture sitting alongside collections of Middle-Eastern rugs, African masks and sculptural carvings, and Modern artworks.

Meanwhile, in Britain, Robin Day was experimenting with the latest man-made materials, particularly new plastics, and he finally fixed his attention on polypropylene. Building on the development of polyethylene (also known as polythene) in the 1930s, polypropylene evolved in the 1950s as a material that was flexible, yet more rigid than many plastics. It also demonstrated a very high resistance to fatigue, which made it incredibly durable. Day had a long-held ambition to create a chair that was light and strong and could be cheaply mass-produced. In 1963 he launched his low-cost Polyprop stacking chair, which was made with a new injection-moulding process. Inspiration came from Charles and Ray Eames in America who, a decade earlier, had been working on a single-shell chair made from fibreglass-reinforced plastic. Day's understated design has a seat and back that are moulded as one piece and fixed to a base with metal legs. It finally put Modern design at the heart of everyday life throughout Britain – thousands of the chairs were produced by manufacturer Hille every week and found a wide range of uses from schools and community halls to hospitals and factory canteens. It has been estimated that more than 14 million Polyprop chairs have been sold worldwide and Hille International continues to make them at a rate of 500,000 a year. The success led Day to produce more designs in this material, including the elegant Poly armchair in 1967 and the Polo in 1973, which is distinctive because of the pattern of holes featured in the shell. The Polo was relaunched in 2000 by the company Loft and is now available with a choice of leg configurations and in a range of a dozen colours.

In the same year as the Polyprop, another British designer created a storm with his own first design – Peter Murdoch (1940–) launched his novel paper chair called Spotty. This fantastic piece of innovation is based on a cone of laminated cardboard, which becomes rigid and strong enough to hold a child's body weight when the top is folded down to make a scooped-out seat and back. Decorated with huge red, green or blue polka dots, Spotty found instant mass-market success and has become a genuine 1960s icon. As part of the 'disposable' culture of the time, this can lay claim to being the first piece of throw-away furniture. Ironically, the very fact that it was disposable now makes this chair rare and highly collectable.

Alongside work in new materials came innovations with existing products. Fascination with plywood has never dulled for designers,

and furniture that demonstrates fresh ways of using this ever-popular material continues to appear every few years. In the early 1960s, it was the turn of Danish designer Grete Jalk (1920–) to make her contribution to the continuing story of plywood with her numerous and beautiful designs. The most elegant is her Lounge chair of 1963 (see also page 59). With a strong Japanese flavour, the piece bends plywood in an extreme way that had never been achieved before – Jalk has literally folded the material. Her chair is made in two pieces: vertical planes form the legs with the seat appearing to be slung in between, like a broad band of ribbon frozen in space. The back continues the folded, ribbon-like appearance. Along with one-off pieces, she also became interested in whole-room environments, and as early as 1947 created a room set for a 'self-supporting woman's den'. Created for a professional woman it comprised a bed, wall storage unit and a desk. Her later works include the 1963 Watch and Listen living-room unit, which was an early example of furniture for the modern living room as a place to relax rather than entertain guests. Produced in pine, her living-room unit featured built-in compartments for an extensive home-entertainment system – with the television as the centrepiece, she designed shelving for storing and accessing a stereo system, tapes, records and even a small film projector. The unit was flanked by openly displayed speakers, demonstrating one of the ways in which industrial design was becoming considered more seriously as part of the home landscape. While Jalk is not that well known, she was prolific and her pieces were expertly made, which makes them highly collectable.

right

Spotty Chair

As part of the disposable culture, this 1963 chair was made in laminated cardboard that, once folded, was rigid and strong enough to hold the weight of a child. The designer is Peter Murdoch. The very fact that it was disposable now makes this chair rare and highly collectable.

below

Ribbon Chair

An elegant flourish, the Ribbon chair, designed by Pierre Paulin in 1965, is made from a tubular metal frame covered with a tensioned rubber sheet, latex foam and upholstery. It balances on a central stem that concludes in a lacquered wood base.

above

Djinn

With a strong anthropomorphic design, the Djinn s
eries of seating by Oliver Mourgue, originally made for
Airborne International in 1965, is sculpted and friendly-
looking. The soft, upholstered forms found their way into
film when they appeared in Stanley Kubrik's 1968 cult
movie *2001: A Space Odyssey*.

In France, two great designers rose to prominence in this
decade: Pierre Paulin (1927–) and Olivier Mourgue (1939–).
Paulin worked closely with the Dutch company Artifort and
experimented with fibreglass, steel, foam and elasticized fabrics
to create highly sculptural forms. Among the most instantly
recognizable is the Ribbon chair of 1965, which is formed from
a folded band of rubber sheeting that is stretched over a metal
frame and then upholstered and covered in textile. The shape
grows up from a central stem base, and has a seat and back that
loops in a sculptural flourish. Even more abstract in design is
Paulin's Tongue chair of 1967. The wave shape is formed from a
tubular steel frame, which is upholstered in foam and covered in
textile. Meanwhile, Olivier Mourgue's most memorable furniture
is his Djinn series from 1965. Sculptural and rounded, with
anthropomorphic shapes, the furniture is made from bent steel
frames covered in polyurethane foam and then covered in fabrics.

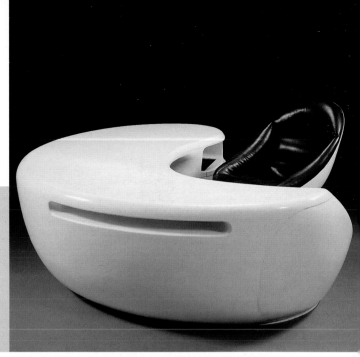

Boomerang Desk and Chair

A 1969 fibreglass desk and leather-upholstered swivel chair by Maurice Calka and Jean Leleu-Deshays, commissioned by the prestigious firm of Leleu-Deshays. The rounded form and curving, sculptural shape has come to epitomize the playful technological imaginings and aesthetics of late-1960s design.

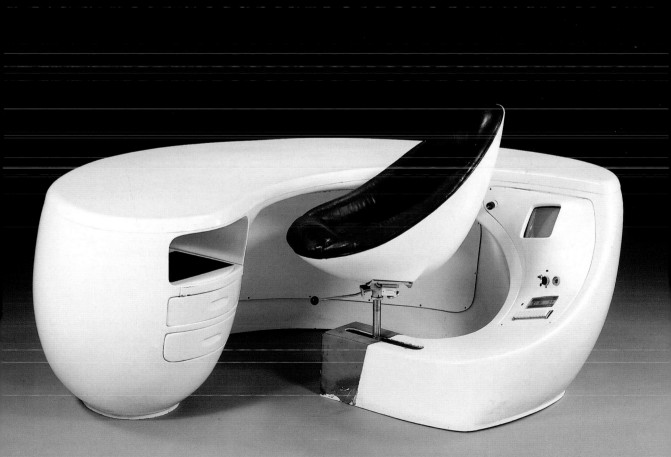

Verner Panton (1926–98)

The father of Pop design, Verner Panton is best known for his colourful, futuristic, exuberant, sensual and experimental designs. His most famous piece is the iconic and curvy, brightly coloured plastic Panton chair that was both a design and technological breakthrough. He also created a portfolio of groundbreaking seating designs, along with lighting, textiles and colourful, psychedelic whole-room environments.

Born in Denmark to parents who ran an inn and restaurant, Panton had an early yearning to be an artist. He trained as an engineer and architect and spent some of his formative years, from 1950–2, working in the Copenhagen office of Modernist giant Arne Jacobsen at a time when was Jacobsen's famous Ant chair, made from moulded plywood, was being developed.

In 1955 he set up his own office and in the same year produced his first chair, the Bachelor chair, for Fritz Hansen. In true Scandinavian style it is restrained and understated, based on a bent-metal frame and with simple panels of canvas for the seat and backrest. In the same year came the Tivoli chair, metal-framed again, but this time with a seat and back in woven plastic cord. It wasn't long, however, before Panton broke into his more expressive designs; in 1958 he produced the Cone chair for the Komigen, his parent's new restaurant in Fünen, Denmark, which he had given an all-red interior. The chair was based on a piece of sheet metal that was twisted into a cone shape, padded, covered in fabric and sat on a cross-shaped metal base. Danish businessman Percy von Halling-Koch of the company Plus-Linje saw the design at the restaurant's opening and offered to put the chair into production. It soon found its way onto magazine covers and is reputed to have caused a stir when it first went on show in a shop window in New York – the designs distracted car drivers and the crowds, who had to be moved on by the police. A heart-shaped version of the Cone was also produced and the shape appeared again in a modified form in Panton's Peacock lounge chair (1960), this time made from wire mesh and given multicoloured circular pad cushions. The company Plus-Linje also produced this, and early versions are highly collectable.

Panton travelled extensively through Europe in his Volkswagen van and, after a brief spell in Cannes in 1962, moved to Basel in Switzerland, where he spent much of the rest of his life. Here he worked closely with the manufacturer Vitra. The company continues to produce a range of Panton furniture designs. Among their first collaborations was the Flying chair (1964), a curvy upholstered shell that was suspended from the ceiling on wires. Typical of Panton's quest for new ways of sitting and lounging, it stole the show at the 1964 Cologne Furniture Fair. A year after this, in 1965, he unveiled his S chair, the first cantilevered design made from moulded plywood and produced by Thonet. This was quickly followed by his most famous piece, the Panton chair. The visionary idea of producing a chair made from a single piece of material had been pursued by others, but after years of experimenting with the manufacturer Vitra, Panton finally succeeded. First produced in 1967, the curvy, cantilevered design was made from cold-pressed, fibreglass-reinforced polyester. Launched the following year at the Cologne Furniture Fair, it was soon being made in a new material

above

Heart Chair

Launched in 1958, this was a futuristic design triumph – the curvaceous outline was achieved by bending sheet metal to form a frame for the strech-knit upholstery. Like his Cone series of the same year, Panton scu;pted an innovative chair outline without conventional legs. In 1994 Polythema reissued it. Very early examples have white-plastic glide feet.

right

An example of one of Panton's all-embracing and rather overwhelming interiors, complete with a curious landscape of carpeted seating, an abstract-geometric mirror-wall installation and a ceiling entirely hung with a Spiral chandelier of tiny cream-coloured translucent discs.

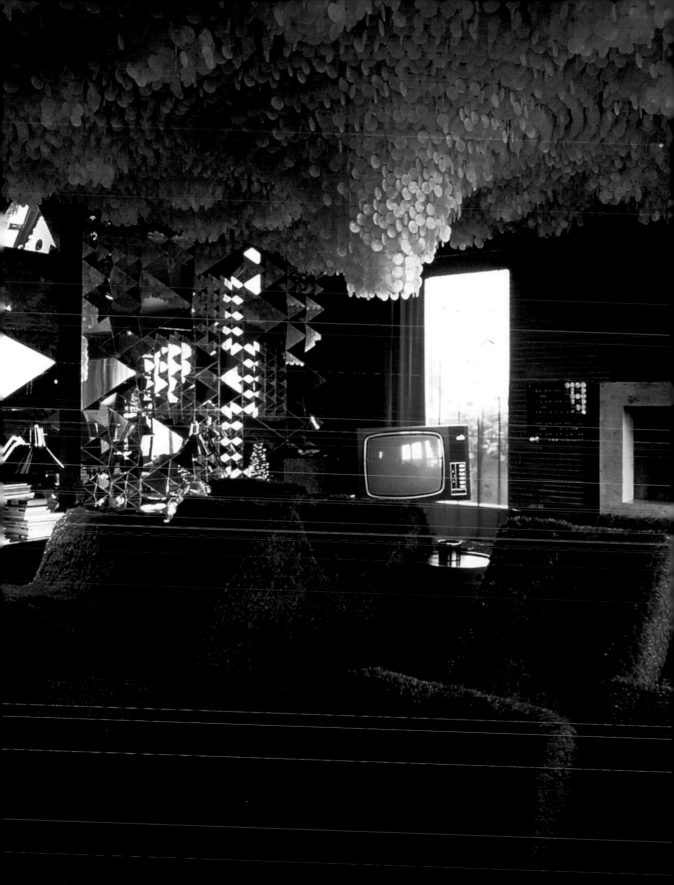

right

Peacock Chair

Experimenting with wire, Verner Panton designed the seating shell of this 1960 chair like a huge bowl. It is upholstered with large, round cushion pads that could be ordered in the same or different colours.

left

Pantower

Panton never ceased in his quest for new forms of furniture. The Pantower from 1969 was one of his wildest concepts. Formed from shaped sheet metal, foam-upholstered and fabric-covered, the idea was to create an environment for perching, sleeping and sitting. It also works as a piece of sculpture.

below

Cone Chair

Sculptural and seductive, the 1958 Cone was a fresh and futuristic design concept based on a piece of shaped metal padded with foam and covered in fabric. Beautifully resolved, the simple shape is pleasing.

called Baydur – polyurethane hard foam. It was a triumph of Pop design combined with the latest manufacturing techniques and has remained a collector's item ever since. Continuing his experiments in seating, in 1969 he created the Pantower. Sitting in and on this highly original design was like lounging in the branches of a tree. The vertical structure was based on a moulded steel frame, upholstered with polyurethane foam and covered in fabric. The marketing material was a triumph, showing Panton stretched and curled up on the different 'branches'.

In addition to these single pieces, Panton always pursued his idea of making whole-room environments. He wanted to blur the lines between floors, walls and ceilings. Among his earliest completed versions of this idea was in the Astoria Hotel in Trondheim, Norway, in 1960, where the walls, floor and ceiling were finished in an Op Art pattern of primary colours. In 1969 he created interiors at the offices of Spiegel Publishing in Hamburg, and in 1970 came his womb-like installation called Phantasy Landscape at the Visiona II exhibition forming part of Cologne Furniture Fair. The idea here was that visitors could sit and lie down in a room that was filled with padded waves of colour. Sponsored by Bayer, it achieved the company's ambition of showing off its synthetic home-furnishing fabrics.

Panton's lighting designs were also highly innovative. He enjoyed a long collaboration with the Danish company Louis Poulsen and explored his preoccupations of creating lighting designs with colour and emotion, while always disguising the source of the light. Among the most unusual designs are his Spiral chandeliers of 1970 – each lamp is made from dozens of small plastic spirals that catch the light as they move and also produce a soft tinkling sound – and his Panthella floor and table lamp from 1971. This unmistakable design is based on a large, semi-spherical shade that sits above a circular base. Panton continued to produce designs through the 1980s and enjoyed renewed interest in his work in the 1990s. With his career back in the spotlight, Verner Panton died in 1998, just 12 days before the opening of a major retrospective exhibition called Light and Colour, which was staged in Denmark.

User-Friendly Design

Throughout the twentieth century, numerous pieces of research were undertaken into the interaction between humans and technology and everyday products. The study of ergonomics, particularly time-and-motion studies, was used to improve efficiency in tasks such as bricklaying and factory production; it was also used to get the best performance from weapons and aircraft controls during the Second World War. Studies involving complex body measurements were used in the home to improve design in areas such as the kitchen and to make furniture as comfortable as possible. Designers became increasingly interested in such things as the optimum height for work surfaces, chair seats and dining tables, and they also explored the different ways in which people sat in chairs – for example, to work, dine or relax – and how they used certain items, such as cutlery and televisions.

One of the areas of concentrated ergonomic research was office furniture. As early as 1973 the manufacturer Olivetti produced an innovative desk chair called the Synthesis 45. Designed by the Italian Ettore Sottsass (1917–), and made in brightly coloured injection-moulded ABS plastic, it is an articulated design – the padded chair seat is on a stem and it has a separate, padded backrest – and was designed to offer office workers a chair that could be adjusted to suit their bodies. Sottsass worked with Olivetti from the late 1950s to help invigorate designs and lift them into a new realm where equipment such as calculators and typewriters could be made visually seductive and highly desirable to younger buyers. Several years later, in 1976, the manufacturer Herman Miller produced its groundbreaking Ergon chair, designed by American William Stumpf (1936–2006). Stumpf was fascinated by the way things worked and how they could be improved. The Ergon is another adjustable chair that is set on a stem and has a padded seat, back and armrests. Stumpf was also part of the team, along with Don Chadwick (1936–), that created the landmark Aeron chair in the mid-1990s, also for Herman Miller. The Aeron is often described as the ultimate ergonomic office chair.

In 1979, British designer Fred Scott (1942–2001) produced his charming and ergonomically sound Supporto chair, made by Hille. It is fully adjustable and was produced as a result of considerable scientific research into how office workers sit and work. With its polished aluminium frame, its distinctive look comes from the elongated backrest and wide-set arms.

below

Ergon Chair

Interest in ergonomics grew in the 1970s, and after establishing his own firm in 1972, William Stumpf created the Ergon chair in 1976, the first ergonomic work chair manufactured by Herman Miller. The Ergon is set on a stem and has a deep, padded seat, large padded back and padded armrests. It is fully adjustable.

In Scandinavia the interest in human-centred design has been particularly strong throughout the twentieth century. Among those specializing in human-centred design is the company Ergonomi, which grew from the collaboration of a group of Swedish designers in the late 1960s. The company has worked on a wide range of products from cutlery and work tools to cameras and medical equipment. One of Scandinavia's leading ergonomic designers is the Norwegian Peter Opsvik (1939–). Among his earliest and timeless designs is the Tripp Trapp child's chair from 1972. This ingenious and simple wooden design features an adjustable seat and footrest, so the chair can be altered as the child grows up. It continues to be made by Norwegian manufacturer Stokke, which also makes Opsvik's 1970 MiniMax adjustable desk, which he designed for both children and adults, and his iconic and unusual Balans chairs from 1979. Based on the idea of distributing the body's weight down the spine and through the knees, the Balans Variable has a padded seat and two padded knee rests, which sit on a curved cradle base, there is no backrest. It is intended for people who are sitting at a desk, but who need to move and change positions while they are working. Additional versions are available with legs and with a backrest.

above right

Supporto Chair

One of the most characterful of all office-chair designs, the Supporto by Fred Scott in 1979 was produced as a result of considerable scientific research into how office workers sit and work. With its polished aluminium frame, its distinctive look comes from the elongated backrest and wide-set arms.

below right

Balans Chair

Introducing an entirely new concept for ergonomic work seating, Peter Opsvik created the Balans chair in 1979 for a kneeling position that is intended to keep the back straight and upright.

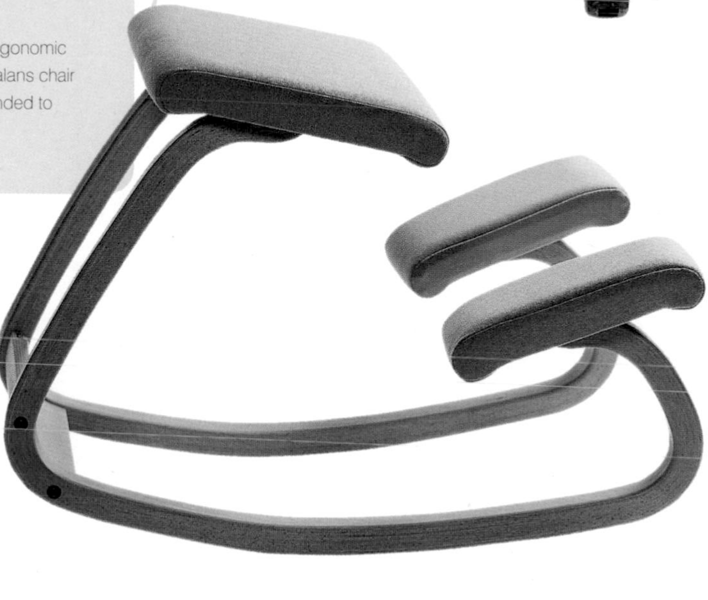

below

Marilyn Sofa

In homage to the surrealist painter Salvador Dalí, who created a 1930s sofa based on the shape of Mae West's lips, Studio 65 updated the story in 1972 with its own sofa based on the iconic actress Marilyn Monroe.

And More Besides

While the design scene of the 1970s was highly fragmented, in addition to the ergonomic chairs it also produced a handful of collectable pieces of furniture. Continuing the stream of brilliant work coming from Italy, the dream team of Gionatan De Pas, Donato d'Urbino and Paolo Lomazzi issued Joe, a massive and sculptural seat made in the form of a baseball glove. Produced in 1970, it was named after the baseball legend Joe DiMaggio. In fact, by appropriating such an iconic piece of design (the glove) and by subverting it and making it large enough to be used as a chair, this stands as an early precursor to the Post-Modern designs that were about to take centre stage during the early 1980s. It can be seen alongside the work of another Italian team, Studio 65, which made such curious objects as the 1971 Capitello chair – based on the sliced-off top of a classical pillar, it resembles a chunk of white stone, but is in fact made of moulded polyurethane foam. The chair was made by the Turin company, Gufram, which continues to produce a series of curious designs from this era including the Marilyn sofa. Designed in 1972, again by Studio 65, it was created in homage to the surrealist painter Salvador Dalí, who in the 1930s modelled a sofa on Mae West's lips. Also in Gufram's collection is the Gruppo Strum's 1966 Pratone seat in moulded polyurethane foam, which looks like a highly magnified chunk of artificial grass. These objects attracted international attention when they went on show in New York at the Museum of Modern Art in the 1972 exhibition entitled Italy: The New Domestic Landscape.

Meanwhile, in the US, the architect Frank Gehry (1929–) added a new twist to the throw-away paper furniture of the 1960s, in his experiments with low-cost designs made from corrugated cardboard. While these designs were inexpensive, they were not intended to be thrown away and could be seen as a response to growing environmental concerns. Unlike the flat-board sheeting used previously, Gehry evolved a system of laminating corrugated cardboard to produce a solid block of material – a similar sort of construction was being used in his office for creating architectural models. In making furniture, the latest die-cutting machinery enabled Gehry to achieve complex, sculptural shapes. Cutting across the grain of the cardboard, the finished pieces left the frayed edges exposed; he described the effect as looking and feeling like corduroy. Among his first pieces was the Easy Edges rocking chair, an all-in-one piece sculpted from cardboard. It formed part of a series of more than a dozen designs produced in 1972. Also from this series was the well-known Wiggle side chair, which, along with a range of side tables and a dining table, are still today made by Vitra.

below

In a clever use of overscaled design, this 1970 Joe sofa is modelled on a baseball glove and made from moulded foam covered with fabric or leather. The designers were Gionatan De Pas, Donato D'Urbino and Paolo Lomazzi. Also shown here is the reinforced fibreglass Karuselli chair, 1965, by Yrjo Kukkapuro.

In Britain, furniture took on a lean and pared-down look. Rodney Kinsman (1943–) designed his extremely popular Omkstak stacking chair in 1971, which was made from a lightweight, tubular steel frame with a broad seat and separate narrow backrest made from colourful epoxy-coated pressed steel sheet pierced with holes. It was a precursor to the hi-tech look that grew popular in the UK in the 1970s. It began in the early architecture of Richard Rogers and Norman Foster, where a building's structure and technical systems, such as central heating and air conditioning, were exposed and celebrated as part of the design. The most famous example of this is the Pompidou Centre in Paris, designed by Richard Rogers (1933–) and Renzo Piano (1937–), which was constructed during the 1970s and opened in 1977. On a smaller scale, industrial products were appropriated for use in interior design for the home. Examples included rubber-stud flooring that was originally designed for factory floors, industrial lamps, industrial kitchen shelving and appliances and aluminium Venetian blinds. The use of these hard materials and industrial-style products can be seen as a reaction against the excesses of the 1960s, and perhaps even a nostalgic backward glance at the functionalism of the early Modernist movement.

Wiggle Chair and Tables

In his first experiments with cardboard furniture, Frank Gehry completed a series called Easy Edges. The collection included this distinctive Wiggle side chair from 1972 and the nest of tables behind, along with a rocking chair and dining table. All are constructed from laminated corrugated cardboard die-cut into shape.

Nanna Ditzel (1923–2005)

Best known for her innovative and brilliant plywood seating, Nanna Ditzel's long career has also included such iconic designs as the woven-cane Hanging chair of 1957 and the Children's Toadstool of 1962, along with textiles, jewellery, tableware and bed linen. As a leading Scandinavian designer, with a career spanning six decades, her work always has a classic, understated and timeless quality.

Born in Copenhagen, Denmark, in 1923, Ditzel trained as a cabinetmaker before studying at the School of Arts and Crafts and then the Royal Academy of Fine Arts in Copenhagen. On graduating in 1946 she established her own design studio with her husband Jørgen Ditzel. From the start of her career, Ditzel relished the

right

Nanna Ditzel, photographed in one of her chairs. She was a hugely prolific designer and was always interested in experimenting with new materials and manufacturing techniques.

below

Bench for Two

One of Nanna Ditzel's best-known designs, this highly unusual bench was made in 1989 from solid maple and aeroplane ply. The eye-catching, hooped pattern is silkscreen-printed. There is a matching wedge-shaped table.

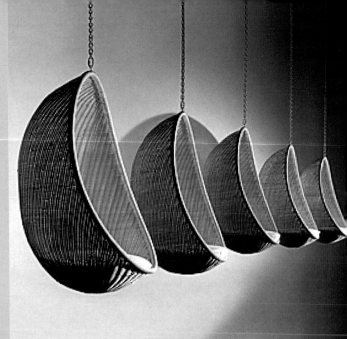

opportunity to experiment with new manufacturing techniques and with materials as varied as fibreglass, wickerwork and foam rubber.

Among her earliest and most memorable designs is the Hanging chair, which she created with her husband Jørgen Ditzel, who died in 1961. The egg-shaped form is incredibly elegant, and because it is made in woven cane, it is also lightweight. The single-shell structure was designed to be suspended from the ceiling and was one of the first such designs. It went on to become hugely popular and iconic during the 1960s and is produced today by the Italian company Pierantonio Bonacina and in Japan by Yamakawa Rattan Industry.

Around the same time Ditzel also produced a series of designs for children's furniture, including the Highchair (1955), an updated and streamlined version of the heavy, old-fashioned designs that were so prevalent at the time, which was made in pine by the company Kolds Savvaerk. There was also the Toadstool, a simple seat made from lathe-turned Oregon pine and made today by Snedkergaarden.

During the 1960s, Ditzel's work diversified into producing exquisite textile designs for Kvadrat and beautiful silver jewellery for Georg Jensen. Early textiles designed for Kvadrat include the Hallingdal Collection from 1964, which is based on a wool fabric with a distinctive weave and composed of rich, saturated colours; it is still in production. More recent collections followed after 2000. Both her corkscrew from 1957 and silver jewellery Surf from 2003 are still made by Georg Jensen.

At the end of the 1960s Ditzel moved to the UK. Between 1968 and 1986 she lived in London; with Kurt Heide, her husband since 1968, she set up the international furniture firm Interspace. Following her return to Denmark, Ditzel entered a period of prolific design work with the manufacturer Fredericia, concentrating mostly on plywood and evolving new ways of working with this intriguing material. Her stream of memorable chairs from this time includes the Bench for

Two (1989), a completely innovative design made from solid maple and airplane ply. Reminiscent of old-fashioned loveseats, it appears as though two chairs have been joined to form a bench. They are given a distinctive silk-screened, black-striped finish, and there is a small table to match.

A year later came the red-and-black-striped Butterfly chair (1990). Again a completely original form, it is made from a cone of folded fibreboard and stands on insect-like, black metal legs. Further experiments with plywood resulted in the Trinidad chair (1993), which is made distinctive by the use of laser cutting to create narrow slits in the back and seat of this stacking chair. In the year she died Ditzel designed the simple folding Concert Hall chair, which was based on the Trinidad and designed for auditoriums.

above

Hanging Chair

Absolutely iconic for the late 1950s and early 1960s, this 1957 ceiling-suspended shell chair made in woven basketwork provided a new seating form and appeared in hundreds of magazine articles and advertisements. It was designed by Nanna Ditzel with her husband, Jørgen, and is still in production.

left

Ring Chair

Originally called the Ring chair, and now known as the Sausage chair, this extremely comfortable armchair was first produced in 1958. Designed by Nanna and Jørgen Ditzel, it is made from laminated beech, maple or cherry and has deep upholstery. .

Beyond Modernism

With western economies recovering from the recessions of the 1970s, the 1980s have come to be remembered as a boom time. In Britain the Conservative politician Margaret Thatcher became the first female British Prime Minister and made it her mission to encourage free-market economics. She set herself against the grip of the unions, most notably in the mining dispute of 1984, and took on the Argentinians in the Falklands War – a battle to save a British dependency that comprised a collection of small islands in the south Atlantic, which were invaded by the Argentinians. In the United States, the Republican President Ronald Reagan promoted his own brand of Conservatism and became Thatcher's close political ally. The era of the rich but young Yuppie was born, and so, too, was the information age and computer technology.

In homes, a mixture of styles proliferated. Among the most popular was a reinvention of a country theme that included floral wallpapers, rag-rolled walls and traditional styles of furniture, while at the other end of the spectrum urban living was on its way back into fashion. In converted factories and warehouses, loft-living evolved. This look was plain, simple and masculine, and was based on exposed brickwork, bare plaster and the tubular-steel and black-leather furniture of the Bauhaus and Le Corbusier, as well as glass-topped tables and photographers' studio lamps.

During the first half of the 1980s, both in furniture design and in architecture, the big story was early Post-Modernism. In architecture, the term Post-Modernism refers to a style of

left

First Chairs

A playful design by Michele de Lucchi, combining simple geometric shapes, and based on a tubular steel frame with circular seat, circular backrest and round armrests. It has been described as symbolizing the electronics age.

building that is considerably more expressive than the streamlined glass-and-steel boxes of the early Modernist decades. It was about rediscovering decoration, mixing in a little irony, perhaps poking some fun and breaking free of the Modernist straitjacket of moderation and restraint.

In furniture, the Italians once again ruled the day. Founded in 1976, Studio Alchimia, with high-profile designers including Alessandro Mendini (1931–) and Ettore Sottsass (1917–), was fascinated by popular culture, everyday objects and by decoration. It became known for its one-off experimental designs, some of which were made in very small editions. There was the famous 1978 version of Marcel Breuer's 1920s Wassily chair, finished by Alessandro Mendini in a splodgy camouflage pattern – heresy to Modernist followers. Also from Mendini, and in the same year, came Proust armchair: a highly ornate period armchair, handpainted with a Pointillist pattern of colourful dots in yellow, blue, green and pink, covering the entire frame and fabric upholstery. The latter piece is now in production with Cappellini.

Following on from this branch of the avant-garde came the Milan-based collective of product and furniture designers called Memphis. In step with like-minded architecture and design colleagues, its aim was to break away from established Modernist notions of good taste. Its members wanted to be irreverent, explore new shapes, and revel in colour and pattern. The group was formed in 1981, and was a powerful and influential force over the following few years. Led by senior designer Ettore Sottsass, the young band of followers included Martine Bedin (1957–), Aldo Cibic (1955–), Michele De Lucchi (1951–), Matteo Thun (1952–) and Marco Zanini (1954–), George Sowden (1942–) and Nathalie du Pasquier (1957–). They were later joined by the American architect Michael Graves (1934–), along with Japanese designers

left

Super Lamp

A colourful and fun design for a floor lamp by Memphis group designer Martine Bedin in 1981. It is reminiscent of a sunburst and, because of the wheels, also resembles a child's toy car.

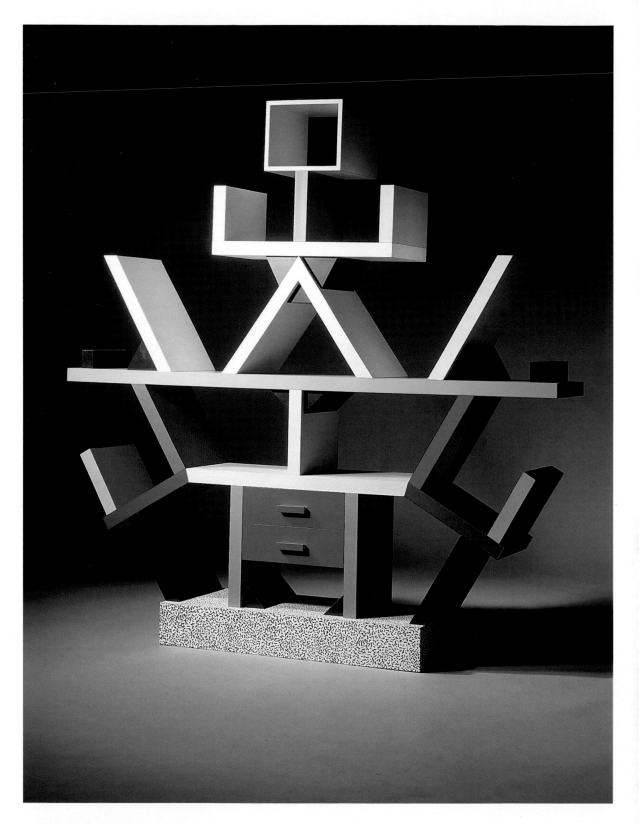

Arata Isozaki (1931–) and Shiro Kuramata (1934–91). The name was borrowed from a Bob Dylan song, *Memphis Blues*, and the group's route to irreverence was to create new and unfamiliar pieces that combined elements from Classical design and kitsch, using cheap, mass-market materials such as plastic laminates, and mixing it all with a dash of Art Deco glamour. These designs fitted perfectly with the latest popular-culture wave of new romanticism.

The tongue-in-cheek works divided opinion right down the middle; there were those who welcomed Memphis as a breath of fresh air, and others who felt threatened and irritated by its juvenile pranks. However, the group's brilliant marketing ensured countless pages of coverage in the latest magazines and it staged exhibitions worldwide from London to Los Angeles and from San Francisco to Tokyo. By 1985 the group was running out of steam and Sottsass announced his departure. It eventually wound down in 1988.

Most pieces of design from the Memphis group are highly collectable and include such key designs as the flamboyant Casablanca sideboard of 1981: a tall cupboard with projecting shelves that make the design almost resemble a robot with arms and legs. It is finished in a colourful combination of red, yellow, black and white. There is also the 1981 Plaza dressing table by Michael Graves – a towering structure, like a piece of fun architecture, with the mirror section sitting on two plinths and climbing to a top capped with a pyramid – and Martine Bedin's Super Lamp from 1981, a semicircle of blue material set on four wheels and studded with six light bulbs.

While Memphis was relatively short-lived, its inheritance is rich and its impact has lived on because it opened the door to freedom for other designers. The Memphis group broke all the Modernist taboos, and showed that it was possible to produce and enjoy more than one prescribed type of design.

Pop and Post-Modern Accessories

For anyone wanting to put together room sets or collect smaller items from this era there are rich pickings indeed. Secondhand shops, retro specialists and auction houses all have plenty to offer. It is also the case that many of the designs have stood the test of time and continue to be produced. Posters are also a quick way of establishing the feel of a period; for example, Andy Warhol's images of Campbell's soup cans are evocative of the 1960s, a James Bond movie poster can sum up the 1970s, and Bridget Riley stripes can help to create an early 1980s feel.

Classic pieces of storage design include Round Up from 1969 by Anna Castelli Ferrieri (1920–2006), manufactured by Kartell. The modular system, made with injection-moulded ABA plastic, is based on circular drums that can be used separately, as stools or low tables, or stacked high into storage towers. From the 1970s, and made by Cappellini, Shiro Kuramata's Furniture in Irregular Forms, including a tall chest of drawers designed in an S shape. Recently reissued by the furniture maker Boffi is Joe Colombo's all-in-one kitchen unit, Minikitchen, from 1963. The cabinet, measuring just 102 by 102 by 66 cm (40 by 40 by 26 in), contains a two-burner

left

Carlton
Probably the most iconic piece of design associated with Memphis, this room divider and shelving unit was designed by Ettore Sottsass in 1981. Irreverent, colourful and quirky, it stood at the other end of the spectrum from rational Modernism.

right

Round Up
Also called the Componibili, this modular storage system in colourful ABS plastic was designed by Anna Castelli Ferrieri in the late 1960s. It comprises shelves and cupboards in circular plastic units.

stove, a fridge, storage space, cutlery drawers, chopping board and a pull-out worktop – everything but the kitchen sink!

In the area of lighting, the choice is endless. Arco is a big gesture from the 1960s; the iconic floor lamp was designed in 1962 for Flos by Achille (1918–2002) and Pier Giacomo Castiglioni (1913–68). Attached to a large slab of marble, the lamp has a dramatic arched stem that cuts through space and terminates in a circular metal shade. For a more delicate piece of design by the same designers, and also for Flos, there is the 1988 Taraxacum pendant lampshade, made from stretched fabric. In 1969 the eldest Castiglioni brother, Livio Castiglioni (1911–79), designed the iconic Boalum lamp in collaboration with Gianfranco Frattini (1926–). Manufactured by Artemide, it was a long, illuminated, translucent flexi-tube that was inspired by the hose of a vacuum cleaner.

In the mid-1960s Joe Colombo designed his elegant Acrilica 281 desk lamp from a single wave of transparent acrylic, which evolved from his work with perspex prisms, and in 1963 Edward Craven-Walker (1918–2000) produced his iconic Lava lamp. From the 1970s comes a range of work from Verner Panton, including his Panthella lamp of 1970 for Louis Poulsen. This is distinguished by its lampshade that is made from half a sphere standing on a circular flared base. In 1972 came the bestselling

Tizio desk lamp from Richard Sapper and made by Artemide. Paper shades by Isamu Noguchi (1904–1988) and Le Klint are also essential accessories from the 1970s.

Beautiful glassware was also produced throughout these years, and among the most exciting and exquisite pieces are those from Scandinavian designers and producers. Look for designer names such as Tapio Wirkkala (1915–85), Oiva Toikka (1931–), Timo Sarpaneva (1926–), and Kaj Franck (1911–89), and manufacturers such as Iittala, Nuutajarvi, Arabia, Orrefors and Boda. Italian glass is of superb quality, too, with producers including Venini and Murano, while in Britain look for the Whitefriars name.

Intriguing everyday items are also numerous. The bright red Valentine portable Olivetti typewriter, designed by Ettore Sottsass in 1969, and consumer electronics including clocks, radios and hi-fi systems from manufacturers such as Braun and Bang & Olufsen are period design icons, as are the first Sony Walkman from 1978 and Richard Sapper's coffee maker of the same year made by Alessi. An undisputed 1960s design classic is the TS 522 portable radio for Brionvega by Marco Zanuso and Richard Sapper. Zanuso and Sapper collaborated on many similar projects during this time such as portable televisions Doney 14 from 1962 and the Algol from 1965, and the 1965 Grillo folding telephone.

left

Panthella

This beautiful lamp, produced in 1970 by Verner Panton, is distinguished by its hemispherical white shade in injection-moulded white opal acrylic, which is supported on a slender stem and flared circular base in steel and injection-moulded ABS.

right

Irregular Forms

Always experimenting with new materials and shapes, here Shiro Kuramata reinvents the chest of drawers. The piece on the left has an appealing vertical wiggle, while on the right the chest has an intriguing rounded 'belly'.

◀ Panton Stackable, 1967
These injection-moulded plastic stacking chairs by Vernon Panton for Herman Miller were unveiled in 1967. The first cantilevered chair to be made from a single piece of plastic, they have since been produced in polypropylene.

▶ Globe or Ball Chair, 1966
By Eero Aarnio for Asko, the fibreglass-reinforced polyester shell with a metal base and support (for stability) offered a protective enclosed seating; his Bubble chair of 1968 was a hanging transparent version.

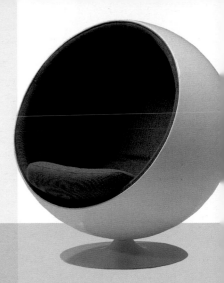

Key icons of

pop & post-modernism

▶ Irregular Forms Cabinet, 1970
Shiro Kuramata produced these unconventional and challenging versions for a tall chest of drawers for Cappellini.

▼ Ribbon Chair, 1965
By Pierre Paulin for Artifort, the Ribbon chair curves and folds towards the central support. Made of a tubular steel frame covered with rubber sheeting and foam rubber padding, it predates moulded plastic.

▲ Djinn Chair, 1965
By Olivier Mourgue for Airborne, the Djinn uses the same materials as Paulin's Ribbon chair – nylon stretch jersey covers the piece and is light in feel and weight.

▲ Carlton Cabinet, 1981
This room divider/bookshelf by Ettore Sottsass embodies his work for Memphis. Sottsass had been experimenting since the mid-1960s with 'superboxes' in bright colours made from inexpensive materials such as plastic laminates.

▼ Karuselli Chair, 1963
Yrjo Kukkapuro's Karuselli chair for Haimi has a white fibreglass shell with a comfortable leather covering. The brushed-metal support allows the sitter to rock and pivot.

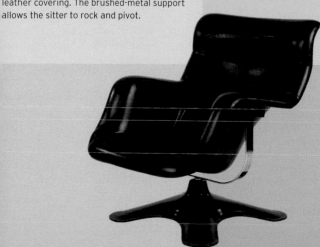

▲ Storage Unit Trolley, 1967
By Joe Colombo for Zanotta, the trolley has 14 layers of laminate in various shapes fixed to four tubular columns. Open storage was a popular concept of the time, and the narrow bottom shelves were for paperwork and magazines.

Late Modernism

Designer decadence: furniture designs from 1985 to 2000

The 1980s has been labelled the 'Designer Decade' – it was the moment when the word 'design' was transformed into an adjective. Here was the era of designer hotels, designer cafés and bars, designer cocktails, designer salad servers, designer ties and designer socks. Design was a marketable commodity: it boasted added value. A designer bowl wasn't any old bowl, but had been given the designer treatment, which meant it was probably made in a modern shape, a modern colour and from a modern material. It was also likely to be credited to a named designer. Everyone could become a design connoisseur and design became collectable, the best (most expensive) design even becoming elevated to the status of an artwork. Much of this outpouring had little or nothing to do with the Modernist ideals of fitness for purpose, or form following function, but was much more about economics.

For a substantial number of people, the Western economies of the 1980s meant that there was plenty of disposable income to lavish on fashion labels and modern furniture. New home-makeover shows appeared on the television and were playing their part in changing tastes and the way we lived. The Swedish home-furnishing emporium Ikea was spreading the word about mass-market, affordable modern design and opening stores all over the world, including Spain in 1980, Saudi Arabia in 1983, Kuwait in 1984, the US in 1985 and the UK in 1987. The burgeoning market for weekend colour supplements with lifestyle pages and home-design magazines included the launch in Britain in 1989 of *Elle Decoration*, which helped to promote ideas for creating and living with contemporary interiors. However, towards the end of the decade the party was drawing to a close and the narcissistic, high-spending yuppie culture was about to get a dose of reality. Following the global stock-market crash of Black Monday in October 1987, the bullish confidence of the money markets turned into a bad hangover and culminated in a recession that lasted into the early 1990s.

In furniture, lighting and homeware design, the tide of idealistic Modernism, which had gathered force almost a century earlier, had ebbed and flowed. Following the explosion of the colourful and patterned designs from the Italian Memphis group and other Post-Modernists in the early 1980s, the second half of the decade saw design ideas ricochet off in different directions. Memphis had blown the lid off the repression of strict Modernism and demonstrated to a new generation of designers that it was possible to pursue ideas that were not enshrined in the preachings of the high priests such as Le Corbusier and Mies van der Rohe.

Design with Attitude

Britain took its turn in the spotlight in the second half on the 1980s with a band of young designers, including Tom Dixon (1959–), Mark Brazier-Jones (1956–), Ron Arad (1951–) and Danny Lane (1955–). These were rebels with a cause, determined to make furniture their own way and to grab plenty of headlines as they went. Interestingly, they shared the fact that they were 'outsiders': Tom Dixon had been born in Tunisia, Mark Brazier-Jones in New Zealand, Ron Arad in Israel and Danny Lane in America. However, by the 1980s they found each other in London, and were enjoying the sense of freedom

overleaf

The fabulous and expressive Hat Trick chairs, 1992, by Frank Gehry and manufactured by Knoll, are made from interwoven flexible strips of maple. The chair is credited with taking its inspiration from the apple crates that Gehry played with as a child.

S Chair

Tom Dixon's S chair, from 1988, is based on a single S-shaped squiggle of steel, which creates a continuous flowing support, cantilevered seat and backrest. It had been made with an assortment of finishes, including woven rush and fabrics. It was put into production in 1992 by the Italian company Cappellini.

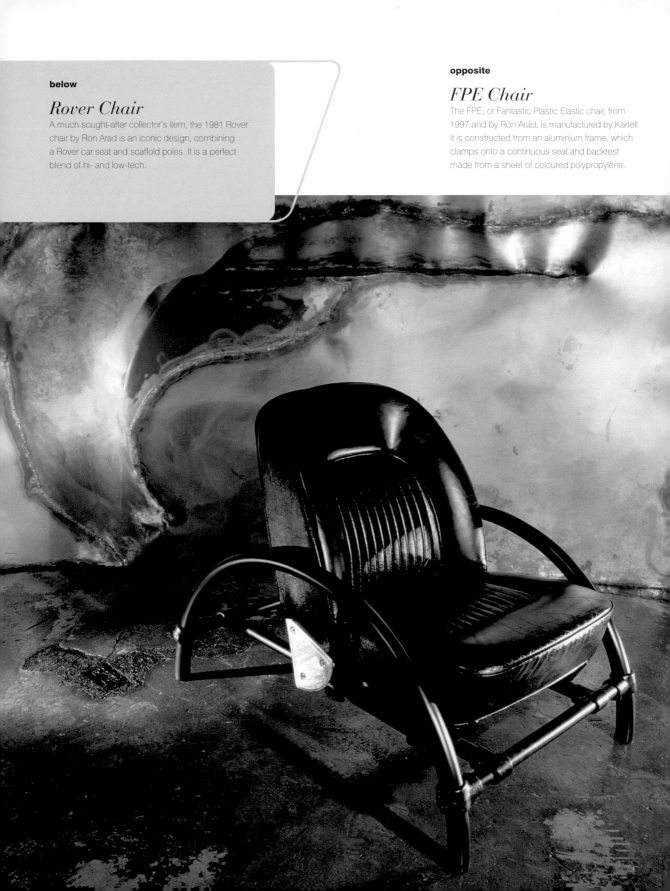

below

Rover Chair

A much sought-after collector's item, the 1981 Rover chair by Ron Arad is an iconic design, combining a Rover car seat and scaffold poles. It is a perfect blend of hi- and low-tech.

opposite

FPE Chair

The FPE, or Fantastic Plastic Elastic chair, from 1997 and by Ron Arad, is manufactured by Kartell. It is constructed from an aluminium frame, which clamps onto a continuous seat and backrest made from a sheet of coloured polypropylene.

created after the Memphis designers had cleared the way for something new. They relished the opportunity to experiment. Unlike the strict functionality of the early Modernists, the rationalism of mid-century designers, the bright lipstick colours and shiny finishes of the Pop era, and the patterned and slick work produced by Memphis designers, their work was rough and ready, ad hoc, handmade, post-industrial, rough-edged, rebellious and charged with energy.

Among the first pieces to emerge from this new wave was Ron Arad's Rover chair of 1981. Using a salvaged Rover car seat, it was put together with a frame of scaffolding poles. The car seat represented a highly accomplished piece of chair production and stood in sharp contrast to the low-tech poles. There were echoes of the past as it bore more than a passing resemblance to a chair designed by Jean Prouvé (1901–84) in 1924, which also had a padded seat and backrest and great semicircular hooped arms made from steel. Arad's design, however, oozed attitude. It appeared in magazines and advertising and grew to be symbolic of the post-punk years and tough urban living. Arad had created a piece of furniture that stood at the threshold of craft and design and it was considered by many to be art. A couple of years after he launched the Rover chair, he set up his own studio/gallery in Covent Garden, London, called One Off, in order to sell his handcrafted pieces.

Scouring skips (dumpsters) and scrapyards and using junk metal, young designer-makers Tom Dixon, Mark Brazier-Jones and Nick Jones started producing strange hybrid pieces of welded sculptural furniture. There was a chair made from Victorian cast-iron railings with a coal-hole cover for its seat, and other pieces made as compositions of bits of welded metals; all of them were conceived as a reaction against the bland mainstream production of furniture design. Like young rock stars or avant-garde artists, these designers became the darlings of the London party scene and, although they were untrained in furniture design, they set up their own company, Creative Salvage, in 1984. This was a rebellious time in Britain. In the same year Prime Minister Margaret Thatcher and her government were involved with the mining dispute, determined to break the power of the unions – this heralded the end of Britain as an industrial society and saw the country entering a new era.

The manifesto for Creative Salvage stated that its members believed the future did not 'lie in expensive, anonymous, mass-produced hi-tech products', but instead required a more decorative and human approach. They weren't interested in the expensive research and development carried out by so many corporations, but instead preferred to turn scrap into stylish and functional artefacts. While the pieces were intended to look raw and handmade, and to be

left

Atlantis Chair

The Atlantis, by Mark Brazier-Jones in 1989, is a beautiful and romantic design with wing-shaped arm supports of cast bronze and fine silk upholstery.

below

Pegasus Chair

Made from a choice of either polished aluminium or bronze, this 1994 three-legged chair by Mark Brazier-Jones is a highly expressive and fantastical design with winged seatback and cabriole legs, which finish in tiny feet.

affordable, they were rarely inexpensive and soon became elevated to collectors' items with huge price tags. One of Dixon's most successful pieces of this time is the S chair from 1988: a big squiggle of mild steel with a cantilevered seat and a narrow back sitting on a circular base. It was available covered in a skin of shiny latex, woven rush or woven cane. After making it himself at first, in 1992 Dixon handed it over for production to the Italian company Cappellini. Meanwhile, Brazier-Jones pursued his interest in functional art and sculpture. Among his key pieces of the 1980s was the 1989 Whaletail, which consisted of a polished cast-aluminium frame with a seatback in the shape of a whale's tail, and, from the same year, his Atlantis armchair, a highly wrought and fantastical design in cast bronze with dainty animal feet, winged arms and floral silk upholstery.

Using metal in an irreverent but quite different way was French designer André Dubreuil (1951–). Working in London in the 1980s, and taught to weld by Tom Dixon, Dubreuil took his inspiration from eighteenth-century France. Appropriating the baroque forms of classic formal furniture, he translated them into metal and gave the pieces decorative finishes. Among the most memorable pieces of the 1980s are his Paris chair from 1988, with its shield-shaped back and cabriole legs that were all in metal and given a spotty, faux leopard-skin finish, and the Spine chair, also from 1988, a whirl of bent and welded steel rods reminiscent of French park chairs. The pieces are poetic and pretty, and there is also an air of decadence about them.

The post-apocalyptic style of design could be found in other areas, too. For a few brief years interior design lost its glossy edge and a number of designers worked carefully to achieve a look of decay and roughness. Floorboards were left in an unfinished state, brick walls were cleaned of their plaster and left exposed, new plaster remained unpainted, industrial lighting was appropriated, and shelving was made from scaffolding boards. The effect was intended to look casual, gritty and urban, when in fact it was highly orchestrated and carefully composed.

Another fellow designer at this time creating his own one-off pieces was American-born Danny Lane. His unique approach was his use of glass – not in smooth, rounded and moulded forms but in great jagged-edged slabs. Among his early pieces is the Etruscan chair from 1984. It has a slab of glass for the seat and another for the back, both of which have nibbled and broken edges, and is held together on a frame of mild steel that is bolted right through the glass. In 1987 he produced the extraordinary Angaraib chaise: a bed of broken-edged glass resting on an arrangement of tree branches. He has gone on to produce other pieces, including the Stacking chair of 1993, made from a stack of glass slabs, along with a series of glass tables and benches and huge glass installations and sculptures, among them his massive 2005 Borealis, one of the world's largest glass sculptures, located at the GM Renaissance Center, Detroit.

below

Etruscan Chair

The Etruscan chair by Danny Lane in 1984 was constructed from a slab of glass for the seat and another for the back, both of which have nibbled and broken edges. It is held together on a frame of mild steel that is bolted right through the glass.

below

Spine Chair

Taking its inspiration from French park chairs, the 1986 Spine chair by André Dubreuil is a whirl of bent and welded steel rods. It is pretty and poetic.

Ron Arad (1951–)

One of the most influential and prolific of contemporary European designers, Ron Arad is well known for his constant stream of experiments with a vast range of materials, most famously with hammered and welded metal. He is also known for his curiosity in reworking familiar designs in new ways. Among his most recent and unusual experiments are those in the realm of rapid prototyping, where objects can be 'grown' directly from designs created on a computer screen. Arad achieved fame with his oversized metal furniture. His famous pieces include the 1986 Well Tempered chair, formed from four sheets of springy tempered steel, and his Big Easy from 1988, a huge armchair made from hammered and welded metal. He has also created numerous interior designs for the Belgo chain of restaurants in London, for the foyer of the Tel Aviv Opera House and most recently for the Y Store in Tokyo for Yohji Yamamoto. Since the late 1990s he has taught at the Royal College of Art in London and is now a professor and head of design products.

Born in 1951 in Tel Aviv to artist parents – his mother is a painter and his father is a photographer – he studied at the Bezalel Academy of Art in Jerusalem before coming to London in 1973 to study at

the Architectural Association. In 1981 he founded the company One Off in London with business partner Caroline Thurman and made his first piece of furniture: a limited-edition chair called Rover made from a scrapyard Rover 2000 car seat set into a frame of scaffolding poles and clamps. This was the start of Arad's exploration of handmade objects using everyday materials. Against the 1980s backdrop of urban decay laced with post-punk anarchy, Arad joined fellow designer-makers in producing rough-and-ready, one-off pieces of hand-built furniture. In 1983 he turned his hand to chunky slabs of concrete, which he transformed into stereo systems in a brilliant hi- and low-tech collision. He then worked with furniture-maker Vitra to make the Well Tempered chair. This is a fresh and economical design, using just four sheets of tempered steel bolted into place to make a large armchair form. While metal is rarely associated with comfortable seating, the use of tempered steel gave the design an appealing springiness. The design was reissued by Vitra in 2002, this time made from four sheets of a new plastic material made with glass and carbon-fibre laminate, and called the Bad Tempered chair.

It emerged early in his career that Arad's preferred medium was metal, ideally hammered and welded sheet material. In 1988 came the limited editions of his Tinker chair and, more famously, the Big Easy. Both were large metal objects that had been hammered into shape. This was sculpture to sit on; the chairs looked crumpled and lumpy and hard, as far from the traditional, upholstered armchair as it was possible to imagine. The Big Easy became a chair form that Arad experimented with for many years; it has been produced in smooth, highly polished versions, as an upholstered chair in 1990 by the Italian company Moroso, and in 1999 it was made of pigmented layers of polyester and renamed New Orleans.

Another of his well-known pieces is the Bookworm bookshelf. Produced in 1993 as an experiment in using tempered steel, the early models continued to be made of metal and were designed to be fixed to the wall in virtually any shape from a coil to a snake. In 1994 the shelf was produced in PVC by Kartell and instantly became a bestseller. In the same year Arad set up a production workshop in Italy making a range of his limited-edition pieces.

Towards the end of the decade Arad worked again with Vitra, this time on a 1997 mass-production model called the Tom Vac chair. Composed of a body shell and separate legs, the body section is a squashed, rounded and ridged shape made from polypropylene. The chair is named after Arad's American photographer friend Tom Vack, who has produced beautiful images of his furniture. This was followed a year later by the highly experimental design for Kartell of the FPE (Fantastic Plastic Elastic) chair, a piece composed of two tubes of extruded aluminium and a seat and back made from a piece of plastic membrane. When the membrane is fitted into the tubes, the chair locks together without the need for fixing screws or glue.

During the late 1990s Arad worked for the homewares manufacturer Alessi, producing intriguing designs for a CD rack, a sculptural felt hat, cocktail shakers, hors d'oeuvres sets and a watch. By the millennium, Arad had become fascinated by the possibilities of rapid prototyping. Using a laser process, particles of polyamide powder are fused together to 'grow' computer-generated designs. As the name suggests, this process was designed for creating prototype models, but Arad has adapted it for making one-off and small-edition pieces. Among his most intriguing experiments are the jewellery pieces from his 2000 series called Not Made By Hand, Not Made In China. The designs are based on signatures and handwriting, which are then formed into three-dimensional shapes.

In the years since the millennium, Arad has been dividing his time between teaching and an increasing number of architecture projects. Two of his most recent buildings include the new design museum at Holon in Israel and the headquarters for the domestic products manufacturer Magis in Treviso, Italy.

A Star Is Born

The late 1980s also saw the flowering of one of the most prolific, influential and certainly one of the best-known designers of all time: Philippe Starck (1949–). Where earlier designers such as Charles and Ray Eames or Robin and Lucienne Day might have been held up as famous for their glamorous modern lifestyles, Starck was a one-off, iconic design personality. His design approach was quite different from that of the Mid-Century Modernists, too; while they held on to the idealistic notion of improving the world through design, Starck, interested in functional design, was promoting joyful, delightful and decorative products. He swiftly became a modern design phenomenon with rock-star status.

Starck burst onto the stage in the 1982 with his Costes chair for the Café Costes in Paris. Here he produced a reworking of the tub chair with a curved mahogany-faced plywood frame, and it was hailed as an immediate design classic. Typical of much of his work that followed, it features quirky and thoughtful touches, including a finger hole in the back to make it easy to move and three legs rather than four so that busy waiters wouldn't trip over it as much.

Throughout the decade Starck produced an almost endless stream of eye-catching furniture designs, always with big personalities and names to match. In 1986 came the Ed Archer chair, which looked like a strip of folded leather with its back supported on a single, shiny tapering fin of aluminium. Dr Glob, in 1988, was part plastic and part tubular steel with a curved tubular-metal backrest, and in the same year came the Lola Mundo chair, with its black seat and backrest sitting on cast-aluminium cabriole legs.

Starck's great skill has been in putting fun into functionalism. His designs are witty, original, highly sophisticated and intended for mass production. In his drive to popularize contemporary design, Starck was fascinated by materials and the process of reducing costs. One of his goals was to halve the cost of his chairs every two years. The Café Costes chair sold for around $700, this was followed two years later by Mr Blob at $300, then by Lord Yo at $140 and Dr No at $100. The sequence concluded with La Marie, the world's first transparent chair in polycarbonate and made by Kartell, which went on sale for a mere $50.

above right

Lola Mundo

One of Philippe Starck's most playful designs, the Lola Mundo, 1988, is a modern-style chair with ebony seat and back on cast-aluminium cabriole legs. The seatback folds down flat to turn the piece into a stool.

below right

Lord Yo

This 1994 chair by Philippe Starck is ideal for indoor or outdoor use and is constructed from a lightweight aluminium frame with all-in-one polypropylene shell seat. It is available in a wide range of colours.

Philippe Starck (1949–)

Bearing the title of the most famous modern designer in the world, Philippe Starck has had an immense influence on contemporary design. Rising to international prominence in the 'Designer Decade' of the 1980s, he has been an inspiring and unstoppable force in the creative world for almost three decades. His work schedule is punishing and his output unequalled – it is not unusual for him to turn up at the annual international design fest in Milan with as many as 30 new product launches. Worldwide, his work embraces every aspect of design, from large-scale architecture projects to the design of a toothpick. His portfolio includes new factory buildings, restaurants, hotels and homes, luxury yachts, motorcycles, lamps, a toothbrush, a lavatory brush and a lemon squeezer, pasta shapes, door handles, clothing, and furniture, including beds, sofas, tables, stools and chairs… literally dozens of chairs. While it is clear that Starck can turn his hand to designing just about anything, it is difficult to ascribe a particular style to him. The work is in the Post-Modern vein and is often glamorous, theatrical, kitsch and humorous; many pieces take their inspiration from historical precedents, while others are utterly new and inventive.

Born in 1949 in Paris, Philippe Starck counts among his earliest memories the times he spent as a young boy under his father's drawing board as the latter worked designing aircraft. The streamlined aerofoil shapes, hi-tech designs and a fascination with engineering were all elements that appeared in Philippe's early work. After studying design at the École Nissim de Camondo in Paris, he set up his own company in 1968 to produce inflatable objects. By the 1970s he had moved into interior design and completed two hugely popular Parisian nightclubs. These won him the attention

of French President François Mitterrand, who commissioned Starck to decorate his apartments in the Elysée Palace, completed in 1982.

His first international recognition came in 1984 with the glamorous and Post-Modern interiors of the Café Costes in Paris, for which he created the now-iconic Café Costes chair that is still in production with Driade. With its glamorous central staircase flanked by massive columns, an oversize clock and sleek furniture, the place was splashed across design magazines around the globe. Starck had succeeded in breathing new life into the very idea of the Parisian café, which had become tired and worn, and in doing so inspired an entire generation of new cafés, bars and restaurants. He had begun his jet-propelled ascent to fame. Soon afterwards he worked his magic on another tired realm – the hotel. Working alongside US hotelier Ian Schrager, he created hugely dramatic landmark interiors for two New York hotels: the Royalton in 1988 and the Paramount in 1990. The theatrical lobbies were filled with wild furniture and curious new lighting designs; he created novelty lavatories and luxurious modern guest rooms. These were destination hotels where guests came not just to stay but also to become part of a theatrical event. In a world that is now filled

right

Miss Sissi

One of Starck's bestselling designs, the all-in-one moulded plastic 1991 Miss Sissy lamp is a truly affordable design classic made in a wide range of colours by Flos.

with designer hotels, it is difficult to imagine the impact of these interiors when they were first unveiled.

Meanwhile, work was always underway on his chair designs. In 1984 came the J chair that looks like a regular leather armchair from the front, but which, at the back, is poised on a single aluminium fin. The following year came the fold-away Mrs Frick, a three-legged design with triangular backrest, and in 1986 the pretty Lola Mundo, with the seat and backrest sleek, black and modern, and in complete contrast with the cast-aluminium cabriole-shaped legs. In 1987 came Romantica, an S-shaped chair with exaggerated splayed legs at the rear; then, based on the same design but with a slatted seat, was Dick Deck. In 1988 came one of his most popular pieces, the Dr Glob, made from a metal frame, rear legs and hooped backrest and a plastic seat and front legs. In more recent years his most popular pieces, both for Kartell, include the transparent 1999 La Marie and the 2004 Louis Ghost; the latter has been described as one of the first design classics of the twenty-first century.

With every design comes a new twist of the chair story, always experimental and unfailingly novel. The same is true of every piece of Starck's work. Among his most famous lighting designs are Ara from 1988, a desk lamp in the shape of a shiny metal horn; Miss Sissy from 1991, the colourful plastic table lamp; and the Romeo Moon series of lamps and pendants from 1998. These were accompanied by dozens of everyday objects, including the 1998 Dr Kiss toothbrush with its quirky tail and his reinvented egg-shaped computer mouse from 2004 for Microsoft.

While Starck's workload continues undiminished, we can be sure of ever-more inventive designs. Along with his astonishing output, he has found a place in modern design history as the person who achieved the ultimate Modernist ideal of democratizing design and making contemporary design affordable for all.

right

Café Costes Chair

This is the chair that put Philippe Starck on the international map. His reinvention of the French café at Café Costes in Paris included the design of this fantastic tub chair from 1982. With its curved mahogany-faced plywood frame and modern legs, it was hailed as an immediate design classic. Original designs had three legs.

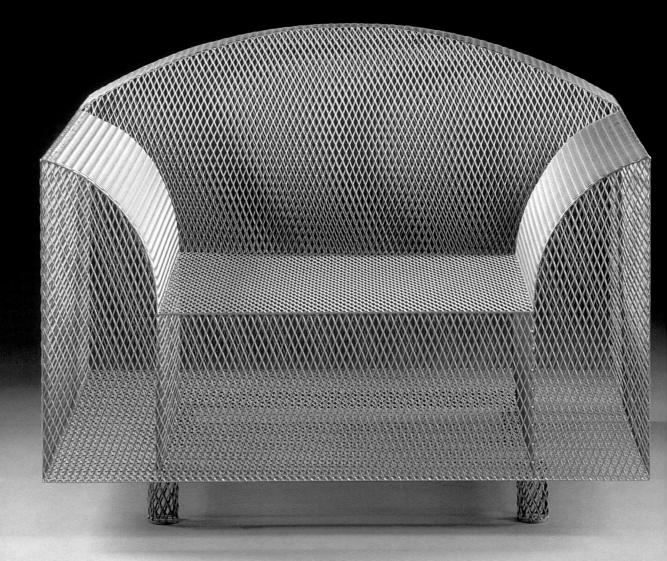

above

How High The Moon

Shiro Kuramata was fascinated by the contrasting and complementary concepts of size and bulk, hardness and softness, lightness and transparency. They all meet here in this chair design from 1986, named after a piece of music by Duke Ellington.

right

Getsuen Chair

Dating from 1990, the Getsuen by Masanori Umeda is in the shape of a massive flower head, thought to be based on the *kikyo*, or Chinese bellflower. The petals are made from velvet-covered polyurethane foam on a complex steel frame. The chair has a wheel at the back to make it easy to move.

New Romantics

Starck was certainly a romantic, taking delight in prettiness, softness, mysticism, the beauty of nature and charming detail. With strict Modernism in retreat during the early 1980s, decoration was enjoying a renaissance – there was romance in the air. In furniture design it became possible to unleash fantasies. Czech artist/designer Borek Šípek produced his Bambi chair in 1983, a whimsical design redolent of the Disney character, poised on fragile, awkward legs, and with a textile-covered backrest. Meanwhile, in France, Elisabeth Garouste (1949–) and Mattia Bonetti (1953–) produced Prince Imperial in 1985, a curious chair in painted wood and raffia, which looks like an African chief's throne. Also taking inspiration from more primitive forms of construction, British designer/maker Julienne Dolphin-Wilding (1960–) turned her hand to rough-hewn tree trunks, telegraph poles and great slabs of trees, combining them with rope and twine to make over-size fantasy furniture, including her landmark Gulliver's chair of 1987, which is distinguished by its towering back with rope lashing. Like Dixon, Brazier-Jones and Lane, Dolphin-Wilding's work also has an underlying theme of recycling and sustainability.

In Japan, romantic designers made highly poignant and poetic pieces. Shiro Kuramata (1934–91) designed a wide range of products from complete interiors for Issey Miyake fashion stores to his chest of drawers and a simple vase. The pieces have a haunting, dreamlike quality and reflect his concern that the modern world, and Japan in particular, had lost its sense of romance. One of his earliest internationally known designs was How High The Moon from 1986,

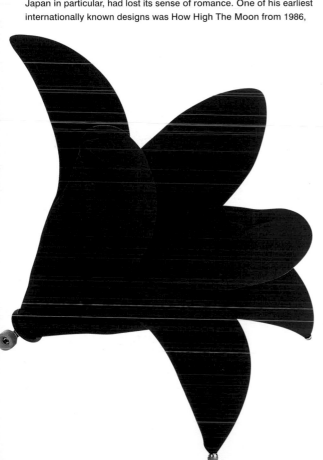

a large armchair made from wire mesh. It plays with notions of size and bulk, hardness and softness, lightness and transparency, and is now made by Vitra. Again exploring spatial ideas, in 1989 came his chair called Miss Blanche (see page 165). Taking its name from the central character in Tennessee Williams' play *A Streetcar Named Desire*, this armchair is made from cast acrylic resin, its seat and arms containing artificial roses 'frozen' into the acrylic. It is incredibly delicate and charming.

Fellow Japanese designer Masanori Umeda (1941–) was also exploring frailty and nature and was concerned that economic and technological success was being offset by the destruction of the natural world. His desire to reintroduce nature into Japanese homes came through a series of chair designs in the form of oversize flowers. Dating from 1990, the Getsuen chair, in the shape of a massive flower head, is thought to be based on the *kikyo*, or Chinese bellflower. The huge petals are made from fabric-covered polyurethane foam on a steel frame. The chair has a wheel at the back to make it easy to move. Umeda's Rose chair again uses the same materials and is formed into the shape of a huge red or white rose, where the sitter occupies the middle. Both flower chairs are made by Edra.

Shiro Kuramata (1934–91)

One of the few Japanese furniture designers to forge an international career, Shiro Kuramata was best known for his whimsical, dreamlike and poetic designs, and for transforming and elevating everyday materials. He was fascinated by Western culture and also felt passionately that the modern world has lost the sense of romance. Among his best-known pieces are the 1986 metal mesh chair called How High The Moon and his work in acrylics, including the 1988 chair called Miss Blanche, with its floating red roses. Not interested in the Modernist fixation on form following function, he became a firm admirer of Italian design giant Ettore Sottsass and collaborated with the influential Post-Modern Memphis group of designers in the 1980s. His playful attitude to design and materials provided inspiration for an entire generation of Post-Modern designers, including Philippe Starck and Ron Arad. Because so much of his work was made in small editions, it is highly valuable and collectable.

Shiro Kuramata was born in 1934 and after school studied traditional woodcraft at Tokyo's polytechnic before taking a job in a furniture factory in the early 1950s. By the mid-1950s he was training in interior design and set up his own office in Tokyo in 1965. A pioneering contemporary designer, he worked across a spectrum of disciplines, including interiors, furniture and lighting, and produced a range of shop fit-outs during the 1980s in Tokyo, Paris and New York for Japanese fashion designer Issey Miyake. Along with experiments in materials, Kuramata liked to play with ideas of balance and tension, solidity and transparency, and with gravity and scale.

His experiments with furniture took shape in the late 1960s and 1970s with works such as Furniture in Irregular Forms. This series of designs include his Revolving Cabinet, made from a very tall stack of drawers held upright on a single pole; the Pyramid, a tapering tall stack of drawers; and Side 1, a tall chest of drawers in an S shape. All of these are now made by Cappellini. He explored transparency with his 1976 Glass chair, using six simple planes of glass to create an armchair. Looking almost ephemeral, the work was made possible by a new type of super-strong glass glue.

Among his pieces which started to attract attention outside Japan was the Kyoto table for Memphis in 1983. It is a small side table with a circular base and a circular top made from terrazzo

left

Acrylic Stool with Feathers

Typical of Shiro Kuramata's playful approach, this acrylic stool from 1990 plays with ideas of mass and weight and looks as though it might be as light as one of the feathers it encapsulates. It is in fact incredibly heavy. It was designed for Spiral, a boutique in the Axis shopping complex in Tokyo.

right

Miss Blanche

Taking its name from one of the central characters
of the Tennessee Williams' play *A Streetcar
Named Desire*, this 1989 armchair, Miss Blanche,
is made from cast acrylic resin, its seat and arms
containing artificial roses 'frozen' into the acrylic.

concrete sprinkled with coloured glass pieces. Kuramata called
this material 'Star Piece Terrazzo' and used it lavishly in his
designs for the Issey Miyake boutiques. His first design to win
true international recognition, however, was How High The Moon.
Named after a piece of music by jazz musician Duke Ellington, its
huge armchair form is constructed from nickel-plated steel wire
mesh and embodies many of Kuramata's experiments with form
and mass. The use of an unexpected material like wire mesh for a
chair attracts attention and yet it is also functional and comfortable.
Like many of his pieces, it is intended to blur the boundary between
functional objects and art – it is abstract and see-through. The chair
is now made to order by Vitra.

Transparency emerges again as a theme in his chair Miss Blanche;
this time it is made of clear acrylic resin in which are suspended
artificial red roses. The name Miss Blanche refers to Blanche DuBois,
played by Vivien Leigh, who wore a corsage with a red-rose pattern
in the film *A Streetcar Named Desire*. In the chair, the floating roses
look as if they are effortlessly suspended in space, but the process
of casting them took numerous experiments to get right. In the end,
the flowers were held in place individually with tweezers as the resin
was poured into the moulds. One of Kuramata's last designs was an
all-glass washstand with circular basin called Coup de Foudre, for
the Italian manufacturer Rapsel. It was produced in 1991, the year of
his death at the age of just 56.

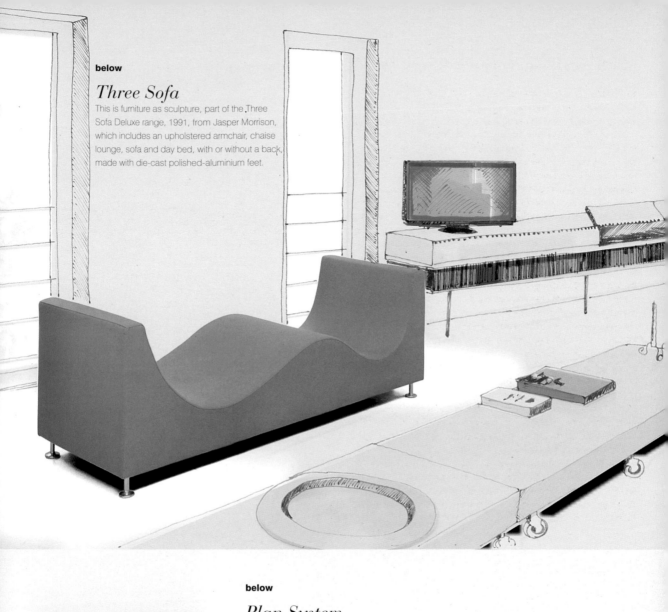

below

Three Sofa

This is furniture as sculpture, part of the Three Sofa Deluxe range, 1991, from Jasper Morrison, which includes an upholstered armchair, chaise lounge, sofa and day bed, with or without a back, made with die-cast polished-aluminium feet.

below

Plan System

In characteristic pared-down style, Jasper Morrison created his colourful Plan system, 1999, based on a range of cabinets. The pieces are made in natural oak, ebony-stained oak, macroter-lacquered and polished. Bases are in satin stainless steel with rubber feet and handles are in satin stainless steel.

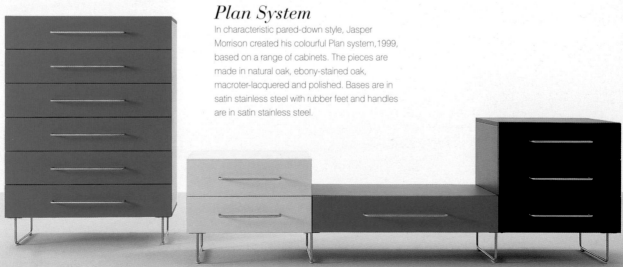

Modernist Renaissance

The global recession of the late 1980s and early 1990s, coupled with the Gulf War of 1991, resulted in plenty of belt-tightening in the western world. Economic confidence was low and consumers were reluctant to spend, so furniture and homewares manufacturers were forced to cut back on their investments. Following the exuberance and profligacy of the 1980s, this new caution and parsimony seemed to rub off on the design world, where the extrovert 1980s were left behind and restraint ruled. A new type of Modernism emerged.

Once again British designers were in the vanguard, with Jasper Morrison (1959–) leading the charge. London-based Morrison had already attracted attention during the 1980s with his clever reuse of everyday objects. He combined bicycle handlebars and sheet glass to make a table; placed a glass disc on top of a stack of terracotta flowerpots and made another table, which was later put into production by Italian firm Cappellini; and he took the bases of two office chairs and a length of tubing to create a coat stand. In 1988 he created a room set called Some New Items for the Home, Part 1 for a German gallery. He then created Some New Items for the Home, Part 2 in 1989 for the Milan Furniture Fair. It was shown sponsored by Vitra. In both cases, Morrison created a theatrical-style set furnished with plywood tables, a day bed, and chairs of such pared-down simplicity that they were almost like cartoon drawings. This body of work joins the long history of Modernist experimentation with plywood, and the understated elegance of the designs was immediately spotted and snapped up by Vitra. While the company was best known for its production of office furniture, it was also keen to promote the talents of individual designers and more experimental designs, so in 1987 it introduced the Vitra Edition series. This encompassed designs of furniture and other objects by such high-profile international names as Coop Himmelblau, Frank Gehry, Shiro Kuramata, Alessandro Mendini and Ettore Sottsass. Two years later, the company opened its own Vitra Design Museum in Germany, which was designed by Frank Gehry.

Balzac Armchair

The iconic Balzac armchair, 1991, by Matthew Hilton is a reinterpretation of a classic club chair. The design exaggerates the rounded corners, producing a more sensual and organic form. It is in production with British manufacturer SCP.

Loop Chaise Longue

This elegant day bed, 1999, by Edward Barber and Jay Osgerby is deeply upholstered and extremely comfortable. The legs are made of satin stainless steel with rubber feet.

Jasper Morrison continued throughout the decade to produce his exquisite and spare pieces of furniture and lighting designs. For him the decade concluded in 1999 with his designs for the High-Pad and Lo-Pad upholstered chairs made by Cappellini; the super-lightweight Air chair made by Magis using the latest technology for gas-injected polypropylene; and the Tate chair of 2000, which he designed for the opening of the Tate Modern gallery in London. This last piece was his latest exploration of moulded plywood and is produced by Cappellini.

Fellow Brit Matthew Hilton (1957–) was experimenting with wood too. His Auberon dining table from 1991 is made of solid oak with fold-down flaps – when in the open position, the table has a pleasing shape with the long sides given a gentle outward curve. In a similar vein to Morrison, the designs took existing and familiar everyday design types and reinvented them with a subtle twist. In this way, Hilton's iconic Balzac armchair from 1991 takes a classic club chair and exaggerates the rounded corners, producing a more

Loop Table

By Edward Barber and Jay Osgerby, who together
form the company Barber Osgerby, the Loop
table, 1996, is among their first designs. Made
by Isokon Plus, it continues the line of plywood
experiments that made the company famous
through designers like Marcel Breuer in the 1930s.

Loop Bench

In the same series as the chaise longue opposite,
this 1999 bench by Edward Barber and Jay
Osgerby is also extremely comfortable and is sold
in a range of brightly coloured upholstery fabrics.

sensual and organic form. It remains in production with British
manufacturer SCP.

From the hothouse of the Royal College of Art in London, which
produced Jasper Morrison, new young designers were emerging,
including Edward Barber (1969–) and Jay Osgerby (1969–), who
together formed the company Barber Osgerby. Among their first
designs to find a manufacturer was the minimalist Loop table
from 1996, made by Isokon Plus. Continuing the line of plywood
experiments that made Isokon famous through designers like Marcel
Breuer in the 1930s, Barberg Osgerby produced the Loop table
from bent plywood. It was followed by a shelving unit called Loop
shelves, also 1996, and then the Portmouth bench, from 2002, a
wooden seat in solid oak. Isokon was also responsible for producing
work by London-based Japanese couple Shin (1965–) and Tomoko
Azumi (1966–) when it started making their reinterpretation of the
small bookcase called the Penguin Donkey, originally designed
by Egon Riss in 1939 (see also page 42). The Azumis' version is

Donkey 3 from 2003. The Azumis achieved their first taste of
fame with their Table = Chest design in 1995; a transformer
design, it can be folded and changed from a tall chest of
drawers to a low-level table.

By the 1990s, the Americans had all but dropped out of
the international picture in making furniture and furnishings.
Occasionally, a design emerged that had global sales potential,
such as the great Aeron office chair of 1992 from William Stumpf and
Donald Chadwick for Herman Miller, but for the most part America
was enduring a period of introspection and producing designs that
often lacked international lustre and were only for the home market.
In mainland Europe, Philippe Starck reigned supreme in France,
while brilliant young designer Maarten van Severen (1956–2005) rose
to fame in his native Belgium for his highly refined designs. Among
his best-known pieces are the Model No. 2 chair from 1992, a birch-
faced, plywood, all-in-one seat and back with aluminium frame, and
the Aluminium chaise of 1996, made from a folded ribbon of metal.

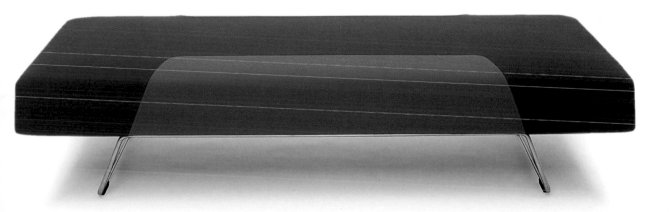

In Scandinavia, meanwhile, the revival of Modernism was embraced wholeheartedly. Nanna Ditzel (1923–2005) continued her experiments in plywood with Danish manufacturer Fredericia, and following her innovative Bench for Two in 1989 produced the expressive Butterfly chair in 1990, followed in 1993 by the finely detailed Trinidad chair with its decorative laser-cut slits in the seat and chair back. The young Swedish designers Thomas Sandell (1959–) and Thomas Eriksson (1959–) both produced streamlined and minimal storage units and chairs for Cappellini and Asplund. They also joined the group of well-known designers working from the mid-1990s on Ikea's PS limited-editions range. Among Eriksson's most iconic Ikea pieces are the PS clock, called Klocka, and the simple Television table on four wheels, both from 1995.

In Italy, the huge furniture industry was also responding to the proliferation of the new stripped-down look with its references to early Modernism. For example, Pietro Arosio (1946–) designed Mirandolina in 1992 from a single sheet of aluminium – it has a perforated back and seat and is made by Zanotta. Again with an air of nostalgia, this pays homage to the early Modernist metal chairs, most particularly to the Landi, designed in 1938 by Swiss designer Hans Coray (1906–91). This was followed a few years later in 1996 by the elegant and austere aluminium Aprile chair by Piero Lissoni (1956–) for Cappellini. This is like a café chair, but had been reduced to a delicate minimal frame with slim seat. In the same year, Ricardo Blumer (1959–) created his LaLeggera chair for Alias. Stripped to its very essentials, the chair has a core of polyurethane foam that is veneered in pale maple and formed part of a series that included several chairs, stools, benches and tables.

Throughout the story of modern furniture, most attention is focused on chair design. It was through the 1990s, however, that

Charles Large Sofa

A modern classic sofa by Antonio Citterio for B&B Italia, this is like a piece of interior landscaping and offers a comfortable refuge for sprawling and snoozing. It forms part of the Charles furniture series, which has been evolving since 1997.

Charles Bed

A beautiful bed and headboard by Antionio Citterio as part of his Charles family of furniture designs for B&B Italia.

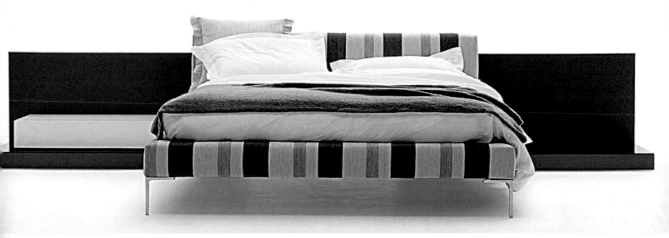

many furniture designers also turned their hand to other products, including lighting, storage and large pieces of furniture, particularly sofas. The great proliferation of modern sofa designs include a number of new classics, often based on rectangular forms, such as Jasper Morrison's Vitra sofa of 1993 for Vitra and his modular seating system, including a sofa, called Orly from 1998 for Cappelini. Piero Lissoni created the Met modular sofa in 1996 for Cassina, David Chipperfield (1953–) the hm991 from 1998 for Hitch Mylius, Antonio Citterio (1950–) the Charles sofa in 1998 for B&B Italia, and in the same year came Philippe Starck's Lazy Working sofa, complete with built-in shelving and lighting for Cassina.

The late 1990s was the height of minimalism. Here was furniture that was so reduced and modest it was almost too shy to raise its head and be noticed. It became clear that a new generation of Italian designers was not emerging to replace such high-profile names as Sottsass, Mendini and Castiglioni, so the major manufacturers like Cappellini, Kartell and Casina were trawling the globe for outside talent. Cappellini, for example, featured the works of designers including Brits Jasper Morrison, Tom Dixon and Ross Lovegrove (1958–), along with Swede Thomas Eriksson, Australian Marc Newson (1963–), Dutchman Marcel Wanders (1963–), and more besides. In an increasingly global market, it was a trend that would continue.

above

Model No. *hm991*

A sofa from the modular seating system, including a day bed, 1998, by British architect David Chipperfield for British manufacturer Hitch Mylius.

Marc Newson (1963–)

With his sensual, organic, blobby, futuristic designs, Marc Newson's work merges the fantasy/science-fiction world of Buck Rogers with the hi-tech engineering of Buckminster Fuller. Like many contemporary designers, he has demonstrated that he can work without boundaries across a wide spectrum of design areas on projects from chairs and tables to watches and even prototype cars and jet planes. He rose to fame with his Lockheed in 1986, a biomorphic-shaped lounger made from a fibreglass shell with riveted aluminium skin. This was followed by the Orgone series of furniture, distinguished by its fluid shapes and nipped-in waists, including the Embryo chair of 1988 and the Felt chair and Orgone lounge, both 1989.

Born in Sydney in 1963, Newson studied jewellery design and sculpture at the Sydney College of Arts. This training has led him to produce work with an intricate attention to detail, which is also highly tactile and sculptural. His range of influences is broad, from the expressive and colourful Post-Modernism of the Italian Memphis group and specific designers, including Ettore Sottsass, to vintage

above
The Australian designer Marc Newson has taken the world by storm with his innovative and often unexpected forms. He has worked all over the world and is currently based in London.

below

Bucky Chair
The 1995 Bucky by Marc Newson is based on an original three-cornered blobby shape. The multicoloured plastic seat is formed from injection-moulded polyurethane foam.

Aston Martin cars and the film sets of Ken Adams, who worked on such cult movies as *Moonraker*, *Thunderball* and *Dr No*.

Like a giant blob of mercury, the Lockheed lounge instantly attracted media attention and was widely published in international magazines. It made a guest appearance in Madonna's video for 'Rain' and also took pride of place in the groundbreaking Paramount Hotel in New York designed by Philippe Starck, where it was featured in the lobby. In these early days of success Newson was making limited-edition versions of his designs through his company, Pod.

In 1987 he moved to Tokyo when entrepreneur Teruo Kurosaki of the company Idée offered to put his designs into production. Key pieces included the Felt chair, a big, body-hugging wave of felt dented in the middle to form a seat and back – the textile is wrapped around a frame of fibreglass-reinforced polyester and is now made by Cappellini. Also made by Idée was the 1988 Black Hole table, a piece of sculptural cast black polyurethane on three legs, each terminating at the top in a mysterious black hole.

In 1991 Newson set up a studio in Paris where he designed lighting, including the tall and slender Helice lamps in 1993 with their UFO-shaped lampshade for manufacturers such as Flos, and furniture, including the 1993 blobby Gluon chair for Moroso. In the same year he produced the Seaslug watch made by his own company Ikepod. The company also produced limited editions of his furniture, including the Orgone chair in sleek and shiny cast aluminium. The word 'orgone' is borrowed from an early twentieth-century physician and psychoanalyst called Wilhelm Reich, who used the term to describe a type of life energy that he believed was all around us – he believed that a lack of orgone caused illness. It works well in the context of Newson's furniture, including the Orgone chair, which often features hollows and mysteriously sculpted cavities.

During the mid-1990s, Newson's work expanded into interior design, with such high-profile restaurants as Coast in London and Mash & Air in Manchester, along with the Komed restaurant in Cologne and Syn recording studio in Tokyo for Simon Le Bon. By 1997, Newson had set up shop in London and was joined by business partner, collaborator and computer expert Benjamin de Haan. The design work had moved away from small-batch and limited editions to mass production of items, including glassware for Iittala, kitchen and bathroom accessories for Alessi, and furniture, lighting and household objects for Magis, B&B Italia, Idée and Dupont Corian. In 1999–2000, Newson also designed vehicles, such as a bicycle, the MN01, for Danish firm Biomega; a concept car, the 021C, for Ford; and the interiors of a Falcon 900B private jet. In 2002–3 he designed interiors for the Lever House Restaurant in the landmark Lever House Building in New York, a business-class seat called a Skybed for Qantas, a cookware range for Tefal and a bathroom range, the Newson Suite, for Ideal Standard. He also opened a second studio in Paris.

In most recent years Newson has branched into clothing with G-Star and a series of footwear designs for Nike. In 2006 he was appointed creative director of Qantas airways, where he set to work on plane interiors and airport lounges.

below

Orgone Chair

One of Marc Newson's trademark designs is this cast-aluminium Orgone chair from 1993, a curious piece in rounded organic shapes with a mysterious and brightly coloured interior.

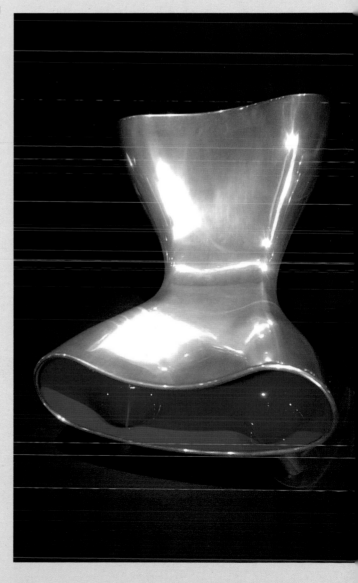

above

Knotted Chair

By Marcel Wanders, the Knotted chair, designed in 1996,
is reminiscent of a hammock frozen in space. The chair
is made from rope, with a carbon thread at its centre.
Once knotted, macramé-style, into shape, it is soaked
in epoxy resin and hung on a frame to set rock-hard.
After first being made by Droog, it was picked up for
production by Cappellini in 2005.

The Nineties Nonconformists

In reaction to any mainstream movement, there is always a band of nonconformists and the 1990s was no exception. Among the most intriguing was the Dutch outfit called Droog Design. Founded in 1993 by art historian Renny Ramakers (1946–) and designer Gijs Bakker (1942–), Droog (meaning 'dry') is a manufacturer, gallery, design collective, publisher and marketing company all in one. It is based on wit, irony and whimsy – all the things that the new minimalists avoided – and it is also about the Dutch interpretation of design.

Among the early pieces to emerge under the Droog umbrella was the S(h)it on It bench designed by Richard Hutten in 1994. Made from steel and MDF, this looks at first like a version of a park bench, but on closer inspection it becomes clear that the top rail of the bench is formed in the shape of a swastika. The four seats place their sitters in an unsociable format with their backs to each other. Next came the Cow chairs of Niels van Eijk (1970–) in 1997. At first they look as if they are made from some sort of injection-moulded or formed plastic, but they are in fact stiffened and translucent cowhide. In the same year came a quirky porcelain stool by Hella Jongerius (1963–), which is formed like a narrow slice through a stool. At the core of Droog's work is its lab, where experimental works are always under way and projects are hatched to study how people relate to furniture, design and everyday products. One of the key names to emerge through Droog is Marcel Wanders. His Knotted chair, designed in 1996, is reminiscent of a hammock frozen in space. Building on his interest in traditional crafts skills, like crochet and basket-weaving, this chair is made from rope with a carbon thread at its centre. Once knotted, macramé-style, into shape, it is soaked in epoxy resin and hung on a frame to set.

Other great nonconformists from this time are the 'Blobby' designers – a series of people who refused to knuckle down to the conventional shapes of the Modernists and the minimalists. With their roots in space-age futurism and the more expressive designs from the 1960s and 1970s by such designers as Pierre Paulin and Olivier Mourgue, the new generation in love with rotund and organic shapes is headed by Australian Marc Newson. Among his early designs are the Felt chair from 1989 and Wicker chair of 1990, the latter with its big, swelling forms and nipped-in waist, followed the next year by his Orgone table, again with an asymmetrical and amoeba-like form. In 1993 came his Orgone lounge, a type of day bed in flowing metal with a hollow interior, painted in bright colours including flame red. Britain's Ron Arad can be included here, too, with his great armchairs and free-form tables, all made in metal but with large, rounded shapes. Among his best-known pieces is his Big Easy chair, first made in the late 1980s but revisited and developed in the 1990s. In 1993 he created the revolutionary Bookworm bookshelf, first produced in steel in his own workshops, and from 1994 manufacture began with Kartell, where it was made from a snaking piece of PVC material that can be fixed to the wall in many different configurations. Then in 1997 came the Tom Vac shell chair, first made in Arad's own workshops in a limited edition of aluminium, and then from the same year made by Vitra in injection-moulded plastic.

Experiments with plastics led Tom Dixon to produce his Jacklight in 1996; a big and blobby shape, like a huge, six-pointed star, it doubles as a light or a stool and is made in rotation-moulded polythene – the same material and process that is used for making traffic cones. A similar manufacturing system was used by the Glasgow designers at One Foot Taller to produce their fluid-shaped Canyon chair in 1999.

below

Lockheed Lounge

This was the piece that brought Marc Newson to international attention in the mid-1980s. It is a reinterpretation of a classic day bed and is finished in beaten and riveted aluminium panels.

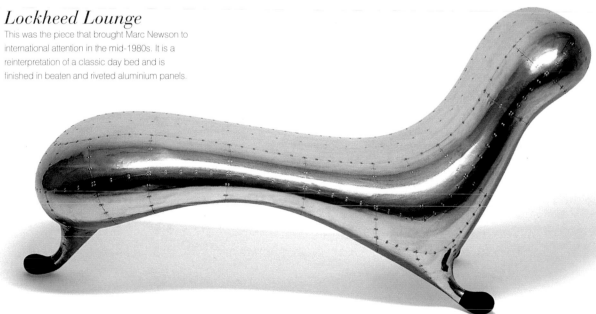

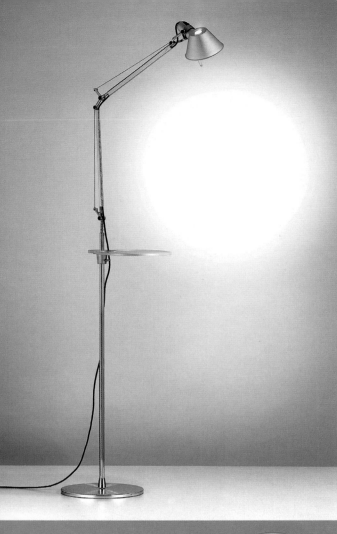

Get the Look

The arrival of Post-Modernism in the design world in the early and mid-1980s was like pulling a cork from a bottle: it had the effect of releasing pent-up energy and expressionism that was poured into fantastic glassware, lighting, fabrics and product designs. As with furniture, most of the freshest work in homewares and furnishings came from Italy, but there were brilliant exceptions, too.

From the late 1980s came such eye-catching classics as the Taraxacum 88 by Achille Castiglioni in 1988. It is a surreal pendant lamp in the shape of a sphere that is made from dozens of naked light bulbs. Then, in 1991, came Miss Sissi, the colourful table lamp by Philippe Starck, which is formed – base, stem and lampshade – from one piece of plastic (see also page 161). In 1996 came the Fuscia pendants, also by Achille Castiglioni, who bunched together conical-shaped, glass light fittings to make a modern chandelier, and, by contrast, Jasper Morrison's wonderfully simple 1998 Glo-Ball, a spherical white-glass light shade on a slender stem with a circular base – it was available as a floor or table lamp or, using the shade alone, as a pendant. All of these very different designs were, and are, produced by the Italian manufacturer Flos.

One of the greatest lighting designers of this period is the prolific German designer and maker Ingo Maurer (1932–), whose designs are poetic and sometimes almost verging on kitsch. Among his best-known small pieces is the delicate and charming Lucellino from 1992, a naked light bulb with wings attached that can stand on a stem to make a table lamp or is used as a wall light. In the Netherlands, young designer Tejo Remy (1960–) experimented with recycled materials in the 1993 Milk Bottle lamp. This comprises 12 sandblasted bottles, each with a small light bulb inside, which are ceiling suspended in a crate-like formation; it is made by Droog Design. Equally intriguing is Michael Sodeau's (1969–) woven-cane lamp series called Bolla from 1999. These are huge, sculptural and handcrafted pieces up to 2 m (6½ ft) in height and with a large, bulbous base tapering to a narrow stem; the light source is in the belly of the design and produces

Glo-Ball

These floor lamps form part of the extensive family of handblown, opal-glass diffuser lamps, designed in 1998 by Jasper Morrison. The range includes pendant lamps and table lamps. The large globe shade is not quite a perfect sphere, which gives it an interesting sense of weight. The base is made in stainless steel.

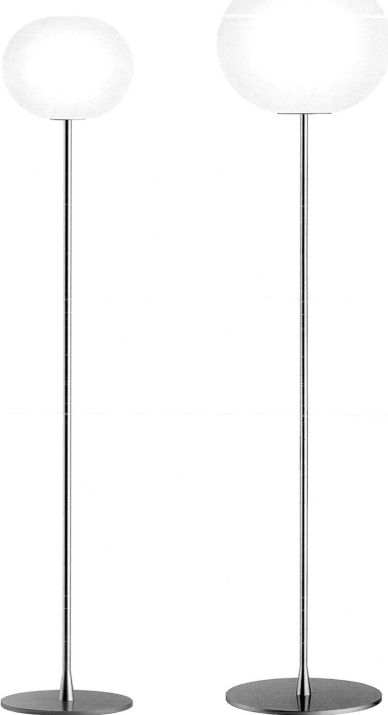

Bombo Stool

One of the most iconic bar stools of the 1990s
and early millennium, the colourful Bombo, 1997,
by Stefano Giovannoni was an instant success.
The rounded shape makes it extremely tactile and
the design with its generous base is very stable.

right

The 1985 metal Settimanale cupboard by
Matteo Thun with, perforated cut-out motifs.
Other notable cabinets were the Golden
Settimanale and the Cassettiera. An original
member of Ettore Sottsass's Memphis group,
Thun also designed the iconic Tam Tam stool.

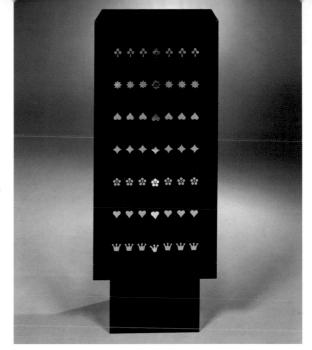

patterned light-fall through the cane weave. At the minimal end of the
scale, the aluminium Tolomeo table, floor and desk lamp with neat
spun-aluminium shade by Michele de Lucchi (1951–) from 1987 has
easily won its place as a design classic (see page 178).

Meanwhile, in storage and other types of furniture, the hi-tech
theme continues with Norman Foster's (1935–) Nomos table from
1985–7 for the furniture manufacturer Tecno. A strongly architectural
design, it has a metal base that stands on circular pad feet and a
rectangular glass top. And to prove that eclecticism was alive and
well, this was accompanied a year later by Ron Arad's handmade
tables in hammered steel and acrylic and by Philippe Starck's
Miss Balu, a classically styled side table made from thermoset
polypropylene for Kartell. Storage ideas were particularly fertile at
this time. One outstanding example is the Bookworm book shelving
by Ron Arad in 1994 for Kartell (see page 156), which is a wavy
strip of PVC that can be fixed to the wall in any shape. From the
same year also came the Mobil cabinets by Antonio Citterio and
Glen Oliver Low (1959–) also for Kartell. These translucent, colourful
units with drawers and doors were set on wheels to make them
easier to move around. In characteristic pared-down style, Jasper
Morrison created the Universale storage system in plywood in 1990
and followed it at the end of the decade with his colourful Plan system,
based on a range of cabinets (see page 166); both were for Cappellini.

By the late 1990s, the sideboard had made a comeback and
dozens of designers played their part in its reinvention. Memorable
examples include a low-level, sleek, black sideboard by Swiss
designer Alfredo Haberli (1964–) for Zanotta, and the Art-Deco-
inspired Wing unit, 1999, in a variety of finishes, including walnut
veneer and blond birch-faced plywood with distinctive curved ends
by Michael Sodeau for Isokon Plus.

In home and tablewares, the late 1980s and 1990s were a time
of great creativity for the Italian manufacturer Alessi. With a band
of high-profile designers, including Philippe Starck, Michael Graves,
Stefano Giovannoni (1954–), Alessandro Mendini and Enzo Mari
(1932–), Alessi produced a stream of brilliant designs for bowls and
plates, coffee sets, storage jars and the famous lemon squeezer –
Starck's spider-shaped cast-aluminium Juicy Salif from 1990. The
aim of reinventing everyday objects was also a source of brilliant
work from the American kitchenware company Oxo International,
founded in 1990 and working with Smart Design. Among its
best pieces is the ergonomic range called Good Grips, featuring
reworkings of equipment such as corkscrews and vegetable peelers.

Ceramics and glass enjoyed a creative flourish, too. Royal
Copenhagen in Denmark was among ceramic producers
interested in reinventing and updating its productions with
designers including Ursula Munch-Petersen (1937–). Meanwhile,
in glass, Czech designer Borek Šípek (1949–) produced highly
decorative and colourful wineglasses in 1991 for Alterego in the

Netherlands, and in 1994, for the same company, David Palterer
(1949–) made vases in organic shapes and bright colours. Venini
in Italy produced designs by Italian Mario Bellini (1935–), and
Marc Newson used Murano glass for his beautiful red, blue
and green blobby-shaped plates called Progetto Oggetto for
Cappellini. The pieces echo the seductive shapes of his furniture
and are very collectable.

Mobil

As the name suggests, these colourful
translucent plastic cabinets are on wheels
and can be moved from room to room.
They were designed for Kartell by Antonio
Citterio and Glen Oliver Low.

Key icons of

late

modernism

▲ Loop Table, 1996
One of the first collaborative projects of Edward Barber and Jay Osgerby, this deceptively simple coffee table, with a birch plywood top looping around the base, was produced first by Isokon Plus, then by Cappellini.

▶ Quinta Chair, 1985
A high-tech design by Mario Botta for Alias, the Quinta (meaning 'fifth') chair is a slender steel-rod frame supporting two bent, perforated sheet-metal components.

▶ Lo-Pad, 1999
By Jasper Morrison for Cappellini, the Lo-Pad is formed of a solid stainless-steel base supporting a plywood body and upholstered in polyurethane foam that is covered in leather.

◀ Felt Chair, 1994
When creating the compound curved form of his 1988 Felt chair, Marc Newson applied the origami principle of working from a flat piece of thick felt; he later worked with Cappellini to remake the Felt in the model shown here, a fibreglass-reinforced polyester shell.

◀ Nomos Table, 1987
This table was part of the office furniture system by Norman Foster for Tecno and an example of the hi-tech movement. The pieces were constructed from chromium-plated steel tubing and glass.

▶ Magic Chair, 1997
Ross Lovegrove's light and minimalist Magic chair for Fasem is a graceful moulded polyurethane seat on tubular aluminium supports – two uprights support the seat and create the arms.

▼ Three Sofa, 1991
Jasper Morrison's pared-down undulating sofa form for Cappellini is constructed of polyurethane foam on an aluminium frame.

The New Millennium

The end of Modernism is nigh: collectables from 2000 and after

The opening years of the new millennium saw the world change forever. With the destruction of New York's World Trade Center twin towers in 2001 and the subsequent series of terrorist attacks in Western cities, the mood of the times changed irrevocably from new-century optimism to a more closed and defensive stance. The ensuing recession shattered business confidence for a while. At the same time, growing concern about global climate change has also taken its toll, with its effects being wrought on many economies, industries and the way we live.

In the world of architecture, a new breed of iconic buildings have continued to rise. American architect Frank Gehry's hugely expressive, metal-clad Guggenheim Museum put the Spanish city of Bilbao on the map in 1997 and demonstrated the power of design, with architecture acting as a catalyst to economic renaissance. In Britain, the 2004 office tower known affectionately as the Gherkin in the City of London, designed by Norman Foster, renewed faith in tall buildings and indicated a change in tastes. In Germany, too, experimental architecture has drawn praise, not least with the 2005 Phaeno Science Centre by Zaha Hadid (1950–), with its free-flowing, dynamic structure. In cities all around the globe, it has become clear that design and construction have moved beyond building just rational and rectilinear blocks.

In furniture design, it seems that all things are possible. After a century of preaching a mantra that 'form follows function' and that the pursuit of good design improves lives, the Modernist movement appears to have almost run its course. The job is done, in the Western world at least. With our amassed body of technical, scientific and social knowledge, improved manufacturing techniques, new hi-tech materials, and mass-produced cut-price products, the original goals of the Modernist pioneers now seem to have been achieved and even surpassed. However, we are far from the end of the design story. The world of furniture continues

to produce star designers; their names take top billing above brands, their creations are often compared with works of art and they are increasingly collectable. The exciting news is that the design of furniture and other items for the home is enjoying a tremendous surge of creativity and energy. Modest Modernism stands alongside pieces of great ebullience, wit and charm, exploring new materials and the endless possibilities and delights of decoration.

Fast-Forward into the Future

While the key Modernist goals may have been achieved, there is always room for better design, and countless challenges remain to improve lives in poor countries, to tackle global concerns such as climate change, and to keep the wheels of commerce turning. Designers and manufacturers continue to be driven to experiment with new concepts, materials and manufacturing techniques. The pace of technological advance has shown no signs of slowing in recent years, and even in the short time since the millennium, great strides forward have been made.

One of the areas of rapid change has been in computer-aided design and computer-aided manufacturing (CAD, CAM). Where designers throughout the twentieth century would sketch and then make models and prototypes of their furniture ideas, now almost all

overleaf
For sheer exuberance, it's difficult to beat the work of designer Karim Rashid. Here his Wavelength sofas, from 2000, appear in plain black for the two-seat versions, and black and white for the three-seaters at the Semiramis Hotel on the outskirts of Athens. Rashid has designed everything for this hotel, right down to the slippers under the bed.

above

Kloud Sofa and Chair

With its soft and sensual aura, the body-hugging Kloud chair and sofa, 2006, was designed by New York-based Karim Rashid in response to an evolving trend towards organic, softer and more fluid forms. The chair has a swivel base.

right

Orgy Sofa

'Why sit when you can lie down?' asks designer Karim Rashid, who designed this all-enveloping, brightly coloured sofa and stool called Orgy in 2003. The huge piece, almost 3 m (10 ft) in length, is designed as a room centrepiece where friends can lie back and chill out. With the stool slotted into the curved niche, the sofa doubles as a bed.

left

Sax Chair and Footstool

Part of the Sax series of seating and tables, 2002, this is a comfortable and welcoming armchair with matching footstool by Terence Woodgate. The Sax range is designed to evoke the laid-back spirit of smoky jazz clubs and relaxed decadence.

Rainbow Chair

A life-enhancing piece by Patrick Norguet,
the Rainbow chair, 2000, is made entirely
from acrylic resin as a structural material.
The transparent and translucent slices
of multicoloured resin are bonded together
using ultrasound.

designers rely on computers as part of the work process. Along with providing invaluable help in technical areas, such as understanding where stresses and tensions may affect a particular type of material, the use of the computer has had an influence on the look of twenty- first-century design. The most visible aspect of this is the use of rounded corners in so many designs as the shape is best suited to manufacturing processes such as moulding. Nonetheless, it has proved to be a pleasing aesthetic and distinctive of the new era. The other area of rapid change has been in hi-tech manufacturing processes.

Fusing sensual curves, innovative use of materials and technical prowess, French designer Patrick Norguet's (1969–) Rainbow chair of 2000, made by Cappellini, is a delight. It is also a piece of great accomplishment, being made entirely from acrylic resin as a structural material – the transparent and translucent slices of multicoloured resin are bonded using ultrasound. Norguet works as an industrial and interior designer with companies such as Christian Dior and Louis Vuitton.

Working with curves of a very different sort, and in characteristically anarchic fashion, Tom Dixon combined hi-tech materials with handcrafted production in his Fresh Fat series of chairs, tables and bowls, which began in 2001. Experimenting with a new clear plastic gel called Eastman Provost, a PETG co-polyester, the objects are formed from the warm, soft material that is extruded from a nozzle, which is manipulated by hand. Built up in a series of hoops and squiggles, the material adheres on contact and solidifies when cold into a glassy, transparent, hard plastic to make intriguing, glistening objects.

Using hi-tech production, but in a break away from the sleek, highly sophisticated, rounded-corner aesthetic, in 2003 German-born Konstantin Grcic (1965–) worked with the manufacturer Magis to explore the use of die-cast aluminium in furniture. The process is based on injecting molten metal into a mould. Grcic has evolved a distinctive style based on open-weave, angular framework structures that look like pieces of engineering. Chair One, from 2004, has a shell body composed of slender struts in a geometric, triangular grid – the design is reminiscent

below

Extendable Screen

A light and bright room divider designed by Tom Dixon. The highly flexible and translucent Extendable Screen, from 2004, is made from Provista, PETG co-polyester. It glows in the light and is produced in a range of bold colours.

of computerized line drawings. The chair's lightweight shell body sits on a concrete cone base. Working as an industrial designer across many disciplines, Munich-based Grcic has produced a range of distinctive products, from pedal bins and a ballpoint pen, to tableware and many other furniture pieces.

Experimenting with lightweight materials has become one of the current preoccupations of many designers. Carbon fibre was deployed by Dutch designer Bertjan Pot (1975–) for his Carbon chair, 2004. Taking its inspiration from the Charles and Ray Eameses' Plastic dining chair from the 1950s, the Carbon chair uses the same outline shape, but is made entirely of carbon fibre that has been woven into shape, even forming the space-frame-style legs, and then the whole piece is frozen rigid with epoxy resin. The resulting piece is a captivating mesh of intersecting lines, it is extremely lightweight and, with the helping hand of Marcel Wanders, is now in production with Moooi.

The latest great technological leap has been in the close coupling of computer design and production. One entirely new area is rapid prototyping. This process, using either powders or liquids, can be used to create one-off products that are 'grown' by the use of lasers, and it opens up the intriguing possibility of producing more customized designs. Among the most striking examples to appear so far is the Solid chair from 2004 by French designer Patrick Jouin (1967–). Working with the Belgian company Materialize, Jouin created the Solid chair from liquid resin. The piece was 'grown' from a tank of liquid resin with the use of a laser beam that solidified the material following directions from the design on screen. The process is called stereo lithography and is inspiring a new kind of organic-based aesthetic.

Another area that is opening up new production possibilities is the use of a machine called a computer numerically controlled cutting mill or CNC mill. Once again using the close link between computer and production, a laser cutter translates a screen-based design into

above

Chair One

An intriguing design by Konstantin Grcic made from die-cast aluminium with a concrete base. In Chair One, 2003, Grcic has evolved a distinctive style based on open-weave, angular framework structures which look like pieces of engineering.

right

Solid Chair

Patrick Jouin created the Solid chair, 2004, from liquid resin. The piece was 'grown' from a tank of liquid resin with the use of a laser beam in a process called stereolithography and is inspiring a new kind of organic-inspired aesthetic.

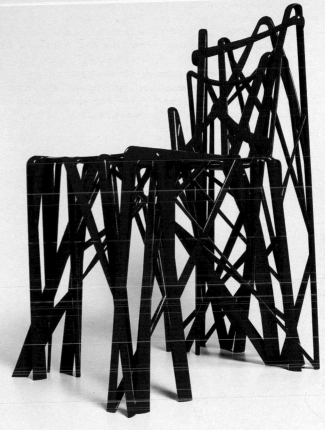

a three-dimensional object. Starting with solid blocks of material, this mill can cut three-dimensional shapes from it. The most high-profile piece of furniture created using this process so far is the Cinderella table, which was part of the 2004 Industrialized Wood series from Dutch designer Jeroen Verhoeven. He is part of the studio called Demakersvan ('the makers of'), which includes his twin brother Joep Verhoeven (1976–) and Judith de Graauw (1976–). The table, made from laminated sheets of plywood, is an incredibly complex hollow form based on multiple and asymmetrical curves and flourishes inspired by eighteenth-century furniture designs. Quite contrary to the long-held perception of mechanized mass production as lacking any soul, part of Verhoeven's idea behind this project was to show that computer-aided design and computer-aided manufacturer can be a new type of craft. It is an intriguing philosophy, and this innovative piece stands among those marking the threshold of a new approach to design and manufacture.

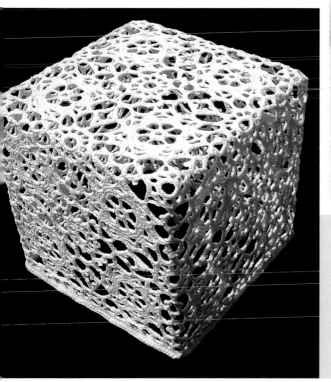

left

Crochet Table

This highly decorative table called Crochet, 2001, is by Dutch designer Marcel Wanders. The lacy, filigree design is made from cotton dipped in epoxy resin, which sets hard to form the shape.

Women Are Doing It

Of course there have always been talented women involved in the design and production of modern furniture, such as Charlotte Perriand, Eileen Grey, Florence Knoll and Ray Eames, but the list is short. The old reasoning used to be that women were not attracted to a male-dominated industry with such a strong technical bias. However, in recent years the cast of women designers has broadened considerably. It is difficult to pinpoint precisely why this change has come about. Some commentators suggest that more women are joining design courses and are also going on to work in the field. Others reason that the industry itself has evolved, with furniture design becoming part of a general 'lifestyle' industry. While women have long been interior designers and worked in areas such as ceramics and textiles, it should come as no surprise that some would want to transfer to furniture. Whatever the reason, the twenty-first-century roll-call of high-profile female designers is a new phenomenon in the furniture world.

One of the most prolific of these is Patricia Urquiola (1961–). Born in Spain but now based in Milan, she works for leading manufacturers, including B&B Italia, Driade and Moroso. Her design style is modest, modern and highly varied, ranging from a reinvented wicker chair called Pavo, in 2006 for Driade, to indoor/outdoor furniture in soft, rounded shapes called Nido, from 2006, designed with Eliana Gerotto (1951–) for manufacturer Paola Lenti. She has also designed accessories, including lighting and rugs. One of her best-known works is the 2002 Fjord chair for Moroso. With echoes of Arne Jacobsen's Swan and Egg chairs from the 1950s, this design stands on a central stem and is based on a

above

Black Magic Chair

Made from humble MDF and laser-cut to produce decorative incised patterns on every surface, the Black Magic chair, 2002, is by Ineke Hans. Mixing the latest technology with folksy design, the chair is given a standard finish in black, but other colours can be requested.

below

Fjord Chair

An unusual asymmetrical chair design called Fjord, 2002, by Patricia Urquiola. The high back, rounded seat and stem base are reminiscent of Arne Jacobsen's Swan and Egg chairs from the 1950s.

rounded seat and back shell, but this time the form is asymmetrical, with one half of the backrest rising tall and the other remaining low. The V-shaped gap between the two parts of the backrest give the chair its name Fjord. The piece is given a slimline layer of upholstery and finished in either fabric or leather. More recently, Urquiola produced her Lazy collection for B&B Italia. Launched in 2004, it is based on a slender, bent tubular steel frame with a sleigh-style base and slimline upholstery in expressive shapes. The chairs feature extra-wide seats with low backs, or narrow seats with tall backs, and are finished in an interesting palette of fabric colours, including sage green, rust orange and raspberry pink. The metal frame and intriguing types of covering fabrics are recurring motifs in her work.

Meanwhile, in the Netherlands Ineke Hans (1966–) has been cutting a dash with her intriguing work and is now recognized as one of the country's leading designers. After studying at the Royal College of Art in London, she worked for in the UK for five years in the mid-1990s for the homeware store Habitat and returned to Holland to set up her own studio in 1998. Eye-catching recent pieces include the Black Magic chair from 2002, which is based on a simple dining-chair form that features intricate lacy patterns in the seat, and back and legs that have been created by laser cutting – the chair is constructed in MDF and painted black. An almost child-like theme is recurrent in her work and appears again in her Ordinairy Furniture from 2005. Again predominantly in black, these chairs are formed from slabs of recycled plastic that is given a wood-grain finish and are conceived to look undesigned, as though they have been very roughly assembled from

below

Lazy Chair

With their crisp silhouettes and laid-back design, the Lazy series of chairs, 2004, by Patricia Urquiola is finished in an interesting palette of fabric colours, including sage green, rust orange and raspberry pink. The metal frame and intriguing types of covering fabrics are recurring motifs in her work.

below

Lem Stool

Stylish, comfortable and finding almost instant success when it was launched in 2000, the Lem bar stool is among the best-known early pieces from design team Shin and Tomoko Azumi.

chunks of timber. The series includes chairs, tables and benches and, because the plastic is virtually indestructible, can be used inside or out. While Hans produces much of her own furniture, she has recently started an association with the manufacturer Cappellini, which in 2007 launched her Fracture range of chairs, stools and tables. For Hans, these pieces are made in an unusually bright palette of red, pink, white and black. Once again these are based on simple, rustic-style forms, but are made from lightweight polystyrene that has been wrapped with a modern bandage material, which sets rock hard.

In France, among the emerging band of women designers is Inga Sempe (1968–), who works for forward-looking manufacturers such as Cappellini and Edra. Intriguing recent pieces include her Brosse storage units for Edra from 2003. The unusual designs are based on an idea of open and closed shelving. Units are constructed from a stack of shelves that are then given a screen of plastic frond curtains. In the UK, Jane Atfield (1964–) was among the women designers to achieve recognition in the mid-1990s with her experiments in using recycled materials. Her best-known design is the RCP2 chair from 1994, which is made from a recycled coloured plastic sheet material and manufactured by her company Made of Waste. Again with a highly experimental approach is Clare Page (1975–), a founder in 2001 of the design company Committee with Harry Richardson (1975–). Renowned for their recycling of junk materials and objects, their best-known pieces include the 2004 standard lamps called Kebab. This series of lamps is distinguished by the stem, which is used as a kind of skewer for all manner of found objects and trinkets. The designers even recycled their experience of scavenging through rubbish by producing a wallpaper called Flytip, which features disturbing images of broken dolls, discarded drinks cans and mobile (cell) phones.

Among the high-profile female designers who have made Britain their home is Tomoko Azumi. She arrived in England in the early 1990s and studied at the Royal College of Art before setting up a design studio with her husband, Shin. Their company, Azumi, soon acquired cult status for its witty, delightful and highly seductive designs, working for high-profile clients such as Muji, Authentics and Keen. Among their best-known designs is the 2000 Lem bar stool for Lapalma, and the delightful 1999 Snowman salt and pepper pots, on which the holes for the salt and pepper form snowman faces. Following the couple's separation, Tomoko opened her own studio, TNA Design, in 2006.

Finally, and unquestionably the most famous woman designer in the world, is London-based and Iraqi-born Zaha Hadid (1950–). While she is certainly best known for her visionary deconstructivist buildings, such as the Phaeno Science Centre in Germany, Hadid has recently experimented with a number of smaller-scale designs, including furniture for the luxury brand Sawaya & Moroni. Called the Z.scape, she has been developing a series of seating designs since 2000 with the first four pieces called Stalactite, Stalagmite, Glacier and Moraine. The concept is based on a landscape of irregularly shaped forms, like huge rock formations, which can be used in a variety of configurations. Glacier and Moraine are a pair of sofas in upholstered foam with printed fabric coverings, while Stalactite and Stalagmite are two complementary tables made of wood with natural or lacquered finishes. One of her best-known pieces is the huge table, more than 4 m (13 ft) in length, called Aqua by British manufacturer Established & Sons. Featuring Hadid's trademark free-flowing abstract forms, the monumental table stands on three sculptural legs and is made from laminated and matt polyurethane resin with silicone. Each piece is extremely expensive and extremely collectable – truly, here is furniture as artwork.

right

Ice Storm

There's no shortage of drama and intrigue in this seating design by Zaha Hadid. Taking its inspiration from the wind-sculpted forms of snow and ice, it was conceived as part of a digitally-designed, whole-room installation called Ice Storm on show at the MAK exhibition in Vienna, Austria, 2003. The idea was to create a flowing living and lounging environment.

below

Aqua Table

One of Zaha Hadid's best-known furniture pieces is the huge Aqua table, more than 4 m (13 feet) in length. Made by exclusive British manufacturer Established & Sons, it features Hadid's trademark free-flowing abstract forms and is made from laminated and matt polyurethane resin with silicone.

Ineke Hans (1966–)

Borrowing from folklore, vernacular design, pictograms and children's drawings, Ineke Hans has evolved a highly distinctive personal style in her short career. Describing herself as being 'down-to-earth', she is interested in archetypes, function and utility, along with the history and roots of products. She also likes to explore the power of objects and environments on our imagination and behaviour. Best known for her all-black furniture and tablewares, and for the use of humour and irony, her work has a powerful charm. After years of manufacturing many of the pieces at her own studio, she has recently also started to work with larger furniture producers and has made the transition from one-offs and small batches to mass production.

Born in 1966, Hans did not follow the path that has been chosen by so many of her fellow Dutch designers: attending the Design Academy Eindhoven and then creating conceptual pieces for Droog. Instead, she pursued her own course, attending the Hogeschool voor de Kunsten in Arnhem in 1991 and the Royal College of Art in London in 1995. In another unusual move for a designer of her generation, on graduating she accepted a job with the homeware store Habitat in London and worked on designs for its furniture and product collections. Among her best-selling items was a flatpack, folding metal table with a handle hole cut out of the tabletop.

In 1998, she returned to the Netherlands and set up her studio, Ineke Hans/Arnhem. In a reaction against her years in the high-pressure commercial world, her early pieces from this time appear almost non-designed – she says she took her inspiration from furniture she discovered in folk museums. Her experiments started with black, recycled plastic that was made to look like planks of wood from which she made several tables, stools and other items. Gradually the numbers of designs grew and began to form her Ordinairy collection. Assembling collections is her preferred way

above
One of the fast-rising stars of Dutch design, Ineke Hans has produced a considerable portfolio of work from furniture to textiles. The pieces are often imbued with an almost childlike simplicity, which belies the technical complexity and sophistication.

above

Elephant Chaise Longue

With its very simple outline, almost like a child's drawing, this 2002 chaise is made from plywood wrapped in soft wool. It forms part of Ineke Hans's Under Cover chair series.

left

Ordinairy

From 2005, this collection of furniture by Ineke Hans looks like big planks of wood roughly assembled and nailed together. It is in fact made from recycled plastic and is extremely durable, whether used inside or out.

of working; she is a prolific designer and admits to having problems deciding where to make the edits.

Working in black soon became a theme for Hans. There followed her Black Beauties range of children's furniture, which includes pieces like the Happy Horse from 2001, a black plastic rocking horse, and from the same year Crash Car, a black plastic toy car. It was an unusual and quirky move to make designs like this in black when most people opt for bright, primary colours when designing for children. Like so many of her designs, these have an appealing, naïve quality and look like children's drawings.

The following year, black emerged again as the colour of choice in Hans's Black Gold porcelain series that was made at her studio. These large, chunky pots and containers, candelabras and tablewares are constructed from just five repeated elements and look almost as if they were made out of soot-blackened metal. Extra interest is added by the fact that the black pigment weakens the porcelain, which means the objects tend to warp and bend.

In 2002 came her intriguing Laser chairs, made from laser-cut MDF and painted black. She takes these traditional chair shapes and then covers the entire surface with lacy, folksy, laser-cut decoration. Most recently, her work has moved into upholstered furniture with the Elephant series of sofas, and has become more colourful, too. Big splashes of colour feature in her 2006 Fracture furniture for Cappellini. Moving her work into other areas, she has also designed fabrics, lighting and tablewares for Alessi, and a blissfully simple to use and clean garlic crusher in stainless steel for the manufacturer Royal VKB, both in 2005.

Into the New Age

Of course it is too early to identify a new direction in design for the twenty-first century, but there are several clear strands of fresh ideas under investigation. While the cool, rational Modernists will continue to produce ever-more refined and elegant designs, they will be working in an increasingly eclectic marketplace. The dominance of Modernism has evaporated along with the dictates of the Modernist pioneers. Form no longer needs to follow function; things have loosened up and moved on. Meanwhile, the ripples of the aftershock of Post Modernism continue to be felt with a clear sense of design freedom. Of course the Post-Modernist philosophies have changed, evolved and become transformed, but present in many contemporary designs are echoes of their wit and appropriation, a wild and adventurous colour palette and the ravishing use of decoration.

Standing on the line where Modernism meets the new age are the French Bouroullec brothers, Ronan (1971–) and Erwan (1976–). Their interests are diverse and they've worked on furniture and tableware, interior design and office furniture. The designs are usually restrained and always modest, and while they rarely delve

right

Facett Sofa

The result of two interests, Facett, 2005, by Ronan and Erwan Bouroullec, combines ideas on structure and comfort with an interesting cover. The pieces are made from foam without any visible structure or feet, and the padded cover was achieved after research into sewing and pleating.

below

Brick

Originally designed as an exhibition backdrop, this storage system, 2000, by the Bouroullecs, was first made from laser-cut polystyrene. The modular system comes in small elements, which can be stacked high and constructed like a brick wall. More recently, it has been produced in wood.

left

Nest

Made from rotation-moulded plastic, this pretty chair called Nest, 2006, is designed by Tord Boontje. The decorative skin has a raised flower-and-leaf pattern, which is a Boontje trademark.

into decorative effects, they do embrace colour. A recurring theme is their fascination with modular systems for furniture and shelving that suit modern nomadic lifestyles, where people move regularly in pursuit of education or work. Among their best-known pieces is the Brick shelving system from 2001, produced by Cappellini. It is composed of horizontal slabs, like a squashed honeycomb, which can be piled on top of each other to build a storage unit. The epitome of flexibility and modularity is their Joyn office system for Vitra from 2002. Starting with a simple, plain white trestle table, the kit includes primary-coloured accessories, including lighting, screens and desk mats. And among their most recent works is the 2005 Facett seating for Ligne Roset, which includes upholstered armchairs and sofas that look like big pieces of angular and faceted sculpture.

One of the most exciting exponents of the new freedom to delight in decoration is Dutch designer Tord Boontje (1968–). Among his early work is the groundbreaking Wednesday lamp, part of the Wednesday collection, which began in 2000. Utterly reinventing the idea of a lampshade, Boontje has stamped a delicate filigree pattern of flowers and leaves on a very fine sheet of stainless steel, which is then twisted and draped, rather like a garland, around a naked light bulb, where the fine steel glitters and shimmers and filters the light. A mass-produced paper version of the lampshade proved to be a bestseller at British homeware store, Habitat. His large collection of work, embracing projects from wallpapers and textiles to ceramics and furniture, has always borne his trademarks of delicacy and floral patterns. Among the most recent works is his Petit Jardin garden bench and armchair series, 2007, a twisted tangle of branches and leaves made from laser-cut steel and finished in white.

Subversion is also a major contemporary theme, and again the Dutch are the masters. Among the key players is Maarten Baas (1978–), who in 2002 produced his landmark Smoke series of burned and blackened furniture – the initial collection was based on antique furniture, including a decorative chandelier, eighteenth-century dining chair, a traditional chaise longue and chest of

drawers. Interested in exploring ideas about beauty, the patina of use and damage, he set to work setting fire to the furniture, then encapsulating the burned piece in a coat of resin, reupholstering where appropriate. The result is both shocking and intriguing. In 2004, Baas took the work a step further for a New York exhibition called Where There's Smoke, where he showed 25 pieces of burned modern classic chairs by designers including Gaudí, Eames, Rietveld, Sottsass and the Campana brothers. Whereas originally the pieces were created in Baas's studio, several items, including an armchair and the chandelier, are now made by Moooi.

Subversion of traditional furniture also features in the work of Dutchman Marcel Wanders. His New Antiques collection of 2004, produced by Cappellini, is sure to guarantee a double take. At first glance, the pieces, including chairs and tables, look like fine antiques – they have decorative lathe-turned legs, leather upholstery and a glossy finish. But look again and it becomes clear that, with their exaggerated lines and deep seats, the proportions of the chairs are far from traditional and the side tables have smoked-glass tops. In true Wanders spirit, the designs are witty and smart.

below

Jenette Chair

From 2005, Jenette, by Fernando and Humberto Campana, is moulded from rigid structural polyurethane with a metallic core. The backrest is composed of hundreds of PVC stalks.

Finally, leading the way for a new design wave from South America, another team brimming with promise and with a highly original vision are the Campana brothers from Brazil. Taking their inspiration from everyday life mixed with the vibrancy of carnival culture, the brothers Humberto (1953–) and Fernando (1961–) are producing furniture that defies all categorization. Among their first key designs was the Favela chair, originally produced in 1991 and then put into production in 2003 by Edra. Made from offcuts of waste wood, it is reminiscent of a piece of homemade furniture that might be found in a slum-dweller's shack. It speaks volumes about universal issues such as a scarcity of resources. More recently their work has taken on a surreal edge, in particular with their chairs. These include the Banquette chair from 2002, which is made from a metal frame, upholstered with children's fluffy toy animals, and the Corallo chair from 2004, which is a chaotic cloud of woven steel-wire squiggles formed to make a seat and is in production with Edra. Always experimenting with humble materials, and finding a balance between craft and high technology, the work is refreshing, unusual and exuberant.

above

Bottoni Sofa

The idea for this simple, geometric Bottoni sofa, 2002, came from an exploration of upholstery. The designer Marcel Wanders has likened it to a quintessential designer suit: stylish, sexy and fit for every occasion. It is available in a range of covers, including combinations of plain and patterned fabrics as shown here.

left

Favela Chair

Evoking the make-do-and-mend way of life in the poor *favela* districts of South America, this chair from 1991 by Fernando and Humberto Campana is made from wood offcuts. Junk furniture is raised to an art form.

Ronan (1971–) and Erwan Bouroullec (1976–)

It has taken a long while for France to find design successors to the great Philippe Starck, but in the twenty-first century a new generation of exciting contenders has emerged. Rising to stardom faster than the rest are the Bouroullec brothers, Ronan and Erwan – even in a short space of time, their joint output is impressive. A reflection of their individual interests, Ronan possesses greater technical knowledge, while Erwan trained as an artist; their work fuses technical know-how and modesty with a poetic approach. It has been described as micro-architecture. However, while they have different attributes, they stress that every project is a joint effort and emerges as the result of hours of experiment and discussion. Their work reflects a young, contemporary lifestyle. Pieces are often modular and easy to assemble and dismount – ideal for a modern nomadic way of living. Key pieces include the 2000 Lit Clos sleeping cabin, a raised bed 'box' ideal for creating privacy in open-plan apartments; their modular shelving systems, including Brick from 2001, Self from 2004 and Spring Clouds from 2003; and many chair designs.

Born in Brittany to parents who both worked in medicine, elder brother Ronan left for Paris in his teens to study industrial design

above

Brothers Ronan and Erwan Bouroullec combine their complementary design and technical skills to produce fresh and inspiring pieces which have brought them international attention and injected new life into the French design scene.

below

Spring Chair

The first chair designed by Ronan and Erwan Bouroullec for the Italian firm Cappellini. Spring, 2000, is manufactured in a traditional way with a foam-covered shell, which is then upholstered. The footrest is articulated on a spring that responds to the movement of the legs. The headrest is adjustable, as is found in cars.

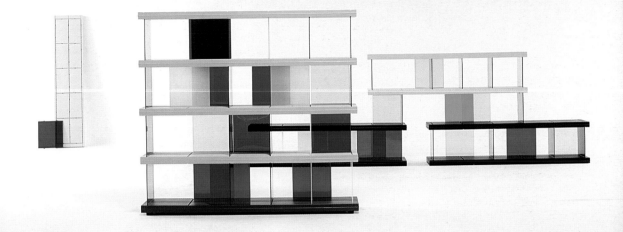

and then furniture design. Later, Erwan followed his brother to the capital to study art. Among the first pieces to win attention were Ronan's designs for Combinatory vases, made in white ABS plastic in 1997. The eight-piece set was conceived to be used separately or in a variety of combinations, even arranging all eight pieces together to make a single unit. Around the same time he was working on prototypes for his modular kitchen units called Cuisine Desintegre. The idea was that buyers could piece together worktops, drawers, cupboards and shelves to construct their own bespoke kitchen, which could be dismounted and taken away when they moved. While on show at a Paris trade fair, both projects were spotted by Giulio Cappellini of the Italian firm Cappellini. He suggested putting a range of Ronan's existing and new designs into production, and so, in order to keep up with the work, Ronan asked Erwan to join him. From 1999 the brothers have worked in collaboration.

The new century began with creations for Cappellini, including the Lit Clos sleeping cabin and the Hole chair, both 2000. This latter design is ultra-lightweight, made from sheet aluminium that is cut by laser then stamped, folded and lacquer-painted to become a completed three-dimensional object. In 2001 they produced their Glide sofa for Cappellini: a laidback design featuring a slimline upholstered seating shell on a metal, sleigh-style base. The back of the sofa has two shelves and there is an optional footrest that turns one of the seats into a chaise longue. The same year saw the launch of the Brick shelving system, which is based on a horizontal section of three oval, honeycomb-like forms from which it is possible to create a tall shelf or room divider by stacking the horizontal strips on top of each other. Originally an exhibition backdrop and made in laser-cut polystyrene, the pieces are now made from a wooden honeycomb, which is given a hard-wearing, macretor-lacquered

above

Self Shelf

This is a truly modular and flexible shelving system created from colourful horizontal boards and supports, which are made from ABS polycarbonate. From 2004, the Self is reminiscent of classic student shelving improvised from wooden planks and bricks.

right

Lit Clos

Ideal in contemporary open-plan living spaces, this 2000 bed box, called Lit Clos, provides privacy without claustrophobia. It is conceived as a cross between a room and a piece of furniture and is made from painted plywood, steel and aluminium.

finish.

Around this time, as their fame was growing rapidly, work was under way for a wide range of clients. The brothers completed the interior of Issey Miyake's Paris A-POC boutique, tableware for the homeware store Habitat and designs for a two-tone document case in ABS plastic called La Valise, 2003, for Magis. Also came the start of an important relationship with the furniture manufacturer Vitra, with whom the brothers first devised the Self shelving system. Ideal for anyone who regularly moves home, this design is based on the old student solution of creating shelves from bricks and planks. The considerably more sophisticated Bouroullec version is based on blown-polypropylene shelves and vertical dividing walls made from polycarbonate, plus steel fixing rods. Devised to be assembled without tools, the units work as shelves, display cabinets or room dividers. Extensions can be added when required.

Developing these modular ideas, the Bouroullecs began work on the Joyn office system for Vitra. It was launched in 2003 and is based on a long, trestle-table-style white desk, to which brightly coloured accessories can be fixed, including low-level screens, lighting and storage boxes. The single table idea is conceived so that people can work together in task groups, while the screens and storage units also create separate and bespoke workstations. A domestic version of this idea has since been produced, also called Joyn, by Vitra.

More schemes for Cappellini include the Spring chair from 2000 and the Spring Clouds shelving system in high-density polystyrene from 2002. Spring Clouds is another development in modularity, this time a cloud-shaped form containing eight cut-out circles into which can be placed books or objects for display. Several 'clouds' can be fixed together to make an extended unit. The Spring chair has a polyurethane seat and stainless-steel base and is available in a range of colours, including black and bright yellow.

By 2007, the brothers expanded their work further into new realms and began working on the design for the Floating House, a scheme completed with architects Jean-Marie Finot and Denis Daversin to create a floating barge-like studio for resident artists. It is moored at the Impressionists' island of Chatou on the Seine in Paris.

right

Slow Chair

A lightweight chair, Slow, 2006, is a reinterpretation of a classic armchair with matching ottoman. With its mesh covering, it is shown here as part of the Floating House artists and writers studio project created by the Bouroullec brothers with architects Jean-Marie Finot and Denis Daversin.

left

Late Sofa

A sofa with bolt-on accessories including a shelf and lamps by Ronan and Erwan Bouroullec. Late, 2004, is extremely comfortable and is designed for long evenings of lounging.

New Millennium, New Collectables

In addition to the brilliant crop of new furniture, it is increasingly the case that today's designers are turning their hand to every area of three-dimensional creativity, from architecture and interiors to the humble toaster. Twenty-first-century lighting designs are eclectic and playful, with a particular emphasis on pendant lamps, including the renaissance of the chandelier. Outstanding designs in this area include the Random light from 2002 by the Monkey Boys – Bertjan Pot (1975–) and Daniel White (1975–) – for Moooi. This pendant shade is made from fibreglass string, frozen with resin into a sphere. In the same year came the highly memorable Smoke chandelier by Maarten Baas. Here, pieces of traditional design, including a wooden chandelier with four arms, have been partially burned with a blowtorch, fixed with epoxy resin and then, in the case of the chandelier, rewired for use. Baas made the initial pieces himself, but the items are now in production with Moooi. Following the retro trend, Kenneth Grange (1929–) was called upon to update the classic British Anglepoise desk lamp, originally designed in the early 1930s by George Carwardine; his version, called the Type 3, was launched in 2003. Two years later, to mark the seventieth birthday of the original classic, the company issued a floor lamp in a model three times the size of the original – the effect is surreal. Playing with scale has been a recurrent theme of late; Piet Boon (1958–) launched his Square Boon with Moooi in 2002: a pendant lampshade that is black on the outside and white inside and has sides almost 1 m (3¼ ft) in length. It looks very stylish over a dining table.

The kitchen and bathroom have been the focus of considerable design attention in recent years. Piero Lissoni created the ultra-sleek Case system, a modular kitchen in stainless steel or glossy snow-white, for Boffi in 2000. This was followed two years later by the equally sheer LT system in matt black for the same company. Both kitchen-unit designs have a strong architectural feel with a grid system of doors and drawers and no protruding handles. Also in 2000 came the fantastic, all-in-one kitchen unit called K2 from German designer Norbert Wangen (1962–). This freestanding, stainless-steel-clad rectangular chest features all the usual appliances, services and storage space, and, best of all, the top slides to one side to form a dining table. When it is closed, the kitchen becomes a mysterious stainless-steel block. The series, which now includes larger units up to K12, is today made by Boffi. Even

above left

Random Light

A pretty, filigree lamp shade called Random, 2002, by Bertjan Pot. It is made from fibreglass strands which have been dipped in epoxy resin, they are wound around a large balloon-like sphere and then set hard.

left

Cornflake Chair

A stylish, stackable and pared-down design, this laminated-plywood Cornflake chair, 2002, is designed by Mårten Claesson, Eero Koivisto and Ola Rune. It is available in a range of colours and with or without an upholstered finish. The series includes a Cornflake bar stool and table.

Beckham

The Swedish company David Design features a range
of projects all related to the name David. Beckham, 2000,
by Claesson Koivisto Rune, is a classic stainless-steel
clothes' rail. The pared-down design includes two tiny
raised pegs on the top rail to prevent clothes slipping off.

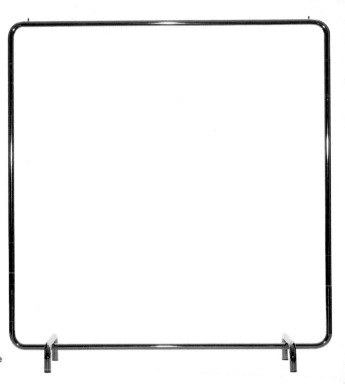

Zaha Hadid has been lured into the kitchen with her intriguing and
sculptural Z.Island, unveiled in 2006. In sweeping shapes with sensual
curves it is made for DuPont using its composite material, Corian. The
design comes in two pieces: Fire for the cooking area and Water for
washing. On a smaller scale, Hadid also designed her sculptural Tea
and Coffee Towers for Alessi in 2003 and Vortex chandeliers in 2007 for
Zumtobel. Jasper Morrison has created a series of exquisite electrical
appliances, including a kettle, toaster and coffee maker for Rowenta in
2004, and a typically understated and restrained set of cookware called
Pots and Pans in 2006 for Alessi.

Meanwhile, in the bathroom, following the examples set by such
designer heroes as Arne Jacobsen and his classic Vola taps (faucets),
Philippe Starck has enjoyed a long relationship with Duravit producing
designs for bathroom suites and furniture. Among his classic pieces
is the freestanding, double-ended bath called Oval from around 2000.
Other beautiful twenty-first-century baths include those by an impressive
roll-call of leading designers. There's the Il Bagno, 2003, a chubby tub
by Stefano Giovannoni (1954–) for Alessi; the sleek, rectangular block
called Mood, from 2000 and by Claesson Koivisto Rune for Boffi; I Fiumi
Po, a super-luxurious, solid limestone bowl-shaped bath by Claudio
Silvestrin (1954–) in 2000, also for Boffi; and Newson, a sculptural,
freestanding 2003 design based on a rectangle with rounded corners
and designed by Marc Newson for Ideal Standard.

Other miscellaneous designs of note include several good storage
ideas: the simple stainless-steel clothes-hanging rail called Beckham
by Swedish trio Claesson Koivisto Rune – Mårten Claesson (1970–),
Eero Koivisto (1958–) and Ola Rune (1963–) – for David Design in 2000,
followed in 2002 by the City System cabinets by Marcel Wanders for
Moooi. This modular system of storage cabinets, made in powder-
coated steel, is based on a collection of abstract geometric shapes; in
fact, when they are grouped together they can make an intriguing mini
cityscape of towers and blocks. Most recent innovations include the
2007 Make/Shift shelving by British designer Peter Marigold (1974–) for
Movisi. This is an intriguing concept, based on interlocking triangular
wedges formed from a type of polypropylene. The pieces, which
come in black, white or shocking pink, can be put together to make
freestanding units or wall-fixed shelving.

Make/Shift

An ingenious and flexible concept for modular shelving,
Make/Shift, 2007, was designed by Peter Marigold and
is made from ARPRO expanded polypropylene. The
wedge-shaped pieces, available in black, white or
pink, can be pieced together to fit different spaces
and it is assembled and dismounted in minutes,
making it highly portable.

◀ Favela Chair, 1991 and 2003
Every piece of this chair, designed by the Campana brothers and manufactured by Edra, is hand-glued and nailed. It is constructed piece-by-piece from the same wood used to build the homes in Rio de Janeiro's slums, called *favelas*.

▶ Miura Stool, 2004
Konstantin Grcic's one-piece stackable stool is manufactured by Plank and features a faceted seat with a pleasing visual connection to the raked vertical supports. Made of polypropylene, it is fully recyclable.

Key icons of
the new
millennium

◀ Cornflake Table and Chairs, 2002
By Claesson Koivisto Rune for Offecct, this stylish table and stackable dining chairs are made with laminated plywood and chrome legs.

◀ Thin Table, 2001

With his glass-top table on a frame of American walnut, Matthew Hilton has created a skeletal structure. The distinctive leg detail is visible through the inset glass tabletop.

▼ New Antiques, 2004

A stunning take on period furniture, Marcel Wanders references historical design in his New Antiques furniture for Cappellini. Detailed, turned objects are made modern by slender proportions and lightness; the pieces are available in matt black or white lacquered wood.

Fjord Chair, 2002

atricia Urquoila has created a soft, smooth
up with just one armrest for manufacturer
oroso. Inspired by Arne Jacobsen's well-
nown Egg chair, the Fjord consists of
olyurethane foam, upholstered in black
ather, on a steel swivel base.

Ordinairy Furniture, 2005

table and two benches from Ineke Hans's
rdinairy Furniture line. Created to resemble
ugh, found wood, this furniture is,
eceptively, made from recycled plastic.

Buying & Collecting

In a recent frenzy of bidding activity, auction houses on both sides of the Atlantic have seen new, all-time records set for pieces of collectable Modern furniture. In New York in 2006, a 1948 trestle-leg glass table by Italian designer Carlo Mollino made a staggering $3.8 million, the highest price paid for any work of Modern design. A few months later, a prototype table, just one year old and designed by Zaha Hadid, sold for $296,000; this was followed by bidding for the aluminium-wrapped 1985 Lockheed by Marc Newson, which peaked at $968,000 in 2007. This impressive bid became the highest price ever paid for a piece of furniture by a living designer – Newson

was just 42 years old at the time. Along with its unusual sculptural beauty, the piece's rarity – it is a prototype for an edition of just 13 – was certainly at the root of the astronomical price it reached. Zaha Hadid summed up the astonishing flurry of sales by pointing out that auction houses and buyers were now treating editions of designs as pieces of art, and it is certainly true that many art collectors have broadened their scope to include great pieces of design.

There is no doubting then, that the Modern furniture market is enjoying buoyant times. While collecting Modern design is a relatively new phenomenon, it has clearly gained enormous appeal.

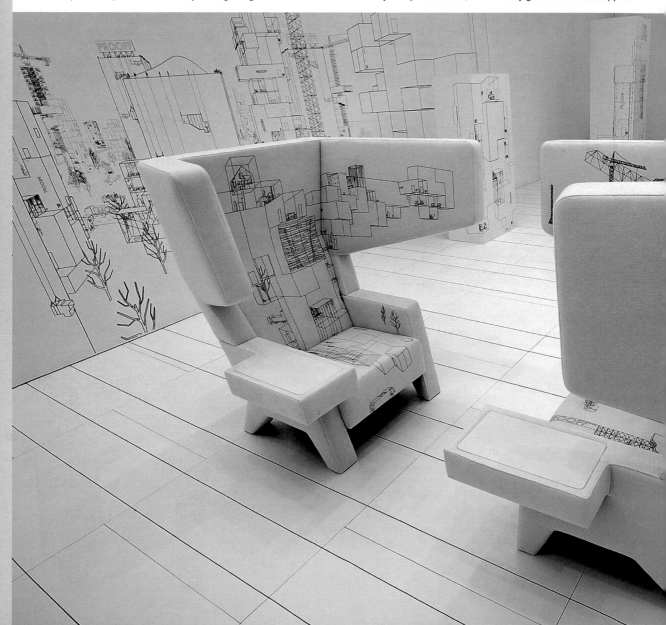

Since more and more people are now furnishing their homes in a contemporary way, there is far more information about the realm of Modern furniture classics available, and as a result such pieces are becoming highly sought after, along with ceramics, glassware, posters and paintings, clocks and other home accessories. Interior design and lifestyle magazines are brimming with picture stories about collectors and new furniture pieces, making architects and designers, from Marcel Breuer to Marcel Wanders, household names. Plenty of today's designers have even achieved superstar status, attracting crowds to launches of their new products.

Collectors come in many guises and pursue different themes. There are those who follow the fortunes of particular designers: Charles and Ray Eames perhaps, Ettore Sottsass or Jasper Morrison. They might be interested in particular pieces of furniture or in everything that their chosen designer has produced. Others hunt for period pieces, collecting anything in the glamorous Art Deco style, or the futuristic Mid-Century or exuberant Pop eras. Some collectors are specialists in particular materials: plywood furniture is ever-popular, as are plastics; or perhaps they prefer to piece together a home furnished with Scandinavian design. Whatever you decide to concentrate your efforts on, however, be aware that there is never any guarantee that your items will increase in value. Make sure you choose items because you enjoy living with them; the secret of creating a great collection is simply to buy the pieces you want to live with.

When deciding what to collect, the best starting point is to visit exhibitions, museums, galleries, shops and auctions. One of the great advantages of becoming a collector of modern design these days is that there is not only plenty for sale on the market, but there are also still great bargains to be found. There are plenty of provincial auctions, junk shops and car-boot (garage) sales where vendors will be only too pleased to part with furniture and other items that would, even recently, be considered of little or no value. Don't be afraid to haggle about the price; in the secondhand market there is always room for good-humoured negotiation.

Because the scope for collecting is so vast, it is wise to specialize in a relatively small area and to do as much research as possible about the items that you are interested in. Collecting modern furniture can present plenty of challenges, so to avoid wasting money it is always best to be armed with as much knowledge as possible. One of the most common pitfalls is to buy a piece of furniture that turns out to be a cheap reproduction. Some classic designs, including those by Le Corbusier, Marcel Breuer and Arne Jacobsen, have been the subject of low-cost copies for many years. Some of the copies are very good, but plenty are badly made and use inferior materials and poor manufacturing techniques. They also often look strange because they are made to inaccurate and odd proportions. As a general rule, the truly collectable items are made by licensed manufacturers who hold the design copyright.

Always look for a manufacturer's name. The best-quality pieces usually have some sort of stamp, label or mark to denote the maker. Bear in mind that some furniture designs have been produced by different manufacturers through the years; for example, some of

left

The Ear chair 2002 by Jurgen Bey is a modern version of the traditional wing chair and was designed for the insurance company Interpolis. The chair was conceived for use in the reception area so it could be used for small meetings and interviews. The big wing or 'ear' provides privacy for those seated and the in-built table is ideal to rest on while taking notes. It looks just as handsome and sculptural in a home setting.

Gerrit Rietveld's early designs and prototypes were made by him, some were made in relatively small batch editions at the workshops of Gerard van de Groenekan, and most recently, the best-selling designs are produced by Cassina. Just to confuse matters, there are plenty of copies around, too. Not surprisingly, Rietveld's own prototypes will be the most sought after and attract the highest prices. There are plenty of versions of this scenario. For example, many contemporary designers, including Ron Arad, Ineke Hans and Maarten Baas, make their own experimental, one-off and limited-edition pieces that, either immediately or even years later, begin to be mass produced by big-name manufacturers. It is really only those collectors who have done their research and homework who will know how to tell the difference.

Before you buy, also look closely for any other identifying marks; these can make designs more unusual and collectable. For example, some of Alvar Aalto's early plywood chairs, designed for the Paimio Sanatorium, have stencilled Roman numerals on their underside to denote the ward number they were intended for – this makes these pieces extremely valuable. If an item is sold with original paperwork, including a bill of sale, perhaps a magazine advertisement, or a product brochure, this also helps to add to the item's story and credibility.

The condition of furniture pieces can be crucial in assessing their value. Large areas of damage or very obvious and poor-quality repairs will have an adverse effect on value. This is true unless a piece is very rare. When it comes to upholstery, the serious collector will prefer well-worn original material to recent, replacement upholstery. There is a fine line to be drawn here between the collector who simply wants to own and admire the pieces and someone who wants to use them.

Auction Houses

Along with scouring bargain shops and special sales, auction houses are worth visiting as they provide a reliable source of high-quality furniture pieces. Buying at auction is an art in itself. Most of the mainstream high-profile houses, like Sotheby's and Christie's, now have sales specializing in Modern furniture and artifacts. While the auction experience can be intimidating at first, once you are familiar with the process it can be great. Although it is the huge price tags that make the headlines, there are plenty of more humble items selling for very competitive prices.

The first step to buying at auction is to visit the sale houses' websites to find out when their next sale is scheduled. Before buying, go along to a couple of sales just to watch. The atmosphere can be tense and it is a good idea to get a feel for the process rather than plunging in head first. Close to the auction date, actual items may be shown on the website and there will also be a catalogue released that you can browse through. There may be colour catalogues available for specialist auctions, and although these have to be paid for and can be expensive, they are a good record and a useful future reference for prices; an estimated guide price is printed alongside each item. There will also be details of the dates and times when the auction items are on public view, making it possible to take a look at and check items thoroughly before deciding what to bid on and what price you think it is worth. Experts are usually on hand to discuss the items. Every auction house will draw on the experience of its experts to verify that the item descriptions are as accurate as possible. While there will always be the occasional exception, this is usually a guarantee of reliability.

On the day of the sale, it is advisable to arrive early, as you will need to register your name and address and credit-card details. In exchange you will be given a card, sometimes called a paddle, bearing a bidding number. Your number will be used during bidding in place of your name. Hold up the card or paddle for the auctioneer to see as you make a bid. As the auctioneer makes his or her way through the lots, bids will be made by people in the room, but it is also possible to take part if you can't attend in person. One option is to leave a written bid; this will be given to the auctioneer and used against potential buyers in the room. You can also make a phone bid – as your chosen lot approaches, you will be called by an auction house representative who will bid on your behalf. It will be possible to hear the action as it takes place in the room and you will be invited to make bids by your representative.

If you are lucky enough to have beaten off the competition and won the bid, the piece must then be paid for. There will be a premium to pay to the auctioneer and you may also have to pay a tax. It is best to check all of this in advance, as it can add as much as 20 per cent to your bidding price. The payment is usually completed on the day, or you will be given a time limit to complete the transaction. Once the money is paid, you are free to take the item away. In some instances, if you are unable to collect an item immediately, you may be charged for storage – auction houses are busy places with a high turnover of goods so they can't afford the time and space to hold items.

Internet Auctions

A similar system is in place with Internet auction sites, the best known of which is eBay. Here, as a buyer or seller, you need to register your contact details. Most people also find it is helpful to join the electronic payment system PayPal. The disadvantage of Internet-based auctions, however, is that you cannot view the items in person, but the best sellers will show plenty of photos and give a good description of the item – it is possible to contact the vendor by email if there are any outstanding questions about the item for sale. It is also a good idea to check the vendor's reliability through the feedback system, which will have been completed by pervious buyers, before you start to bid.

When you find an interesting item, follow the screen procedure to leave a bid. This can be tracked electronically, issuing you with an email close to the end of the sale period so you will be given every opportunity to improve your bid. Once the sale is complete, the payment will be taken automatically and you can exchange emails or calls with the vendor to arrange postage, delivery or collection of the item. As with all purchases, the watchword is 'buyer beware'. The more information and knowledge you have, the more you will be assured of a great deal. Happy hunting.

opposite

This family of designs by Warren Platner was created for Knoll and first produced in 1966. It's now called the Platner Collection and comprises the glass-topped dining table and smaller coffee table, a stool and upholstered chairs. Platner's intriguing use of steel wire rods produces a graceful shimmering effect, which changes as you walk around the pieces. The rods are held in place with neat steel hoops, top and bottom.

Care and Repair

In common with traditional antiques, the contemporary view on conservation repair and care of vintage furniture is that all interventions should be as minor as possible. In general, to keep Modern design classics looking their best and to ensure the longest life in the best condition, pieces should be protected from extreme dryness and damp. Both will have very detrimental effects, especially on the more experimental early materials such as plastics. Dryness will also cause damage to materials such as leather, which will become flaky and fragile. Air-conditioning is particularly harsh. Meanwhile, damp will encourage mould and will rot and ruin upholstery foams and fabric covers; it will also cause metal frames to rust. A medium level of humidity is ideal.

Temperature is also a consideration. Most materials do not respond well to extremes of hot or cold, or big fluctuations, which can cause many materials to expand and contract, which in turn promotes cracking. Experts recommend a temperature of just under 20°C (65°F). It is also a good idea to keep furniture and furnishings away from bright and direct sunlight, as this will speed up chemical reactions in materials and cause items to rot. Daylight will bleach colour from fabrics and plastics. So a cool room, with the heating turned down and some shade, is the perfect spot for showing off your collection.

For cleaning your piece, use natural and old-fashioned cleaning methods and materials where possible. Avoid modern cleaning agents, such as scouring powders and creams, detergents and bleach or polish that contains silicone. Many of these contain damaging chemicals. Where possible, use clean water and a sponge to wipe surfaces; a little washing-up (dishwashing) liquid can be added to the water. Natural wax polishes are good for wood, and use leather polishes and cleaners such as saddle soap for leather upholstery.

On the business of repair, all work should be carefully considered. The first decision you have to make is whether you have bought the piece of furniture for use or investment, or a bit of both. In most instances, very rare items are best left alone and pretty much untouched. If you are lucky enough to have an early item by one of the Modernist heroes such as Marcel Breuer or Mies van der Rohe, it is unrealistic to expect this to become a piece of everyday furniture, so treat it as you might a piece of sculpture. Repairs, if absolutely necessary, are best carried out by experts. If a piece is less rare and you are expecting it to be used, then more robust repairs can be carried out. However, it is still a good idea to take advice and find someone with a sensitive approach. A car-repair workshop will be well equipped to weld and solder metals for example, but you need to ensure that they will be good at the detail. A jewellery repairer, for instance, may be better able to treat vintage metalwork.

For the repair of upholstery, similar guidelines apply. If the piece of furniture is rare, it is likely to hold its value better if left with its original leather or fabric cover. However, if the piece is for everyday use, feel free to upholster to your taste. In some cases it may be possible to find reproductions of the original materials.

The Directory

KEY DESIGNERS

Arad, Ron (1951)
Aaino, Eero (1932)
Aalto, Alvar (1898–1976)
Azumi, Tomoko and Shin (1965)

Bellini, Mario (1935)
Bertoia, Harry (1915–78)
Botta, Mario (1943)
Bottoni, Piero (1903–73)
Bouroullec, Erwan (1976)
Bouroullec, Ronan (1971)
Brazier-Jones, Mark (1956)
Breuer, Marcel (1902–81)

Calka, Maurice (1921–99)
Castelli Ferrieri, Anna (1920)
Castiglioni, Achille (1918–2002)
Cherner, Norman (1942)
Chippeffield, David (1953)
Citterio, Antonio (1950)
Coray, Hans (1906–91)

Day, Lucienne (1917)
Day, Robin (1915)
De Pas, Gionatan (1932–91)
Ditzel, Nanna (1923–2005)
Dixon, Tom (1864–1946)
D'Urbino, Donato (1932–91)

Eames, Charles (1907–78)
Eames, Ray (1912–88)
Ercolani, Lucian (1888–1976)
Eriksson, Thomas (1959)

Ferrari-Hardoy, Jorge (1914–77)
Fornasetti, Piero 1913–88)
Foster, Norman (1935)

Gehry, Frank (1929)
Giovannoni, Stefano (1954)
Gray, Eileen (1878–1976)
Gropius, Walter (1883–1969)

Hein, Piet (1905–96)
Herbst, Rene (1891–1982)
Hilton, Matthew (1957)
Hoffmann, Josef (1870–1956)
Hollein, Hans (1934)

Jacobsen, Arne (1902–71)
Jalk, Grete (1920)

Jeanneret, Pierre (1896)
Juhl, Finn (1912–89)

Kagan, Vladimir (1927)
Kinsman, Rodney (1943)
Kjaerholm, Poul (1929–80)
Knoll, Florence (1917)
Kovisto Rune, Claesson (1995)
Kuramata, Shiro (1934–91)

Landels, Willie (1928)
Lloyd Wright, Frank (1867–1959)
Lomazzi, Paolo (1936)
Lovegrove, Ross (1958)

Mackintosh, Charles Rennie (1868–1928)
Mathsson, Bruno (1907–88)
Mendini, Alessandro (1931)
Mollino, Carlo (1905–73)
Morrison, Jasper (1959)
Murdoch, Peter (1795–1871)

Nelson, George (1908–86)
Newson, Marc (1963)
Noguchi, Isamu (1904–88)

Opsvik, Peter (1939)

Panton, Verner (1926–98)
Paulin, Pierre (1927)
Perriand, Charlotte (1903–99)
Pesce, Gaetano (1939)
Pier Giacomo (1928–91)
Platner, Warren (1919)
Ponti, Gio (1891–1979)
Prouve, Jean (1901–1984)

Umeda, Masanori (1941)

Race, Ernest (1913–64)
Rams, Dieter (1932)
Rietveld, Gerrit (1888–1964)
Risom, Jens (1919)
Ruhlmann, Emile-Jacques (1879–1933)

Saarinen, Eero (1910–61)
Stam, Mart (1899–1986)
Starck, Philippe (1949)
Sottsass, Ettore (1917)
Summers, Gerald (1899–1967)

Thonet, Michael (1796–1871)
Thun, Matteo (1952)

Van der Rohe, Ludwig Mies (1886–1969)
Van Severen, Marten (1956–2005)
Volther, Paul

Wanders, Marcel (1963)
Wegner, Hans (1915–2007)
Wewerka, Stefan (1928)
Woodgate, Terence (1953)

Yanagi, Sori (1915)

Zanuso, Marco (1916–2001)

AUCTION HOUSES

UNITED KINGDOM

Bonhams
101 New Bond Street
London W1S 1SR
Tel: 020 7447 7447
www.bonhams.com

Christie's
8 King Street
London SW1Y 6QT
Tel: 020 7839 9060
www.christies.com

Lots Road Galleries
71–73 Lots Road
London SW10 0RN
Tel: 020 7376 6800
www.lotsroad.com

Sotheby's
34–35 New Bond Street
London W1A 2AA
Tel: 020 7293 5000
www.sothebys.com

UNITED STATES

Bonhams & Butterfields
220 San Bruno Avenue
San Francisco, CA 94103
Tel: 415 861 7500
www.bonhams.com

Christie's
20 Rockerfeller Plaza
New York, NY 10020
Tel: 212 636 2000
www.christies.com

Sotheby's
1334 York Avenue
New York, NY 10021
Tel: 541 312 5682
www.sothebys.com

AUSTRALIA
Bonhams & Goodman:
www.bonhamsandgoodman.com.au
New South Wales
7 Anderson Street, Double Bay
Sydney, NSW, 2028
Tel : 612 9327 9900
Victoria
Level 1, 540 Malvern Road
Prahran, Melbourne, VIC, 3181
Tel : 613 8530 3900

Christie's:
www.christies.com
Victoria
Tel: 613 9823 6266
Sydney
Tel: 612 9326 1422

Sotheby's
118–122 Queen Street
Woollahra 2025
Tel: 612 9362 1000
www.sothebys.com

STORES
UNITED KINGDOM
Aram
110 Drury Lane
London WC2B 5SG
Tel: 020 7557 7557
www.aram.co.uk

The Conran Shop
55 Marylebone High Street
London W1U 5HS
Tel: 020 7723 2223
www.conranshop.co.uk

Decoratum
13–25 Church Street
London NW8 8DT
Tel: 020 7724 6969
www.decoratum.com

Habitat
196–199 Tottenham Court Road
London W1T 7PJ
Tel: 08444 99 1122
www.habitat.net

Fritz Hansen
20–22 Rosebery Avenue
London EC1R 4SX
Tel: 020 7837 2030
www.fritzhansen.com

Heals
The Heals Building
196 Tottenham Court Road
London W1T 7LQ
Tel: 020 7636 1666
www.heals.co.uk

Hulsta
22 Bruton Street
London W1X 7DA
Tel: 020 7629 4881
www.hulstastudio.co.uk

IKEA
Tel: 0845 355 1141
www.ikea.com

Ligne Roset
37–39 Commercial Road
London E1 1LF
Tel: 020 7426 9670
www.ligne-roset-city.co.uk

Living Space
53–55 Fulham High Street
London SW6 3JJ
Tel: 020 7731 1180
www.livingspaceuk.com

Purves and Purves
6 Cosmur Close
London W12 9SF
Tel: 020 8838 0200
www.purves.co.uk

Sixty 6
66 Marylebone High Street
London W1U 5JF
Tel: 020 7224 6066

Skandium
86 Marylebone High Street
London W1U 4QS
Tel: 020 7935 2077
www.skandium.com

Twentytwentyone
274 Upper Street
London N1 2UA
Tel: 020 7288 1996
www.twentytwentyone.com

UNITED STATES
Cappellini
152 Wooster Street (Houston Street)
New York, NY 10012
Tel: 212 966 0669
www.cappellini.it

Domus Design Collection
181 Madison Avenue
New York, NY, 10016
Tel: 212 685 0800
www.ddcnyc.com

Design Within Reach
341 Columbus Ave
New York, NY 10024
Tel: 212 799 5900
www.dwr.com

Fresh Kills
50 North 6th Street
Williamsbury, Brooklyn, NY 11211
Tel: 718 388 8081
www.freshkillsforthepeople.com

EBHome
200 East Main Street, Mt. Kisco
New York, NY 10549
Tel: 914 242 7278
www.ebhome.com

Kartell
805 Peachtree Street NE
30308 Atlanta
Tel: 404 601 1275
www.kartell.it

The Magazine
1823 Eastshore Highway
Berkeley CA 94710
Tel: 510 549 2282
www.themagazine.info

MoMA Design Store
81 Spring Street,
New York, NY
Tel: 646 613 1367
www.momastore.org

Moss
150 Greene Street
New York, NY 10012
Tel: 212 204 7100
www.mossonline.com

Totem Design
71 Franklin Street
New York, NY 10013
Tel: 212 925 5506
www.totemdesign.com

AUSTRALIA
Beclau
Unit 15, 198 Young St
Waterloo, NSW 2017
Tel: 612 9698 6422
www.beclau.com

De De Ce
263 Liverpool St, Darlinghurst
Sydney, NSW 2010
Tel: 612 9360 2722
www.dedeci.com

Living Edge
74 Commonwealth Street, Surry Hills
Sydney, NSW 2010
Tel: 612 9212 3542
www.livingedge.com.au

Scandinavium
200 Campbell Street, Darlinghurst
Sydney, NSW, 2010
Tel: 612 9332 4660
www.scandinavium.com/au

Space Furniture
629 Church Street
Richmond, Melbourne VIC 3121
Tel: 613 9426 3000
www.spacefurniture.com.au

MANUFACTURERS
Alessi
Via Privata Alessi, 6
28882 Crusinallo (Vb) Italy
Tel: 0323 868611
www.alessi.com

Artek
Lemuntie 3-5 B
FI-00510 Helsinki
Finland
Tel: 10 617 3430
www.artek.fi

Artifort
Van Leeuwenhoekweg 20
5482 TK Schijndel, Netherlands
Tel: 73 658 00 20
Cassina

Cassina S.p.A.
via Busnelli, 1
I-20036 Meda
Milan, Italy
Tel: 0362372.1
www.cassina.it

B&B Italia
22060 Novedrate (CO) Italia
Strada provinciale 32, Italy
Tel: 031 795 111
www.bebitalia.it

Cappellini
via Marconi, 35 22060 Arosio (CO), Italy
Tel: 031 759111
www.cappellini.com

Edra
via Ciovassino 3
(Brera zone) Milan, Italy
Tel: 0286995122
www.edra.com

Established and Sons
29/31 Cowper Street
London EC2A 4AT
Tel: 020 7608 0990
www.establishedandsons.com

Fasem
Via Francesca Nord, 44/46/48
56010 Vicopisano, Pisa, Italy
Tel: 050 799 576
www.fasem.it

Garsnas
Rödbodtorget 2 SE-111 52
Stockholm, Sweden
Tel: 8 442 91 50

Carl Hansen & Son
Holmevaenget 8
5560 Aarup, Denmark
Tel: 6612 1404
www.carlhansen.com

Fritz Hansen
Allerødvej 8 DK-3450
Allerød, Denmark
Tel: 48 17 23 00
www.fritzhansen.com

Magis
via Magnadola, 15
31045 Motta di Livenza (TV) Italy
Tel: 0422 862600

Herman Miller
www.hermanmiller.com

Isokon Plus
Turnham Green
Terrace Mews, Chiswick
London W4 1QU
Tel: 020 8994 7032
www.isokonplus.com

Kartell
Via Porta Carlo, 1
20121 Milan, Italy
Tel: 02 2901 4935
www.kartell.it

Knoll
www.knollint.com

Offecct
Box 100, SE-543 21
Tibrom Sweden
Tel: 504 415 00
www.offecct.se

Moooi
Minervum 7003
4817 ZL, PO Box 5703
4801 EC
Breda, Netherlands
Tel: 76 578 4444
www.moooi.nl

Moroso
Via Nazionale, 60-33010
Udine, Italy
Tel: 0432 577111
www.moroso.it

Thonet
www.thonet.com

Vitra
www.vitra.com

Vitsoe
72 Wigmore Street
London W1U 2SG
Tel: 020 7935 4968
www.vitsoe.com

Zanotta
20054 Nova Milanese
via Vittorio Veneto 57, Italy
Tel: 0362 4981
www.zanotta.it

Index

Figures in italics indicate captions.

2001: A Space Odyssey (film) 70, 73, *126*
A-POC boutique, Paris 204
Aalto, Aino 48, 50, 53, 54, 57
    'Aalto' ridged glassware 73
Aalto, Alvar 8, 31, 42, *48*, 50, 54, *54*, 57, *57*, 58, *58*, 82, 212
    A331 pendant lamp *48*
    Aulatuli chair *52*
    Finlandia Hall, Helsinki 54, 57
    Finnish Pavilion, New York's World Fair 80
    Kakonen chair *52*
    Massachusetts Institute of Technology 57
    Model No. 60 stool *52*, 53, 54, 57
    Model No. 68 chair *52*
    Model No. 69 chair 54, 57
    Model No. 98 tea trolley *74*
    Model No. 100 screen *56*
    Model No. 400 (the Tank) armchair *48*
    Model No. A330 pendant lamps *50*
    Model No. X601 stool *57*
    Model No. X800B coffee table *48*
    Muuratsalo, Finland 57
    Opera House, Essen 57
    Oregon, USA college and library 57
    Paimio chair (Model No. 4) 50, 53, *53*, 54, *55*
    Paimio Sanatorium 50, 53, *53*, 54, 212
    Savoy glass vase 57, 73, *73*
    Savoy restaurant, Helsinki 57
    Tiilimäki studio, Helsinki *54*, 57
    Viipuri Library *52*, 54
    Villa Mairea, Noormarkku, Finland *50*, 57
Aarhus Town Hall, Denmark 62, *62*
Aarnio, Eero
    Bubble chair *123*, *146*
    Globe (Ball) chair *7*, *114*, *122*, *146*
    Pastil chair *7*, *122*
Abstract Expressionism 86
Adams, Ken 175
Airborne International 126, *147*
Albers, Anni 80
Albers, Joseph 80
Alessi 121, 144, 157, 175, 181, 197, 207
Alias 170, *182*
Alitalia 121
Alterego 181
Alvar Aalto: Architecture and Furniture exhibition (Museum of
    Modern Art, New York, 1938) 57
American Abstract Artists group 86
Apelli & Varesio *111*
Appel, Karel 107
Arabia 144
Arad, Ron *7*, 150, 156–7, *156*, 164, 177, 181, 212
    Bad Tempered chair 157
    Big Easy (renamed New Orleans) 156, 157, 177
    Bookworm *156*, 157, 177, 181
    FPE (Fantastic Plastic Elastic chair) *152*, 157
    Holon design museum, Israel 157
    Little Albert armchairs *156*
    Magis headquarters, Treviso 157
    Not Made By Hand, Not Made in China 157
    Rover chair *152*, 153, 157
    Tel Aviv Opera House 156
    Tinker chair 157
    Tom Vac chair 157, 177
    Victoria and Albert sofa *156*
    Well Tempered chair 156, 157
    Y Store, Tokyo 156
Architectural Forum 92
Archizoom Associati 117
    Superonda 118

Arco 144
Arflex *8*, 103
Armour Institute of Technology
    (later Illinois Institute of Technology) 80
Arosio, Pietro: Mirandolina 170
Art Deco *34*, 35, 143, 181, 211
Art Nouveau 13, 17, 32
Artek 57, *57*, 74
Artemide 144
Artifort 126, *146*
Arts & Architecture magazine 89
Arts and Crafts Movement 13, *15*, 25, 43, 49, 50
Asko *7*
Asplund, Erik Gunnar 50, 58, 170
Astoria Hotel, Trondheim, Norway 131
Atfield, Jane: RCP2 chair 193
auction houses 212
Authentics 194
Azumi, Shin and Tomoko 193–4
    Donkey 3 169
    Lem stool *193*, 194
    Snowman salt and pepper pots 194
    Table = Chest design 169

B&B Italia *8*, *172*, 173, 175, 192
Baas, Maarten 212
    Smoke chandelier 206
    Smoke series 200
Badovici, Jean 32
Baker Furniture 59
Bakker, Gijs 177
Band & Olufsen 144
Barber, Edward and Osgerby, Jay
    Loop bench 169
    Loop chaise longue *168*
    Loop shelves 169
    Loop table 169, *169*, *182*
    Portmouth bench 169
Barber Osgerby 169, *169*
Barbican Arts Centre, London 101
Barnes, Edward 31
Barr, Alfred 41
Bätner, Helmut: Bofinger (BA 1171) 118
Bauhaus 7, 8, 21, 22, 25–6, *25*, 29, 31, 41, 42, 49, 50, 54, 62,
    80, 90, 95, 140
Bayer 131
Bedin, Martine 141
    Super Lamp *141*, 143
Behrens, Peter 38, 50
Bel Geddes, Norman 81
Belgo chain of restaurants, London 156
Bellavista apartment building, Klampenborg 65
Bellevue theatre and restaurant complex, Klampenborg
    65, *70*
Bellini, Mario 181
Bernard, Oliver 43
Bernini company 117
Bertoia, Brigitta (née Valentiner) 96
Bertoia, Harry 89, 90, 96, *96*
    Asymmetric chair 96
    Barstool 96
    Bird chair 96, *97*
    Diamond Lounge Chair 95, 96, *97*, *111*
    Side chair 96
Bexhill-on-Sea pavilion 42
Bey, Jurgen: Ear chair *211*
Bieffeplast 121
Bijenkorf department store 107
Biomega 175
Blackie, Walter *16*
Blumer, Ricardo: LaLeggera chair 170

BOAC 101
Boda 144
Boffi 120, 143, 206, 207
Bonacina, Pierantonio 139
Bonet, Antonio *see* Ferrari-Hardoy
Bonetti, Mattia *see* Garouste
Boon, Piet: Square Boon 206
Boontje, Tord
    Nest 2006 *199*
    Petit Jardin garden bench and armchair series 200
    Wednesday lamp 199
Botta, Mario: Quinta chair *182*
Bottoni, Pierre 44
Bouroullec, Ronan
    Combinatory vases 203
    Cuisine Desintegre 203
Bouroullec, Ronan and Erwan 198–9, 202–3, *202*
    A-POC boutique, Paris 204
    Brick storage system *198*, 199, 202, 203
    Facett sofa *198*, 199
    Floating House project 204, *204*
    Glide sofa 203
    Hole chair 203
    Joyn office system 199, 204
    La Valise 204
    Late sofa *204*
    Lit Clos sleeping cabin 202, 203, *203*
    Self shelf 202, *203*, 204
    Slow chair 204
    Spring chair 202, 204
    Spring Clouds shelving system 202, 204
Brandt, Marianne 26, 29
    WA24 (MT8) table lamp 29
Braque, Georges 20
Braun 107, 144
Brazier-Jones, Mark 150, 153, 163
    Atlantis chair 154, *154*
    Pegasus chair *154*
    Whaletail 154
Breuer, Marcel 26, *26*, 29, *30*, 31, 42, *44*, 50, 54, 80, 92, 169,
    169, 211
    B33 chair 26
    B64 chair 26, 31
    Cesca chair (Model No. B32) 26, 31, *45*
    Lattenstuhl (Slat chair) 31
    Long chair 31
    Model No. 301 dining chair 31
    Model No. 313 chaise longue 31
    UNESCO headquarters, Paris 31
    Wassily chair (Model No. B3) *27*, 29, *30*, 31, 53, 141
    Whitney Museum of Modern Art, New York 31
Brionvega 144
Britain Can Make It exhibition (Victoria and Albert Museum,
    London, 1946) 98
British Council of Design 60
Buckminster Fuller, Richard 174
'Butterfly House' (Villa Planchart), Caracas 105
buying and collecting 210–213

Café Costes, Paris 159, 160, *161*
Calder, Alexander 95
Calka, Maurice and Leleu-Deshays, Jean: Boomerang desk
    and chair *127*
Campana, Fernando and Humberto 200, 201
    Banquette chair 201
    Corallo chair 201
    Favela chair 201, *201*, *208*
    Jenette chair *200*
Canvey Island beach-side café 42
Cappellini 141, 143, *146*, *151*, 154, 164, 167, 168, 170, 173,
    175, 181, *182*, *183*, 189, 193, 197, 199, 200, *202*, 203, 204

Cappellini, Giulio 203
care and repair 213
Carwardine, George 206
Case Study Houses project 89
Cassina 20–21, 37, 103, 105, *105*, 173, 212
Castelli, Giulio 118
Castiglioni, Achille and Pier Giacomo
    Arco floor lamp 144
    Sella 108, *108*
    Taraxacum pendant lampshade 144, 178
Castiglioni, Livio and Frattini, Gianfranco, Boalum lamp 144
Castiglioni family 173
Chadwick, Don *see* Stumpf
Chandigarh government buildings, India 38
Chareau, Pierre 35
Chatou island, Paris 204
Chipperfield, David, Model No. hm991 173, *173*
Christie, Agatha 42
Cibic, Aldo 141
Cité Internationale Universitaire, La, Antony, near Paris 102
Citterio, Antonio
    Charles bed *172*
    Charles large sofa *172*, 173
Citterio, Antonio and Low, Glen Oliver: Mobil cabinets 181, *181*
Claesson Koivisto Rune (Mårten Claesson, Eero Koivisto and Ola Rune)
    Beckham 207, *207*
    Cornflake chair 206, *208*
    Mood 207
CNC (computer numerically controlled cutting) mill 190–91
Coast restaurant, London 175
Coates, Wells *see* Pritchard, Jack
Cologne Furniture Fair 118, 128
    Visiona II exhibition 131
Colombo, Joe 120–21, *120*, *121*
    Acrilica 281 desk lamp 144
    Additional Living System 117, 121
    Boby trolley 121
    Elda armchair 117, *120*
    LEM (Lunar Excursion Module) 120
    Living Centre units *121*
    Minikitchen 120, 143–4
    Model No. 4801 120, *121*
    Multi chair 121
    Optic alarm clock 121
    Storage Unit Trolley *147*
    Tube System *116*, 117
    Universale chair (Model No. 4860) 118, 121
Comacina *44*
Comfort 120
Committee 193
Congrès Internationaux d'Architecture Moderne (CIAM) 39
Constructivism 20
Coray, Hans: Landi chair *28*, 170
Craven-Walker, Edward: Lava lamp 144
Creative Salvage 153–4
Cubism 20, 21, 22, 37

Dalén, Gustaf: Aga cooker 73
Dalí, Salvador: Mae West sofa *134*, 135
Dansk Design Centre 50
Daversin, Denis 204, *204*
David Design 207
Day, Lucienne 159
    Calyx fabric pattern 99, 101
    Perpetua 101
    Spectators 101
Day, Lucienne (née Conradi) 7, 100, *100*, 101
Day, Robin 99, 100–101, *100*, 159
    Club Sofa *111*
    Forum sofa *101*
    Hillestak chair 99
    Polo 124
    Poly armchair 124
    Polyprop chair *100*, 101, 124, *124*

Q Stak chair 101
de Graauw, Judith 191
De Lucchi, Michele 141
    First Chairs *141*
    Tolomeo table, floor and desk lamp *178*, 181
De Pas, Gionatan, D'Urbino, Donato and Lomazzi, Paolo
    Blow chair *118*, 119
    Joe sofa 135, *135*
De Stijl magazine 21, 22
De Stijl (The Style) 20, *20*, 21, 22, 31, *44*
Demakersvan ('the makers of') 191
Denver Art Museum 105
DePree, Dirk Jan 92
Design Forum Finland 50
Design in Scandinavia touring exhibition (1954–7) 60
Desta *45*
Deutscher Werkbund (German Work Federation) 13, *24*, 49
Dior, Christian 189
Ditzel, Jorge 138
Ditzel, Nanna *138*
    Bench for Two *138*, *139*, 170
    Butterfly chair 139, 170
    Concert hall chair 139
    Highchair 139
    Toadstool *138*, 139
    Trinidad chair 139, 170, *170*
Ditzel, Nanna and Jørgen
    chair and stool *114*
    Hanging chair 138, *139*
    Ring chair 139
Dixon, Tom 150, 153, 163, 173
    Extendable Screen *189*
    Fresh Fat series 189
    Jacklight 177
    S chair *151*, 154
Dolphin-Wilding, Julienne: Gulliver's chair 163
Domus magazine 104
Dreyfuss, Henry 81
Driade 160, 192
Droog Design 177, 178, 196
du Pasquier, Nathalie 141
Dubreuil, André 154
    Paris chair 154
    Spine chair 154, *155*
Dunand, Jean 35
DuPont 207
    Tea and Coffee Towers 207
Dupont Corian 175
Duravit 207
D'Urbino, Donato *see* De Pas
Dux 58
Dylan, Bob: *Memphis Blues* 143

Eames, Catherine (née Woermann) 86, 89
Eames, Charles 81, 86, 89, 95
Eames, Charles and Ray 7, 8, 65, 69, *78*, 81, *81*, 86, *86*, 89, 92, *95*, 96, 100, 101, 159, 200, 211
    Aluminium Group 92
    Aluminium series of chairs 89
    Case Study Houses project 89
    DAR armchair *88*
    DCW (Dining Chair Wood) 85
    DKR wire chair *89*
    ESU 400 storage unit *83*
    Hang-It-All 107, *107*
    La Chaise *87*, *114*
    LCM (Lounge Chair Metal) 85
    LCW (Lounge Chair Wood) *81*
    Model No. 670 lounge chair *83*
    Moulded Plastic group 92
    Moulded Plywood series 92
    PAC-1 chairs *78*
    Plywood Group 85, 90
    Sofa Compact *85*
    Soft Pad lounge chair *84*
    Time-Life Stool *110*, 122, 124

Eames, Charles and Saarinen, Eero 81-2
    Conversation chair 81, *90*
    Lounging chair 81
    Relaxation chair 81
Eames, Lucia 86
Eames, Ray (Bernice Alexandra Eames; née Kaiser) 81, 82, *84*, 86, 89, *110*, 124, 192
Early Modernism
    brave new world 13
    British Modernism 42–3, *42*, *43*
    fear and loathing 13
    Gerrit Rietveld 22, *23*
    the International Style 40–41, *40*, *41*
    key icons 44–5
    Le Corbusier 38–9, *39*
    Marcel Breuer 30, 31
    the Mavericks *16*, 17, *17*, *18*
    outside influences 20
    putting on a show 32–7
    the shape of things to come 20–21, *20*, *21*
    the start of the dream 12–13, *12*, *13*, *15*
    to Germany and the Bauhaus 25–9
eBay 8, 212
Edra 163, 193, 201, *208*
Eiffel Tower, Paris 20, *88*
Elle Decoration 150
Ellington, Duke *162*, 165
Elysée Palace, Paris 160
Embru-Werke, Switzerland 31
Enterprise Scotland show (1947) 98
Ergonomi 133
ergonomics 12, 58, 132, *132*, 181
Eriksson, Thomas 170, 173
    PS clock (Klocka) 170
    Television table 170
Eskolin-Nurmesniemi, Vuokko 73
Esprit Nouveau, L' magazine 38
Essen Opera House, Germany 57
Established & Sons 194
Établissements Ruhlmann et Laurent 35
Eurostar lounge, Waterloo Station, London 160
Evans Production Company 85
Evans Products Co. 89
Exposition Internationale des Arts Décoratifs et Industriels Modernes (International Exposition of Modern Industrial and Decorative Arts) (Paris, 1925) 32, 35, 37, 39, 68, 104
Exposition Universelle (World Fair) (Paris, 1900) 32
Expressionism 20

Farnsworth House, Plano, Illinois *12*, 80
Fasem *183*
Ferrari-Hardoy, Jorge, Kurchan, Juan and Bonet, Antonio: Butterfly chair (BFK) *30*, *78*
Ferrieri, Anna Castelli: Round Up (Componibili) 143, *143*
Festival of Britain (1951): Homes and Gardens pavilion 99, 101
Finlandia Hall, Helsinki 54, 57
Finot, Jean-Marie 204, *204*
Firma Karl Mathsson 58
Flexform 117
Floating House 204, *204*
Flos 144, *161*, 175, 178
Ford 175
Ford, Henry 12
Fornasetti, Piero 103, 105
    Corinthian Capitello *103*
    see also Ponti, Gio
Fortnum and Mason store, London: Aalto retrospective 53
Foster, Norman 136
    Gherkin, London 186
    Nomos table 181, *183*
Franck, Josef 73
Franck, Kaj 144
    Kilta tableware 73
Frattini, Gianfranco *see* Castiglioni
Fredericia 139, 170
Functionalism 58

G-Star 175
Garouste, Elisabeth and Bonetti, Mattia: Prince Imperial 163
Gatti, Piero, Paolini, Cesare and Teodoro, Franco: Sacco 119, 119
Gaudí, Antoni 200
Gehry, Frank 135, 167
    Beaver chair and footstool 136
    Cross Check chair 167
    Easy Edges rocking chair 135, 137
    Easy Edges series 137
    Experimental Edges series 136
    Guggenheim Museum, Bilbao 186
    Hat Trick chairs 150
    Vitra Design Museum, Germany 167
    Wiggle side chair 135, 137
Gerotto, Eliana see Urquiola
Gherkin, London 186
Giovannoni, Stefano 181
    Bombo stool 80
    Il Bagno 207
Girard, Alexander see Saarinen
Glasgow style 17
GM Renaissance Center, Detroit 155
Good Furnishing Group 43
Grand Hotel Parco dei Principi, Rome 105
Grange, Kenneth: Type 3 desk lamp 206
Graves, Michael 141, 181
    Plaza dressing table 143
Gray, Eileen 35, 192
    E-1027 side table 32
    Roquebrune Cap Martin (E-1027) 32
    Transat chair 32
Grcic, Konstantin 189–90
    Chair One 189–90, 190
    Miura Stool 208
Great Exhibition (Crystal Palace, London, 1851) 32, 98
Gropius, Walter 22, 24, 25, 26, 31, 42, 50, 68, 80, 92, 96
    Bauhaus building, Dessau 29
    Lehmann department store, Cologne 24
Gruppo Strum 117, 135
Gufram 135
Guggenheim Museum, Bilbao 186
Gullichsen, Harry 57
Gullichsen, Maire 57

Haberli, Alfredo 181
Habitat 101, 101, 192, 196, 199, 204
Hadid, Zaha 194, 210
    Aqua table 194, 194
    Glacier sofa 194
    Ice Storm 194
    Moraine sofa 194
    Phaeno Science Centre 186, 194
    Stalactite table 194
    Stalagmite table 194
    Vortex chandeliers 207
    Z.island 207
    Z.scape 194
Hahl, Nils-Gustav 57
Haimi 147
Halling-Koch, Percy von 128
Hans, Ineke 196–7, 196, 212
    Black Beauties range 197
    Black Gold porcelain series 197
    Black Magic chair 192, 192
    Elephant chaise longue 197, 197
    Fracture range 193, 197
    Laser chairs 197
    Ordinary Furniture 192–3, 196, 197, 209
Hansen, Carl 63
Hansen, Fritz 59, 65, 66, 69, 75, 128
Hansen, Johannes 62, 74
Hansen, Søren: DAN chair 59
Hansen Sørensen 60
Heal's department store, London 43, 60, 101
Heide, Kurt 139

Hein, Piet 58
    see also Mathsson, Bruno
Henningsen, Poul
    PH Artichoke 73
    PH5 170
Herbst, Rene: Sandows chair 29
Herman Miller furniture company (now Herman Miller Inc)
    78, 85, 89, 90, 92, 95, 110, 111, 118, 132, 132, 146, 169
Heywood-Wakefield, H & L 35
Highpoint apartments, Highgate, London 42
Hill House, Helensburgh 16, 17
Hille International 101, 124, 132
Hillestak 101
Hilton, Matthew
    Auberon dining table 168
    Balzac armchair 168–9, 168
    Thin Table 209
Himmelblau, Coop 167
Hitch Mylius 173, 173
Hitchcock, Henry-Russell 41
Hoffmann, Josef, Sitzmaschine 15
Holon design museum, Israel 157
Humphreys, Barry 65
Hutten, Richard: S(h)it on It bench 177

Ideal Standard 105, 175, 207
Idée 175
Iittala 73, 144
Ikea: PS limited-editions range 170
Impressionists 20
Industrial Revolution 8, 12
Ineke Hans/Arnhem 196
Institute of Design, Chicago 80
Interiors magazine 63
International Exhibition (Barcelona, 1929) 12
    German Pavilion 40, 41
International Style 65, 114
International Style exhibition (Museum of Modern Art, New
    York, 1932) 31, 41
Internet auctions 212
Interspace 139
Isokon Furniture Company 31, 42
Isokon Plus 169, 169, 181, 182
Isola, Maija 73

Jacob & Josef Kohn 15
Jacobsen, Arne 7, 50, 65–6, 68–70, 211
    3300 sofa 69
    Aarhus Town Hall 62, 62
    AJ floor and desk lamps 73
    AJ Pendant 73
    AJ stainless-steel cutlery 70, 73
    Ant (Myren) chair 65, 69, 69, 75, 128
    Bellavista apartment building, Klampenborg 65
    Bellevue theatre and restaurant complex, Klampenborg
        65, 69, 70
    Cylinda-Line tableware 70
    Drop chair 69
    Egg chair (Model No. 3316) 64, 66, 69, 70, 70, 192, 192,
        209
    National Bank, Copenhagen 68, 68
    Oxford series 70
    St Catherine's College, Oxford 68, 70
    SAS Royal Hotel, Copenhagen 66, 67, 68, 69, 70, 75
    Series 7 chair (Model No. 3107) 65, 69–70, 75
    Swan chair 65, 68, 69, 70, 75, 192, 192
    Vola series 70
    Vola taps (faucets) 207
Jacobsen, Jacob: Luxo-L1 desk lamp 73
Jalk, Grete
    Lounge chair 59, 124
    Watch and Listen living-room unit 124
Jeanneret, Pierre 39, 90
    see also under Le Corbusier
Jensen, Georg 70, 139
Jensen-Klint, Peder Vilhelm 73

John Lewis Partnership 101
Johnson, Herbert 18
Johnson, Philip 31, 41
Johnson's Wax Headquarters, Racine, Wisconsin 17
Jones, Nick 153
Jongerious, Hella 177
Jouin, Patrick, Solid chair 190, 191
Juhl, Finn 6, 48, 49, 59
    Chieftain chair 59–60, 59
    NV44 chair 59
    Pelican chair 60

Kagan, Vladimir
    Moon sofa 110
    Omnibus modular unit 110
    Serpentine sofa 110
    Sloane sofa 110
Kagan-Dreyfuss 110
Kandinsky, Wassily 26, 27, 29, 31
Kartell 118, 121, 121, 152, 157, 159, 161, 173, 177, 181, 181
Keeler, Christine 65, 75
Keen 194
Kennedy, Jackie 73
Kennedy, John F 73
Key, Ellen 50
    Skonhet for Alla (Beauty for Everyone) 50
Kinsman, Rodney: Omkstak stacking chair 136
Kjærholm, Poul
    Model No. PK22 66, 66
    PK22 chair 75
    PK25 chair 66
    PKO chair 66
Klareboderne, Copenhagen 114
Klee, Paul 26
Klint, Esben 73
Klint, Kaare 69
Knoll 41, 45, 78, 80, 80, 90, 91, 92, 95, 96, 110, 150, 212
Knoll Associates 92
Knoll, Florence (née Schust) 90, 90, 91, 92, 95, 96, 192
    Credenza Cabinet 110
Knoll, Hans G 80, 90, 92, 96
Knoll, Hans G and Florence: Rockefeller family offices,
    Rockefeller Plaza, New York 92
Koivisto, Eero see Claesson Koivisto Rune
Kolds Savvaerk 139
Komed restaurant, Cologne 175
Komigen restaurant, Fünen, Denmark 128
Kubrick, Stanley 70, 73, 126
Kukkapuro, Yrjo: Karuselli chair 135, 147
Kuramata, Shiro 143, 167
    Acrylic Stool with Feathers 164
    Coup de Foudre 165
    Furniture in Irregular Forms 143, 144, 164
    Glass chair 164
    How High the Moon 162, 163, 164, 165
    Irregular Forms Cabinet 146
    Kyoto table 164–5, 164
    Miss Blanche 163, 164, 165
    Pyramid 164
    Revolving Cabinet 164
    Sally table 164
    Side 1 164
Kurchan, Juan see Ferrari-Hardoy
Kurosaki, Teruo 175
Kvadrat 139

La Pavoni 104, 105
Lachaise, Gaston: Floating Figure 87
Lalique, René 35
Landels, Willie: Throw-Away armchair 122
Landesausstellung exhibition (Zurich, 1939) 28
Lane, Danny 150, 163
    Angaraib chaise 155
    Borealis 155
    Etruscan chair 155, 155
    Stacking chair 155

Lapalma 194
Larkin Company Administration Building, Buffalo, New York 17, *18*
Larsson, Carl 50, *50*
    Ett hem (A Home) 50
Larsson, Karin 50, *50*
Late Modernism
    design with attitude 150–55
    get the look 178–81
    key icons *182–3*
    Marc Newson 174–5, *174, 175*
    Modern Renaissance *166*, 167–73
    new Romantics *162*, 163, *163*
    Nineties nonconformists 176, 177, *177*
    Philippe Starck 180–81, *180, 181*
    Ron Arad 156–7, *156*
    Shiro Kuramata 164–5, *164, 165*
    a star is born *158*, 159–61
Latimer, Clive 99, 101
Laurent, Pierre 35
Lawn Road apartments, north London 42
Le Bon, Simon 175
Le Corbusier 13, 38–9, 42, 50, 57, 65, 68, 86, 140, 150, 211
    Chandigarh government buildings, India 38
    Maison Domino 38
    Model No. LC6 dining table 39
    Model No. LC7 side chair 39
    Notre Dame du Haut chapel, Ronchamp, France 39
    Pavilion de L'Esprit Nouveau (Pavilion of the New Spirit) 37, 39, 68–9
    Unite d'Habitation tower block, Marseille 38, 39
    United Nations headquarters, New York 39
    Villa Savoye, Poissy 38
Le Corbusier, Charlotte Perriand and Pierre Jeanneret 37
    Basculant chair (Model No. LC1) 37, 39
    chair 224
    Grand Confort armchair (LC2) 37, 39, *39*, 45
    Grand Confort sofa (LC2) *36*, 39
    Model No. B302 dining chair 37
    Model No. B306 chaise longue 37, *37*, 39
Le Klint 73, 144
Lehmann department store, Cologne *24*
Leigh, Vivien 165
Leleu-Deshays *127*
Leleu-Deshays, Jean *see* Calka
Lenti, Paola 192
Leonardi, Cesare *see* Stagi
Lever House Restaurant, Lever House Building, New York 175
Light and Colour retrospective (Panton) (1998) 131
Ligne Roset 199
Lissoni, Piero
    Aprile chair 170
    Case system 206
    LT system 206
    Met modular sofa 173
Lloyd, Marshall Boyd *44*
Loewy, Raymond 81
Loft 124
Lomazzi, Paolo *see* De Pas
Lovegrove, Ross 173
    Magic chair *183*
Low, Glen Oliver *see* Citterio
Lusty, William, Lloyd Loom Chair *44*

Mackintosh, Charles Rennie *16*, 17, *17*
McLaren, Denham 43
Made of Waste 193
Madonna: 'Rain' video 175
Magis 175, 204
Magis headquarters, Treviso, Italy 157
Maison Domino 38
Makers of Simple Furniture 42, 43
Mäkiniemi, Elissa 57
Maples, London 43
Marcel Breuer Associates 31
Mari, Enzo 181

Marigold, Peter: Make/Shift 207, *207*
Marimekko 73
Mash & Air restaurant, Manchester 175
Massachusetts Institute of Technology 57
Materialize 190
Mathsson, Bruno 58, 80
    Eva chair 58, *58*
    Grasshopper chair 58
    Pernilla chaise longue 58
    Pernilla liunge chair 58
Mathsson, Bruno and Hein, Piet: Superellipse table *58*
Matta, Roberto Sebastian: Malitte 118
Maufe, Edward 35
Maurer, Ingo 178
    Lucellino lamp 178, *178*
Memphis group 141, *141*, 143, *143, 147*, 150, 153, 164, *164, 174, 181*
    Casablanca sideboard 143
Mendini, Alessandro 141, 167, 173, 181
    Proust armchair *140*, 141
Meyer, Adolf *24*
Microsoft 161
Mid-Century Modernism
    Charles and Ray Eames 86, *86, 87, 88*, 89, *89*
    on the Continent *102, 103, 103*
    Festival of Britain (1951) 98–9, *98, 99*
    Gio Ponti 104–5, *104, 105*
    Harry Bertoia 96, *96*
    home-grown American talent 81–2, *81, 83, 84*
    key cions *110–111*
    mid-century mature 95, *95*
    Modernist family tree 80
    more than just chairs 107, *107*
    Robin and Lucienne Day 100–101, *100, 101*
    Scandinavians at large 80, *80*
    sculpture for suburbia 85
    the shape of things to come 108, *108*
    the wartime legacy 90, *90*
Mies van der Rohe, Ludwig 7, *12*, 26, 29, 44, 68, 80, 86, 150
    Barcelona chair (Model No. MR90) 40–41, *40, 45*, 66
    Barcelona sofa 41
    Barcelona stool 41
    Farnsworth House, Plano, Illinois *12*, 80
    German Pavilion, International Exhibition, Barcelona 40
    Model No. MR10 chair 29
    Model No. MR20 chair 29
    Model No. MR70 chair *12*
    MR Armchair *41*
    Seagram Building, New York 80
Milan Furniture Fair 167
Milan Triennale exhibitions *8*, 60, 101, 103, 104, 120
Miller Zenith 89
minimalism 173
Mitterrand, François 169
Miyake, Issey 163, 164, 165, 204
Modernism *see* Early Modernism; Late Modernism; Mid-Century Modernism; Post-Modernism
Mogensen, Børge 67
    Spokeback Sofa *74*
Moholy-Nagy, László 26, 29, 42, 80
Møller, Erik 62, *62*
Mollino, Carlo 103, 210
    Arabesco Coffee Table 103, *111*
Mondrian, Piet 20, 22
Monkey Boys *see* Pot, Bertjan and White, Daniel
Montecatini headquarters, Milan 104
Moooi 190, 200, 206, 207
Morley, Lewis 65
Moroso 157, 175, 192, *209*
Morris, William 13, 50
Morrison, Jasper 167, 168, 169, 173, 211
    Air chair 168
    Glo-Ball 178, *179*
    High-Pad chair 168
    Lo-Pad chair 168, *182*
    Orly seating system 173

Plan system *166*, 181
Pots and Pans 207
    Some New Items for the Home, Part 1 167
    Some New Items for the Home, Part 2 167
    Tate chair 168
    Thinking Man's chair *167*
    Three Sofa *166, 183*
    Universale storage system 181
    Vitra sofa 173
Mourgue, Olivier 126, 177
    Djinn series of seating 126, *126, 147*
Movimento Nucleare (Nuclear Painting Movement) 120
Movisi 207
Muji 194
Munch-Petersen, Ursula 181
Murano glassware company 105, 144, 181
Murdoch, Peter: Spotty chair 124, *125*
Museum of Modern Art, New York 63
    Low-Cost Furniture Design competition (1950) *88*, 89, 99, 101
    The New Domestic Landscape 135
    New Furniture Designed by Charles Eames 85, 89
    Organic Design in Home Furnishings competition 81, 89, 90
Muuratsalo, Finland 57

National Bank, Copenhagen 68, *68*
Nelson, George 78, 92
    Atomic (Ball) clock 7, 107, *107*
    Coconut chair *93*
    Kangaroo chair 107
    Marshmallow sofa 92, *92*
    Platform Bench 92, *111*
    Pretzel chair 90
    Thin Edge bed 92
New Bauhaus 80
New Millennium
    fast-forward into the future 186–91
    Ineke Hans 196–7, *196, 197*
    into the New Age 198–201
    key icons *208–9*
    New Millennium, new collectables 206–7, *206, 207*
    Ronan and Erwan Bouroullec 202–4, *202, 203, 204*
    women are doing it 192–5
Newson, Marc 7, 173, 174–5, *174, 175*
    021C concept car 175
    Black Hole table 175
    Bucky chair *174*
    Coast restaurant, London 175
    Embryo chair 174
    Falcon 900b private jet 175
    Felt chair 174, 175, 177, *182*
    Gluon chair 174
    Helice lamps 175
    Komed restaurant, Cologne 175
    Lever House Restaurant, Lever House Building, New York 175
    Lockheed lounge 174, 175, *177*, 210
    Mash & Air restaurant, Manchester 175
    MN01 bicycle 175
    Newson Suite 175, 207
    Orgone chair 175, *175*
    Orgone lounge 174, 177
    Orgone series 174
    Orgone table 177
    Progetto Oggetto 181
    Seaslug watch 175
    Skybed 175
    Syn recording studio, Tokyo 175
    Wicker chair 177
Nike 175
Nixon, Richard 73
Noguchi, Isamu 92, 107, 144
    Cyclone Table *111*
    Noguchi table *94*, 95, *95*
Nordiska Kompaniet exhibition (1959) *67*

Norguet, Patrick: Rainbow chair *188*, 189
Norsk Form 50
Notre Dame du Haut chapel, Ronchamp, France 39
Novo 69
Nuutajarvi 144
Nyman, Gunnel 73

Olbrich, Joseph Maria: Summer Residence of an Art Lover 32
One Foot Taller: Canyon chair 177
One Off studio/gallery, Covent Garden, London 153, 157
Op Art 131
Opsvik, Peter
    Balans chair 133, *133*
    Balans Variable 133
    MiniMax adjustable desk 133
    Tripp Trapp child's chair 133
Oregon, USA: college and library (Aalto) 57
Orrefors 144
Osgerby, Jay *see* Barber
Osozaki, Arata 143
Oxo International 181
    Good Grips 181

Page, Clare 193
Page, Clare and Richardson, Harry
    Flytip 193
    Kebab standard lamps 193
Paimio Sanatorium 50, 53, *53*, 54, 212
Palmqvist, Sven 73
Palterer, David 181
Panton, Verner *117*, 128
    Astoria Hotel, Trondheim 131
    Bachelor chair 128
    Cone series 128, *128*, *131*
    Flying chair 128
    Heart chair *128*
    Panthella *144*
    Panthella floor and table lamp 131, 144
    Panton chair 8, *114*, *116*, 118, 128
    Panton Junior *116*
    Pantonova Wire chair *117*
    Pantower 131, *131*
    Peacock lounge chair 128, *131*
    Phantasy Landscape installation 131
    S chair 128, 131
    Spiegel Publishing, Hamburg 131
    Spiral chandelier *128*, 131
    Stackable *146*
    System 1-2-3 *117*
    Tivoli chair 128
Paolini, Cesare *see* Gatti
Paramount hotel, New York 160–61, 175
Paris International Exposition (1937): Finnish Pavilion 57
Paulin, Pierre 8, *126*, 177
    Ribbon chair *125*, 126, *146*
    Tongue chair 126
Pavilion de L'Esprit Nouveau, Paris Expo (1925) 13
Paxton, Joseph 32
PayPal electronic payment system 212
PEL 43
Perret, Auguste 38
Perriand, Charlotte 39, 108, 192
    see also under Le Corbusier
Pesce, Gaetano: Up series 119, *119*
Phaeno Science Centre 186, 194
Piano, Renzo *see* Rogers
Picasso, Pablo 20
Pirelli 8, *102*, 103
Pirelli Tower, Milan 105
Plank *208*
Platner, Warren: Platner Collection *212*
Plus-Linje 128
Pod 175
Pointillisme 141
Pollock, Jackson 95
Polythema *128*

Pompidou Centre, Paris 136
Ponti, Gio 104–5, *104*
    'Butterfly House' (Villa Planchart), Caracas 105
    Denver Art Museum 105
    Grand Hotel Parco dei Principi, Rome 105
    Montecatini headquarters, Milan 104
    Pirelli Tower, Milan 105
    Rome University mathematics department 104
    Series P sanitaryware 105
    Super Leggera (Super Light) 103, 104, 105, *105*
    Taranto Cathedral, Apulia, Italy 105
Ponti, Gio and Fornasetti, Piero
    Architettura Trumeaux bureau-bookcase 105
    Casino, San Remo 105
Pop & Post-Modernism
    beyond Modernism 140–41, *140*, *141*, 143, *143*
    Italy in the 1960s spotlight 117–19
    Joe Colombo 120–21, *120*, *121*
    key icons *146–7*
    and more besides 135–6, *135*, *136*, *137*
    Nanna Ditzel 138–9, *138*, *139*
    Pop and Post-Modern accessories 143–4, *143*, *144*
    Primitivism, plastic, paper and plywood 122–6, *127*
    user-friendly design 132–3, *132*, *133*
    Verner Panton 128–31
Pop Art 7, 8
Post-Modernism *see* Pop & Post-Modernism
Pot, Bertjan: Carbon chair 190
Pot, Bertjan and Daniel White (Monkey Boys): Random Light 206, *206*
Poulsen, Louis 73, 131, 144, *170*
PP Møbler 62
Printz, Eugène 35
Pritchard, Jack 31, 42
Pritchard, Jack and Coates, Wells, Lawn Road apartments, north London 42
Profumo, John 65, *75*
Prouvé, Jean 103, 153
    Antony chair *102*
Provista *189*
Purkersdorf Sanatorium, Vienna *15*
Pye 101

Qantas 175

Race, Ernest
    Antelope chair 99, *99*
    BA3 chair and table *98*
Race Furniture 99
Radical design movement (Italy) 117
Rams, Dieter: 606 Universal shelving system 107, *107*
Rapsel 165
Rasch 101
Rashid, Karim
    Kloud sofa and chair *187*
    Orgy sofa and stool *187*
    Semiramis Hotel, Athens *186*
    Wavelength sofas *186*
Reagan, Robert 140
Reich, Wilhelm 175
Remy, Tejo: Milk Bottle lamp 178
Richard-Ginori 104
Richardson, Harry *see* Page
Rietveld, Gerrit 22, *23*, 31, 200, 212
    lamp design 22
    Red/Blue chair 20, *20*, *21*, 22, *44*
    Schröder House, Utrecht *20*, 22
    Schröder table 21, 22
    Utrecht armchair and sofa 21
    Van Gogh Museum, Amsterdam 22
    Zig-Zag chair 21, 22, *23*
Rihitie, Helsinki *48*
Riley, Bridget 143
Risom, Jens 90
    Side chair 80, *80*
Riss, Egon: Penguin Donkey 42, *42*, 169

Rockefeller family offices, Rockefeller Plaza, New York 92
Rogers, Richard 136
Rogers, Richard and Piano, Renzo: Pompidou Centre, Paris 136
Roquebrune Cap Martin, South of France (E-1027) *32*
Rosenthal 101
Rowenta 207
Royal Copenhagen 181
Royal Festival Hall, London 99, 101
Royal Hotel, Copenhagen *64*
Royal Institute of British Architects 57
Royal VKB 197
Royalton hotel, New York 160–61
Rudolph, Paul 31
Ruhlmann, Émile-Jacques 34, 35, *35*
Rune, Ola *see* Claesson Koivisto Rune
Ruskin, John 13
Russell, Gordon 43

Saarinen, Eero 7–8, 81, 90, 96, *108*
    Tulip chair 7, 108, *108*, *122*
    Tulip chair and table 108
    Womb chair 90, *90*, *108*
    see also Eames, Charles and Saarinen, Eero
Saarinen, Eero and Girard, Alexander 84
Saarinen, Eliel 96
St Catherine's College, Oxford 68, 70
St Martin's Lane Hotel, London *158*
Salon d'Automne (Paris) 45
Sambonet 107
Sambonet, Roberto 107
Sandell, Thomas 170
Sapper, Richard 144
    Tizio desk lamp 144
    see also Zanuso
Sarpaneva, Timo 144
SAS Royal Hotel, Copenhagen 65, 66, 68, 69, 70, *75*
Savoy restaurant, Helsinki 57
Sawaya & Moroni 194
Scandinavia at Table (British Council of Design), 1951) 60
Scandinavian Design for Living exhibition (Heal's department store, London, 1951) 60
Scandinavians
    Arne Jacobsen 68–70, *68*, *69*, *70*
    building the new Utopia 49–50
    the complete home 73, *73*
    Danish Modernism 59–60, *59*
    early Scandinavian icons 50, *50*, 52, 53, *53*
    the fabulous fifties *64*, 65–6, *66*, *67*
    Hans Wegner 62–3, *62*, *63*
    key icons *74–5*
    national craft societies 13
    Northern Modernism 50
    a period of change 49
    the Scandinavian phenomenon 60, *60*, *61*
    sculptural and beautifully crafted wooden designs 7
    Swedish Modernism 58, *58*
Schräder-Schröder family 20, 22
Schrager, Ian 160
Schröder House, Utrecht 20, 22
Scott, Fred: Supporto chair 132, *133*
SCP *168*, 169
Semiramis Hotel, Athens *186*
Sempe, Inga 193
    Brosse storage units 193
Silvestrin, Claudio: I Fiumi Po 207
Šipek, Borek 181
    Bambi chair *163*
Smart Design 181
Snedkergaarden 139
Sodeau, Michael
    Bolla lamp series 178, 181
    Wing unit 181
Søholm, north of Copenhagen 69
Sony Walkman 144
Sottsass, Ettore 117, 141, 164, 167, 173, 174, 200, 211

Carlton Cabinet *143*, *147*
Ultrafragola Mirror *140*
Valentine portable Olivetti typewriter *144*
Sowden, George *141*
Space 1999 (television series) *121*
Spiegel Publishing, Hamburg *131*
Spiral boutique, Axis shopping complex, Tokyo *164*
Stagi, Franca and Leonardi, Cesare: Ribbon chair *117*
Stam, Mart *26*
Model No. S33 *25*, *26*, *44*
Starck, Philippe *159–61*, *160*, *163*, *164*, *169*, *181*, *202*
Ara *161*
Café Costes chair *159*, *160*, *161*
Dick Deck *161*
Dr Glob *159*, *161*
Dr Kiss toothbrush *161*
Dr No *159*
Ed Archer chair *159*
Elysée Palace apartments *160*
Eurostar lounge, Waterloo Station *160*
J chair *161*
Juicy Salif *181*
La Marie *159*, *161*
Lazy Working sofa *173*
Lola Mundo *159*, *159*, *161*
Lord Yo *159*, *159*
Louis Ghost *161*
Miss Balu *181*
Miss Sissi *161*, *161*, *178*
Mr Blob *159*
Mrs Frick chair *161*
Oval bath *207*
Paramount hotel, New York *160–61*, *175*
Romantica *161*
Romeo Moon series *161*
Royalton hotel, New York *160–61*
St Martin's Lane Hotel, London *158*
stereo lithography *190*
Stile magazine *104*
Stockholm Exhibition of Art and Industry (1897) *50*
Stokke *133*
Studio, The magazine *50*
Studio 65
Capitello chair *135*
Marilyn sofa *134*, *135*
Studio Alchimia *140*, *141*
Stumpf, William: Ergon chair *132*, *132*
Stumpf, William and Chadwick, Don, Aeron chair *132*, *169*
Summers, Gerald *42*, *43*
Bent Plywood Chair *42*, *43*
Superstudio *117*
Svenskt Form *50*
Svenskt Tenn *73*
Sydney Opera House, Australia *60*
Symbolism *20*
Syn recording studio, Tokyo *175*

Taranto Cathedral, Apulia, Italy *105*
Tate Modern gallery, London *168*
Tecno *103*, *181*, *183*
Tecnolumen *29*
Tefal *175*
Tel Aviv Opera House *156*
Teodoro, Franco *see* Gatti
Thatcher, Margaret, Baroness *140*, *153*
Thonet *12*, *13*, *26*, *26*, *44*, *45*, *128*
Thonet, August *13*
Thonet, Michael
bentwood chairs *12*, *13*, *15*, *37*, *59*
Model No.14 café chair (now Model No. 214) *12–13*, *20*, *45*
Thun, Matteo *141*
Cassettiera *181*
Golden Settimanale *181*
Settimanale cupboard *181*
Tam Tam stool *181*

Thurman, Caroline *157*
Time magazine *60*
Time-Life Building, New York City *110*, *122*
TNA Design *194*
Toikka, Olva *144*
Tribune Tower, Chicago *81*
Tugendhat house, Brno, Czech Republic *12*
Tupper Corporation *90*
Tupperware *90*
Turku, Finland *53*

UFO *117*
Umeda, Masanori *163*
Getsuen chair *162*, *163*
Rose chair *163*, *163*
UNESCO headquarters, Paris *31*
Unite d'Habitation tower block, Marseille *38*, *39*
United Nations headquarters, New York *39*
Urquiola, Patricia *192*
Fjord chair *192*, *192*, *209*
Lazy collection *192*, *193*
Pavo *192*
Urquiola, Patricia and Gerotto, Eliana, Nido *192*
Utzon, Jørn *8*
Sydney Opera House *60*

Vack, Tom *157*
van de Groenekan, Gerard *212*
van Doesburg, Theo *21*, *22*
van Eijk, Niels: Cow chairs *177*
Van Gogh Museum, Amsterdam *22*
van Severen, Maarten *169*
LCP (Low Chair Plastic) *170*
Model No. 2 chair *169*
Venini *144*, *181*
Verhoeven, Jeroen
Cinderella table *191*
Industrialized Wood series *191*
Verhoeven, Joep *191*
Viipuri Library *52*, *54*
Villa Mairea, Noormarkku, Finland *50*, *57*
Villa Savoye, Poissy *38*
Vitra *85*, *89*, *92*, *118*, *128*, *135*, *157*, *163*, *165*, *167*, *173*, *177*, *199*, *204*
Vitra Design Museum, Germany *167*
Vitra Edison series *167*
Vitsœ *107*
Vodder, Niels *6*, *59*, *59*
Volther, Paul: Corona Chair (Model No. EJ 605) *115*
Vuitton, Louis *189*

Wagenfeld, Wilhelm *26*, *29*
Waitrose supermarkets *101*
Wanders, Marcel *173*, *190*, *211*
Bottoni sofa *201*
City System cabinets *207*
Crochet table *191*
Knotted chair *176*, *177*
New Antiques collection *200*, *209*
Wangen, Norbert: K2 *206*
Warhol, Andy *143*
Waring and Gillow, London *43*
Wegner Design Studio *73*
Wegner, Hans Jørgen *60*, *62–3*
Flag Halyard chair (Flaglinestolen) (Model No. PP225) *62*, *63*
Ox chair (Model No. EJ100 Pollestolen) *61*, *63*
Peacock armchair *60*, *62*, *74*
PP19 Teddy Bear chair *63*
PP112 chair *62*
PP120 footrest *63*
PP124 rocking chair *63*
Round chair (Model 503) *73*
Round chair (the Chair) (Model 501) *60*, *62–3*, *73*
Valet chair *63*
Wing chair (Model No. 445) *61*

Y-Stolen chair (Wishbone chair) (Model No. CH24) *60*, *60*, *62*, *63*
Wegner, Marianne *63*, *73*
Weimar Academy of Fine Arts *25*
Weimar School of Arts and Crafts *25*
Where There's Smoke exhibition (New York, 2004) *200*
White, Daniel *see* Pot
Whitefriars *144*
Whitney Museum of Modern Art, New York *31*
Wiener Werkstätte (Vienna Workshops) *13*, *49*
Williams, Tennessee: *A Streetcar Named Desire* *163*, *165*, *165*
Willow Tea Rooms, Glasgow *17*, *17*
Wilton *101*
Windsor chair, English *60*, *62*
Wingspread, Wind Point, Wisconsin *18*
Wirkkala, Tapio *73*, *73*, *144*
Woodgate, Terry: Sax chair and footstool *187*
World's Fair (New York, 1939), Finnish Pavilion *80*
World's Fair (St Louis, Missouri, 1904) *32*
Wright, Frank Lloyd *17*, *57*
Aurora desk *17*
Barrel chair *17*, *18*
Fallingwater house *57*
Husser table *17*
Johnson's Wax Headquarters, Racine, Wisconsin *17*
Larkin Company Administration Building, Buffalo, New York *17*, *18*
Robie chair and table *17*
Wingspread, Wind Point, Wisconsin *18*

Y Store, Tokyo *156*
Yamakawa Rattan industry *139*
Yamamoto, Yohji *156*
Yanagi, Sori: Butterfly Stool *108*, *110*

Zanini, Marco *141*
Zanotta *44*, *103*, *147*, *170*, *181*
Zanuso, Marco
Lady Armchair (with Pirelli) *8*, *102*, *103*, *110*
Lombrico sofa *8*
Zanuso, Marco and Sapper, Richard
Algol *144*
Doney 14 portable television *144*
Grillo folding telephone *144*
Model No. 4999/5 stacking chair *118*
TS 522 portable radio *144*
Zenith *89*
Zumtobel *207*

Author Acknowledgements

The author wishes to thank Lisa Dyer, Lara Maiklem, Lucy Coley and Jenny Lord for making this book possible.

Picture Credits

The publishers would like to thank the following sources for their kind permission to reproduce the pictures in this book.

Key: t=Top, b=Bottom, c=Centre, l=Left and r=Right

Front & Back Endpapers: Victoria & Albert Museum/V&A Images

AKG-Images: 12; /Erich Lessing: 44br
Ake E:Son Lindman: 49
Alamy Images: /©Arcaid: 32, 50, 84, 158, 166t; /©Arcaid/©DACS, London 2007: 23; /©Arcaid/©The Isamu Noguchi Foundation and Garden Museum/ARS, New York and DACS, London 2007: 94; /Boe Photography/© FLC/ADAGP, Paris and DACS, London 2007: 38-9; /©Elizabeth Whiting & Associates: 53, 152; /©David J. Green - studio: 44tr; /©Jack Hobhouse: 131; /©Michael Jenner: 157; /©Justin Leighton: 156tl; /©Lourens Smak: 116t
Alias SpA/www.aliasdesign.it: 182tr
Alvar Aalto Museum: /Maija Holma: 46-7, 51, 52t; /Martti Kapanen: 73; /Gustaf Welin 1935: 52b
Arcblue.com/©Jefferson Smith: 5, 134, 224
Artifort: 125b, 146bl
B&B Italia SpA: 4, 8, 172, 173t, 193t
BarberOsgerby: 168b; /©Lee Funnell: 169t&b, 182tl
©Bildarchiv Foto Marburg: / DACS, London 2007: 24
Ronan & Erwan Bouroullec: /©Cappellini: 202; /©Morgane Le Gall: 198, 202t, 203b, /©Paul Tahon: 199t, 203t, 205; /©Vitra: 204
The Bridgeman Art Library: /A DAR (Dining and Desk Chair), designed by Eames, Charles (1907-70) and Ray (1912-88), 1953 (moulded fibreglass and metal rod), Eames, Charles (1907-80) and Ray (1912-88)/Private Collection, Photo ©Bonhams, London: 88; /An Early Butterfly Stool, designed by Sori Yanagi, 1954 (plywood) Private Collection, Photo ©Bonhams, London, UK: 110br;/Antony Chair, designed by Jean Prouve (b.1901) manufactured by Les Ateliers Jean Prouve, Maxeville, Paris, 1950 (laminated birch and steel), Prouve, Jean (1901-84)/Private Collection, Photo © Bonhams, London UK/©ADAGP Paris and DACS, London 2007: 102t;/'Djinn' two-seater sofa, pair of easy chairs and stool, designed by Olivier Mourgue for Airbourne, 1965 (red stretch fabric over polyfoam upholstered metal frame, on metal rails), Mourgue, Olivier /Private Collection, Photo©Bonhams, London UK:126;/Foreground: An Early DKR-2 (Dining Height, K-Wire Shell, R-Wire Base/Rod Iron Base), 1951 (wire and cloth); Background: An Early DKR-1 (Dining Height, K-Wire Shell, R-Wire Base/Rod Iron Base), 1951 (wire & cloth), both designed by Eames (1907-80) and Ray (1912-88)/Private Collection, Photo ©Bonhams, London UK: 89; /Interior view of the Cafeteria, 1992-95 (photo), Gehry, Frank (b.1929)/Energie-Forum des EMR, Bady Oeynhausen, Germany, Wolfgang Neeb: 148-9;/Ladderback chairs, c.1903 (stained oak), Mackintosh, Charles Rennie (1868-1928)/Private Collection, ©The Fine Art Society, London, UK: 17;/Living Tower' seating sculpture designed for Fritz Hansen by Verner Panton, 1969 (textile),/Private Collection, Photo ©Bonhams, London, UK: 130; /Two chairs designed by Verner Panton: Pantonova Waiting Chair 1971 (left) and 1-2-3 system lounge armchair (right),/ Private Collection, Photo ©Bonhams, London, UK: 117
Cappellini: 182bl, 183
Carl Hansen & Søn A: 60, 61t
Centraal Museum Utrecht: /Jannes Linders/© DACS, London 2007: 20
Christie's Images Ltd: 3, 26, 41b, 55, 58t&b, 59t&b, 61b, 75tl&bl, 80, 82, 85, 91t, 98, 99, 103, 105, 107t, 110t, cl, cr,&bl, 111cl, 116b, 120tr, 121tr, 133t, 137, 141t, 141b, 142, 145, 146br, 147tl, bl&tr, 153, 154b, 155l&r, 164b, 181t; /©ADAGP, Paris and DACS, London 2007: 127t&b; /©DACS, London 2007: 2, 15, 40, 41t; /©FLC/ADAGP, Paris and DACS, London 2007: 37
Claesson Koivisto Rune: /©David Design: 207t
Corbis Images: /©Paul Almasy: 38; /©Annebicque Bernard/Corbis Sygma: 165; /©Michael Boys: 68b; /Condé Nast: 6, 7, 48, 78-9, 122b; /©Thomas A. Heinz/©ARS, NY and DACS, London 2007: 18-9; /©Robert Levin: 87; /©Araldo De Luca: 13; /©Francesco Venturi/©DACS, London 2007: 45bl
Danish Design Center: /Arne-Jacobsen: 65, 70, 71
Danish Museum of Art & Design: /©Nordiska Galleriet: 67
Dansk Mobel Kunst: 73b
Eero Aarnio/www.eero-aarnio.com: 146tr
Elizabeth Whiting & Associates/www.ewastock.com: /Mark Luscombe-Whyte: 64; /Ron: 156; /Tim Street-Porter: 9, 93b, 102b, 148; /Friedhelm Thomas/© FLC/ADAGP and DACS, London 2007: 36
Fasem International srl: 183c
Foundation Le Corbusier: /©FLC/DACS, 2007/©FLC/ADAGP, Paris and DACS, London 2007: 45tl
Foster and Partners: /Norman Foster/©Peter Strobel: 183t
Fredericia Furniture: 74t
Gaetano Pesce Studio: 119
Getty Images: /Hulton Archive: 68t; /Daniel Janin/AFP: 174t; /Arnold Newman: 86; /©Gerry Penny/AFP: 160; /Time & Life Pictures: 30, 31, 96b, 104, 108t
Herman Miller Archive: 76-7, 81, 92, 106, /©Dale Rooks: 91b, 93t; /Ezra Stoller/© The Isamu Noguchi Foundation and Garden Museum/ARS, New York and DACS, London 2007: 95; /©Earl Woods: 132
Hitch Mylius Ltd: 173b
Ineke Hans: 192tr, 196t&b, 197, 208b
Isokon Plus: 42
Karim Rashid: 187t&b; /©Jean François Jaussaud: 184-5
Knoll: 78, 90, 111cr, 167b, 213, /©ARS, NY and DACS, London 2007: 96tl, 111tl
Konstantin Grcic: 208tr
Kudos: /Brian Harrison: 33
Kuramata Design Office: 164t
Les Arts Décoratifs Musée des Arts décoratifs: /Paris Fond d'archives photographiques Editions Albert Lévy Conservé à la photothèque Tout droits réservés: 35t
Magis spa: 190
Marc Newson Ltd: /©Carin Katt: 177
Marcel Wanders Studio/www.marcelwanders.com: 209cr; / ©George Terberg: 201r, 206t
Mark Brazier-Jones Ltd: 154t
Michele De Lucchi: /©Miro Zagnoli: 178t
Moooi: /©Henk Jan Kamerbeek: 191l
Morozzi & Partners s.a.s: 192, 200, 201l, 208tl, 209cl; /Edra: 163t&b
Nanna Ditzel Design: 138t, 139t&b, 171; /Schnakenburg and Brahl: 138b
National Portrait Gallery: 100tl
National Trust for Scotland: 16
Offect: 206b, 208b
PP MØBLER: 62t; /Flag Halyard Chair produced by PP Møbler/Photo: ©Jens Mourits Sørensen: 62b; /Peacock Chair produced by PP Møbler 74bl; /Rocking Chair produced by PP Møbler/Photo: ©Jens Mourits Sørensen: 63b; /Teddy Bear Chair produced by PP Møbler /Photo: ©Jens Mourits Sørensen: 63b; /Tønder Watertower, Interior produced by PP Møbler: 72
Patrick Jouin: 191r
Pernille Klemp: 66
Peter Marigold: 207b
Peter Opsvik/www.opsvik.no: /Tollefsen: 133b
Poltronova s.r.l: 140t
RMN/©Photo CNAC/MNAM Dist. RMN: /©Jean-Claude Planchet: 74br, 143, 181b /© Prévost/© ARS, NY and DACS,

London 2007: 97
Redcover.com: /Graham Atkins-Hughes: 27, 83; / Nick Carter: 180; /Gugielmo Galvin: 28; /Gugielmo Galvin/©DACS, London 2007: 21; /Winfried Heinze: 115; / Ken (Architect: James Slade): 123; /James Mitchell: 109; Chris Tubb: 114; /Wayne Vincent: 135
Rex Features: /Lehtikuva Oy: 54
Robin Day: 100br, 101, 111b
Ronan & Erwan Bouroullec: /©Cappellini: 202; /©Morgane Le Gall: 198, 202t, 203b, /©Paul Tahon: 199t, 203t, 205; /©Vitra: 204
S+ARCKNetwork: 159b, 161t&b
SCP/www.scp.co.uk t. 020 7739 1869: 168t, 186, 209t; /©Cappellini: 166b, 167t, 182br, /©Flos: 179
Scala Archives: /Maurer, Ingo (b. 1932): "Lucellino" Wall Lamp, 1992 (manufactured by Ingo Maurer GmbH, Germany). Glass, brass, plastic, and goose feather wings, 10 x 8 x 4 1/4" (25.4 x 20.3 x 10.8 cm). Gift of the Designer. Acc. N. 300.1999. ©2007 Digital Image Museum of Modern Art/Scala, Florence: 178b; /René Herbst. (French, 1891-1982). Sandows Chair. 1928. Nickel-plated steel tube and elastic rubber cord, 26 x 17 x 19 1/2" (66 x 43.2 x 49.5 cm). Gift of Marshall S. Cogan in honor of Barbara Jakobson/ Digital Image, The Museum of Modern Art/Scala, Florence: 29t; /Piero Gatti. (Italian, born 1940), Cesare Paolini. (Italian, born 1937) and Franco Teodoro. (Italian, born 1939). Sacco Chair. 1968. Leather and polystyrene beads, h. 45" (114.3 cm), diam. 33" (83.8cm). Manufactured by Zanotta S.p.A, Italy. Gift of the Manufacturer Digital Image, The Museum of Modern Art/Scala, Florence: 118b; /Starck, Philippe (b. 1949): Lola Mundo Chair, 1988 Collection David Whitney ©2007. Digital image, The Museum of Modern Art, New York/Scala, Florence: 159t; /Thonet, Gebruder Side Chair, 1918. (Manufacturer: Gebruder Thonet, Wien, established 1853. Bentwood with stamped seat 35 3/4 x 16 3/4 x 17" (90.8 x 42.5 x 43.2 cm), seat h. 18 5/8" (47.3 cm). Given anonymously. Acc.n: SC66.1977/Digital Image©2007 The Museum of Modern Art/Scala, Florence: 14, 45; /Van Severen, Maaten (1956-2005): Low Chair, 1993. Aluminum, 24 3/4 x 19 3/4 x 36 1/4" (62.9 x 50.2 x 92.1) Gift of the manufacturer. Acc.n.: 1429.2001. ©2007. Digital image, The Museum of Modern Art/Scala, Florence: 198
Sotheby's Picture Library: 34, 35b, 43, 56, 57, 111tr, 121bl, 140b, 147cr, 162, 175, /Cooper-Hewitt, National Design Museum, Smithsonian Institution Museum purchase through gift of Esme Usdan and from: 29b
Studio Jurgen Bey: /Daria Scagliola & Stijn Brakee: 210-1
Studio Norguet: 188
Studio Tord Boontje: /Courtesy of Moroso: 199b
T.n.a Design studio: 193b
Tecta/www.tecta.de: /©DACS, London 2007: 25r
Thonet: 25l, 44tl
Tom Dixon: 150, 189
Topfoto.co.uk: /Polfoto: 69, 75cr; /David Wimsett/UPPA. co.uk: 174b
Verner Panton Design: 128, 129
Victoria & Albert Museum/V&A Images: 45tr, 124, 125t, 176; /© ARS, NY and DACS, London 2007: 18
View Pictures Ltd: /©DACS, London 2007: 10-1
Image Courtesy Vitra Design Museum: 22, 120l, 136, 144
Vitsoe: /Photograph by Ken Kirkwood: 107b
Zaha Hadid Architects: /courtesy of Helene Binet: 195; /©Daivd Sykes: 194
Zanotta-Italy: 44bl, 108b, 118t,122t

Every effort has been made to acknowledge correctly and contact the source and/or copyright holder of each picture, item of memorabilia and artwork, and Carlton Books Limited apologizes for any unintentional errors, or omissions, which will be corrected in future editions of this book.

below

Launched in 1928 and the result of Le Corbusier's collaboration with Pierre Jeanneret and Charlotte Perriand, an adjustable chromed-steel cradle rests on a black steel base. Broad straps support the ponyskin cushion with attached headrest.